# Linux Program Development

## a guide with exercises

Jerry Cooperstein

Published by:

Jerry Cooperstein
coop@coopj.com
www.coopj.com

# Contents

# List of Figures

# List of Tables

# Preface

## Objectives

**Linux Program Development** is designed to bring experienced programmers up to speed quickly in a **Linux** environment.

You will learn the tools and methods for developing **C** programs and doing systems programming under **Linux**, including:

- Compilers, compiling, linking and loading programs.

- Building and using both static and shared libraries.

- Using **make** and developing Makefiles.

- Version control.

- Debugging techniques.

- How **system calls** are made and the difference with regular library functions.

- The structure of **Linux** filesystems.

- File I/O functions, using both system-level and standard library calls.

- Advanced file operations, including directory and stat functions, and file locking.

- Process management, including **fork**ing and **exec**ing, exiting, process groups, and waiting.

- Pipes, unnamed and named (**FIFO**'s).

- Signal dispatching and handling.

- Writing multi-threaded applications using the **pthreads** (Posix Threads) library and **API**.

- An introduction to network socket programming.

- **System V** and **POSIX IPC**, including shared memory, semaphores, and message queues.

Upon mastering this material, you will have the necessary tools to develop advanced applications on a **Linux** system.

## Target Audience

You are interested in learning how to write applications for or port them to the **Linux** environment. Maybe you are just doing this for fun, but more likely you have this task as part of your job. The purpose here is to ease your path and perhaps shorten the amount of time it takes to reach a level of basic competence in this endeavor.

How much you get out of this and how bug-free, efficient, and optimized your drivers will be depends on how good a programmer you were before you started with the present material. There is no intent or time here to teach you the elements of good programming or the **Linux** operating system design in great detail.

You should:

- Be proficient in the **C** programming language. (You can do the programming exercises in **C++** if you prefer, but all example solutions are in **C**.)

- Be familiar with basic **Linux** (**Unix**) utilities, such as **ls, rm, grep, tar**.

- Be comfortable using any of the available text editors (i.e., **emacs, vi**.)

- Seen the **X**-Window system before.

Experience with any major **Linux** distribution is helpful but is not strictly required. Likewise ambitious readers could be weak on any of the above except familiarity with the **C** programming language.

There is no shortage of books and classes on programming methods. For **Linux** operating system the choices may be fewer, but they exist.

One text that deserves special mention is ***Advanced Programming in the UNIX Environment***, by W. Richard Stevens, published by Addison Wesley; it belongs on every developer's bookshelf and is used as a primary source by virtually every book on the subject.

All major **Linux** distributions come with exhaustive local documentation, and systems programming subjects including functions, data structures, etc. are covered by **man** pages. These can be accessed from the command line (e.g., do `man 2 open` to get documentation on the system call `open()`, which is in chapter 2 of the **man**ual), or from graphical front-ends installed on most distributions.

Some slapped together **Linux** books merely rephrase **man** pages, or even cut, paste and regurgitate them. I've tried to avoid that and will often recommend looking at the **man** page for more details.

While our material will not be very advanced, it will strive to be thorough and complete. It is worth repeating that we are not aiming for an expert audience, but instead for a competent and motivated one.

Much of what we discuss will apply to any operating system that is **Unix**-like and strives to be **Posix**-compliant. However, we will discuss many topics that are particular to **Linux**. Mostly this means features and **API's** that were written for **Linux** and have not been ported to other operating systems. Sometimes it means the **Linux** interpretation of a standard may have some conflict with other operating systems.

We will point out when we are discussing **Linux**-specific material and warn you that any applications you develop that incorporate these features is likely to be non-portable to other operating systems.

## About the Author

By training I'm a nuclear physicist; I have a PhD in theoretical nuclear astrophysics and I did research on dense nuclear matter, supernova explosions, neutrino diffusion, hydrodynamics, shockwaves, general relativity, etc. for a couple of decades and published dozens of papers, review articles and book chapters in the main physics and astrophysics journals. I was on the faculty at a number of major universities and government labs.

I've been teaching in one form or another for more than 30 years. I've taught advanced as well as introductory courses on a wide variety of subjects in physics and astrophysics at both the undergraduate and graduate level as well as supervised a good number of students. And I've been teaching material such as the present subject matter for more than a decade.

While I've never worked primarily as a software or hardware engineer, I've used and programmed for computers for a long time. The first time I sat down at a computer was 1969; the machine was a DEC PDP-9 and the keyboard was an actual teletype with booting done through paper tapes. I've used every operating system and programming language that has been thrown my way over these four decades and fortunately I've been able to forget about most of them as they became deprecated or obsolete.

In 1994 I left academia and entered the business world. I spent the next 5 years working as a consultant with a major petrochemical company, helping with the geophysics and seismic analysis software used for oil exploration and recovery. (Equations are equations whether they describe colliding nuclei, exploding stars, or seismic waves propagating through layers of the earth.)

During this period I began to use **Linux** extensively as it was a **Unix**-like platform which I could use to develop and debug code which would then be run on large supercomputer platforms.

In 1998 a major chips manufacturer approached my employer and asked us to develop materials to train a bunch of **NT** engineers to work with **Linux**. I was tasked with developing materials and teaching from them and I have been doing it ever since.

Eventually this project grew into three main classes. One was on systems programming, a second was on **Linux** kernel internals, and the third was on **Linux** device drivers. My company, **Axian** of Beaverton, OR, funded and deployed these classes. Eventually we franchised the material out, with some modifications, to be used by various **Linux** distributors. In particular all three classes were used by **Red Hat Inc** for about 10 years as their curriculum for **Linux** developers.

Over those ten years I personally taught sessions of these classes at least 100 times and also functioned as the courseware maintainer and contact person for the many other instructors who taught from this material world-wide, and who contributed in a major way to its improvement.

Great efforts were made to keep the material up to date, since the **Linux** kernel morphs rather quickly. New editions were published four times a year, gradually coming into sync with the new kernel release schedule.

Over the years many students had requested that the courseware material be obtainable in bookstores or mail order. Because it was not possible to publish the courseware because of contractual requirements, it was only possible to obtain it by enrolling in a class, a relatively expensive proposition.

In 2009 the **Axian-Red Hat** contract expired and simultaneously I left **Axian**'s staff. I decided (with **Axian**'s generous permission) to find a way to rework the material and publish it.

And that is how we got here. This it not just a repackaging of the courses that were previously marketed and delivered. There has been a rather major rewrite, development of new exercises, addition of new material and deletion of old material.

## Linux Developer Classes Now Available

I don't expect to get rich by publishing this material. I do hope that if you have **Linux** programming training needs you view it as a good advertisement for engaging our services for live in-person training classes.

The following classes are available:

- Linux Program Development
- Linux Device Drivers
- Linux Kernel Internals

Each of these classes are a full five days in length. Customization and combination options are available. Until demand gets out of control your author is expected to be the instructor.

For detailed descriptions and outlines and pricing and logistics visit **http://www.coopj.com** and contact **coop@coopj.com**.

## Acknowledgments

First of all I must thank my employer of over 15 years, Axian Inc (**http://www.axian.com**) of Beaverton, Oregon, for giving me permission to use material originally under Axian copyright and which was developed on its dime. In particular, Frank Helle and Steve Bissel have not only been extremely generous in allowing me these rights, but have been true friends and supporters in everything I've done.

In the more than a decade I supervised **Linux** developer classes for Axian (which were most often delivered through **Red Hat**'s training division), I interacted with a large number of instructors who taught from the material I was responsible for. They made many suggestions, fixed errors and in some cases contributed exercises. Colleagues I would like to express a very strong thank you to include Marc Curry, Dominic Duval, Terry Griffin, George Hacker, Tatsuo Kawasaki, Richard Keech, and Bill Kerr.

I would also like to thank Alessandro Rubini for his warm and generous hospitality when not long after I began teaching about device drivers and **Linux**, I showed up at his home with my whole family. I also thank him for introducing me to the kind folks at O'Reilly publishing who gave me the opportunity to help with the review of their **Linux** kernel books, which has expanded my knowledge enormously and introduced me to a number of key personalities.

The biggest acknowledgment I must give is to the students who have contributed to the material by asking questions, exposing weaknesses, requesting new material and furnishing their real life experiences and needs, which has hopefully kept the material from being pedantic and made it more useful. Without them (and the money they paid to sit in classes and be forced to listen to and interact with me) this presentation would not exist.

I must also thank my family for putting up me with through all of this, especially with my frequent travels.

Finally, I would like to acknowledge the late Hans A. Bethe, who taught me to never be frightened of taking on a task just because other people had more experience on it.

# Chapter 1

# Preliminaries

We'll discuss our procedures and make some comments about **Linux** distributions. We'll also consider standards such as **Posix** and the **Linux Standard Base**.

## 1.1   Procedures

You will need a computer installed with a current **Linux** distribution, with the important developer tools (for compiling, etc.) properly deployed.

The emphasis will be on hands-on programming, with most sections having laboratory exercises. Where feasible labs will build upon previous lab assignments. The solution set can be retrieved from **http://www.coopj.com/LPD**. As they become available, errata and updated solutions will also be posted on that site.

Lab **solutions** are made available so you can see at least one successful implementation, and have a possible template to begin the next lab exercise if it is a follow up. In addition, **examples** as shown during the exposition are made available as part of the SOLUTIONS package, in the EXAMPLES subdirectory. Once you have obtained the solutions you can unpack it with:

```
tar zxvf LPD*SOLUTIONS*.tar.gz
```

substituting the actual name of the file.

In the main solutions directory, there is a **Makefile** which will recursively compile all subdirectories. By default all sub-directories are recursively compiled, but one can narrow the choice of directories:

```
make SDIRS=s_22
make SDIRS="s_0* s_23"
```

The **genmake** script in the main directory is very useful for automatically generating makefiles, and is worth a perusal.

One should note that we have emphasized clarity and brevity over rigor in the solutions; e.g., we haven't tried to catch every possible error or take into account every possible system configuration option. The code is not bullet-proof; it is meant to be of pedagogical use.

If you have any questions or feedback on this material contact us at *coop@coopj.com*.

---

- The provided solutions will from time to time contain functions and features not discussed in the main text.

- This is done to illustrate methods to do more than the minimum work to solve the problem and teach extra material.

- If there is anything that **must** be used and is not covered in the material, its omission is a bug, not a feature, and should be brought to our attention.

---

## 1.2  Linux Distributions

There are many **Linux** distributions, ranging from very widely used to obscure. They vary by intended usage, hardware and audience, as well as support level. A very comprehensive list can be found at **http://lwn.net/Distributions/**.

We have tried to keep this material as distribution-agnostic as possible. For all but the most specialized distributions this won't present any inconveniences.

Occasionally which distribution you are using will matter, but this should only happen when we (reluctantly) descend into system administration, such as when we must describe the location of particular files and directories or how to install certain required software packages. Fortunately, modern distributions differ much less in these matters than they did in the early days of **Linux** and we will rarely have to deal with such inconveniences.

The material has been developed primarily on **Red Hat**-based systems, mostly on 64-bit variants with testing also done on 32-bit systems. But it has also been tested on a number of other distributions.

Explicitly we have used:

- **Red Hat Enterprise Linux 5.4**

- **Fedora 12**

- **Centos 5.4**

- **Scientific Linux 5.4**

- **Open Suse 11.1**

- **Debian Lenny**

- **Ubuntu 9.10**

- **Gentoo**

As far as software installation and control is concerned distributions tend to use either **RPM**-based or **deb**-based package management. In the above list **Red Hat**, **Fedora**, **Centos**, **Scientific Linux** and **OpenSUSE** are **RPM**-based, and **Debian** and **Ubuntu** are **deb**-based. When necessary we will give required instructions for either of these two broad families.

**GENTOO** is based on neither of this packaging systems, and instead uses the **portage/emerge** system which involves compiling directly from source. If you are a **GENTOO** user, and you have successfully accomplished a fully functional installation (which is generally not a task for novices) you won't need detailed instructions in how to install software or find things, and so we won't insult you by offering it.

If you are running any other distribution you shouldn't have any trouble adapting what we are doing to your installation.

## 1.3    Standards and the LSB

There are a variety of different standards (specifications) that are relevant to working on **Unix**-like operating systems such as **Linux**. For example, a typical **man** page (such as the one for **open()** in the following example) might have a statement in its **CONFORMING TO** section such as:

```
CONFORMING TO

    SVr4, 4.3BSD, POSIX.1-2001.  The O_NOATIME, O_NOFOLLOW, and O_DIRECTORY
    flags are Linux-specific. One may have to define the _GNU_SOURCE macro
    to get their definitions.
```

The history of the different standards and specifications is complicated and is much wrapped up in the convoluted **Unix** family tree with its two main branches, **BSD** and **System V**. For the most part **Linux** strives to be **Posix**-compliant, a later standard that incorporates earlier ones and stands for Portable Operating System for Unix. Note, however, **Linux** distributions are not generally certified as **Unix**-compliant as the rapid development pace is not amenable, and the cost is high and the derived benefits would generally be considered marginal.

It is important, however, that software developed for **Linux** be portable across different distributions without much pain, and the **LSB** specification (**Linux S**tandard **Base**) has stepped into that role. It's home page is at **http://www.linuxbase.org** and it is administered by the **Linux Foundation**, **http://www.linuxfoundation.org**.

In addition to coding considerations, the **LSB** also considers matters such as standard utilities and libraries required, where various things are put on the filesystem etc. If one follows the specification, one should be able to develop on any distribution and use on any other if both are **LSB**-compliant.

# Chapter 2

# Compilers

We'll learn about the various compilers available under **Linux**, concentrating on **gcc**. They will learn about the important optimizations available and use of the preprocessor. Other languages (besides **C**) will be briefly considered. A pointer to available **IDE**s (**I**ntegrated **D**evelopment **Environments**) will be given.

## 2.1  GCC

**gcc** is the **GNU C** compiler. (Its proper name is the *GNU Compiler Collection.*) It can also be invoked as **cc**. **gcc** can compile programs written in C, C++, and Objective C.

**g++** is the **C++** compiler. (It can also be invoked as **c++**.)

**gcc** works closely with the GNU libc, **glibc**, and the debugger, **gdb**.

Virtually every operating system you can think of has a version of **gcc**, and it can be used for cross-compilation.

**gcc** also forms the back end for compiler front ends in Ada95 (package **gcc-gnat**), Fortran (package **gcc-gfortran**), and Pascal (package **gcc-gpc**); i.e., first there is a translation to the **C** language, and then a back end (silently) invokes **gcc**.

Tons of documentation can be found at the **gcc** home page, **http://gcc.gnu.org**, including a complete manual, FAQ, and platform specific information. In addition, doing `info gcc` will give very detailed on-line documentation.

Note that invoking **gcc** actually entails a number of different programs or stages, each of which has its own **man** page, and can be independently and directly invoked:

Table 2.1: **Compiling stages**

| Stage | Command | Default Input | Default Output | `-W` switch |
|-------|---------|---------------|----------------|-------------|
| preprocessing | `cpp` | `.c` | `.i` | `-Wp....` |
| compilation | `gcc` | `.i` | `.s` | N/A |
| assembly | `as` | `.s` | `.o` | `-Wa....` |
| linking | `ld` | `.o` | `a.out` | `-Wl....` |

Depending on your **Linux** distribution, details about the **gcc** installation and defaults can be found in the **/usr/lib/gcc**, **/usr/lib64/gcc** and/or **/usr/libexec/gcc** directories.

---

- **Intel** has a mature set of compilers which are described at **http://software.intel.com/en-us/intel-compilers/**. Evaluation copies can be downloaded for free, and a free non-commercial license can be obtained for learning purposes (see **http://software.intel.com/en-us/articles/non-commercial-software-faq/**.

- The **Intel C** compiler works well for compiling applications under **Linux**. It can be used to compile the kernel but it is not a trivial exercise and it is doubtful anyone is using it for this purpose in a production environment.

---

## 2.2   Major gcc Options

The output format for the executable will be **ELF** (**E**xecutable and **L**inkable **F**ormat) which makes using shared libraries easy; the older so-called **a.out** format, while obsolete (although the name survives), may still be used if the kernel has been configured to support it.

Here's a list of some of the **main** options that can be given to **gcc**:

Table 2.3: **Compiler path options**

| -Idir | Include `dir` in search for included files. Cumulative. |
|---|---|
| -Ldir | Search `dir` for libraries. Cumulative. |
| -l | Link to lib; -lfoo links to `libfoo.so` if it exists, or to `libfoo.a` as a second choice. |

Table 2.4: **Compiler preprocessor options**

| -M | Don't compile. Give dependencies for Make |
|---|---|
| -H | Print out names of included files. |
| -E | pre-process only |
| -Ddef | Define `def` |
| -Udef | Undefine `def` |
| -d | Print #defines |

Table 2.5: **Compiler warning options**

| -v | Verbose mode, gives version number |
|---|---|
| -pedantic | Warn very verbosely |
| -w | Suppress warnings |
| -W | more verbose warnings |
| -Wall | enable a bunch of important warnings |

Table 2.6: **Compiler debugging and profiling options**

| -g | Include debugging information |
|---|---|
| -pg | Provide profile information for gprof |

Table 2.7: **Compiler input and output options**

| -c | Stop after creating object files, don't link |
|---|---|
| -ofile | Output is file ; default is `a.out` |
| -xlang | Expect input to be in `lang`, which can be c, objective-c, c++ (and some others.) Otherwise, guess by input file extension |

Table 2.8: **Compiler control options**

| -ansi | Enforce full ANSI compliance |
|---|---|
| -pipe | Use pipes between stages |
| -static | Suppress linking with shared libraries |
| -O[lev] | Optimization level; 0, 1, 2, 3. Default is 1. |
| -Os | Optimize for size; use all -O2 options except those that increase the size. |

A good set of options to use is:

```
-O2 -Wall -pedantic
```

Make sure you understand any warnings and if you obliterate them, you will save yourself a lot of debugging. However, don't use -pedantic when compiling code for the **Linux** kernel, which uses many **gcc** extensions.

## 2.3   Preprocessor

The preprocessor can be run alone either by invoking **cpp** directly, or doing **gcc** -E ....

Pre-loaded defines can be listed by doing

```
touch foo.h ; gcc -E -dM foo.h; rm foo.h
```

and include:

Table 2.9: **Preloaded compiler definitions**

| -D__GNUC__=4 | -D__GNUC_MINOR__=1 | -D__GNUC_PATCHLEVEL__=2 |
|---|---|---|
| -Dunix | -D__unix | -D__unix__ |
| -Di386 | -D__i386 | -D__i386__ |
| -Dlinux | -D__linux | -D__linux__ |
| -D__gnu_linux__ | | |

as well as a lot of minimum and maximum limits.

The default include path can be listed with:

```
gcc -v -E foo.c
```

where `foo.c` should exist (even if it is empty), and on a recent **x86_64 Red Hat** system would be:

```
/usr/local/include
/usr/lib/gcc/x86_64-redhat-linux/4.1.2/include
/usr/include
```

## 2.4    Other Languages

**Pascal** (done with translation to **C**.)

**Fortran** can be invoked with **gfortran**, **f77**, **g77**, or **f95**. Once again the backend is **gcc**.

**Java** support is very full-featured, with a number of options for runtime environments, development kits, compilers, integrated environments etc.

One can also find compilers for other languages, including **Basic**, **Ada** and **lisp**, by searching various **Linux** resources. In addition many commercial compilers are out there and can be purchased.

## 2.5    Integrated Development Environments (IDE)

There are a very large number of **I**ntegrated **D**evelopment **E**nvironment (**IDE**'s) available under **Linux**. These typically include an editor, an interactive debugger with source code navigation, object disassembly, and automatic **Makefile** generation.

Many veteran developers used to working in a **Unix**-like environment prefer to **roll their own IDE**, often with **emacs** or **vi** at the center.

While **emacs** is an editor at the core, it has evolved in to a complete desktop environment. There is a steep learning curve but it is very powerful. Generally a lot of site and user customization is required before it becomes a satisfactory IDE.

If you prefer working with a pre-packaged **IDE**, there are many offered. Some are under open-source licenses, and some are proprietary, or offer versions in either form.

The following list gives a sense of what is available; You'll have to investigate further to see which fits your needs.

Table 2.10: **Linux IDE's**

| Name | URL | Comments |
|------|-----|----------|
| ActiveState's Ac-tivePython | http://aspn.activestate.com/ | for Python |
| Anjuta | http://anjuta.sourceforge.net/ | for C, C++ |
| BlackAdder | http://www.thekompany.com/ prod-ucts/blackadder/ | for Python and Ruby |
| BlueJ | http://www.bluej.org/ | for Java |
| Boa-Constructor | http://Boa-Constructor.sourceforge.net/ | for Python |
| ICS's BX Pro | http://linux.ics.com/ | for Motif/C++ |
| Code Forge's C-Forge | http://www.codeforge.com/ | Multiple Languages |
| Code Blue | http://codeblue.sourceforge.net/ | for Java |
| Code Crusader | http://www.newplanetsoftware.com/jcc/ | with the **Code Medic** debug-ger. |
| Metrowerks's Code Warrior | http://www.metrowerks.com/MW/ Develop/IDE.htm | Multiple Languages |
| Data Display De-bugger (DDD) | http://www.gnu.org./software/ddd | An Interactive Debugger |
| IBM's Eclipse | http://www.eclipse.org/ | An extensible IDE kit, Java, C/C++ in late beta, other plug-ins pending |
| Interactive Software Engineering's Eiffel-Bench | http://eiffel.com/products/bench/ page.html | For Eiffel |
| FLTK Fluid | http://www.fltk.org/ | for C++ |
| fpGUI | http://www.freepascal.org/fpgui/ | for Object Pascal/Delphi |
| FreeBuilder | http://www.freebuilder.org/ | for Java |
| Ginipad | http://www.mokabyte.it/ginipad/ english.htm | for Java |
| Glimmer | http://glimmer.sourceforge.net/ | Multiple Languages |
| **Red Hat** GNUPro | http://www.redhat.com/software/ gnupro/ | Red Hat commercial IDE, built on **gcc**, **gdb**, etc. |
| Guido van Rossum's IDLE | http://www.python.org/idle/ | for Python |
| InfoDock | http://sourceforge.net/projects/ in-fodock/ | for C++, Java, Python. Built on xemacs. |
| IntelliJ's IDEA | http://www.intellij.com/idea/ | for Java |
| Jedi | http://www.markus-hillenbrand.de/jedi | for Java |
| Jedit | http://www.jedit.org/ | for Java |
| Jext | http://www.jext.org/ | for Python |
| Jipe | http://jipe.sourceforge.net/ | for Java |
| JOODA | http://jooda.sourceforge.net/ | for Java |
| KDbg | http://www.kdbg.org | Graphical interface to **gdb** for **KDE**. |

| | | |
|---|---|---|
| KDevelop | **http://www.kdevelop.org/** | Multiple Languages; part of KDE. |
| KDE Studio | **http://www.thekompany.com/ projects/kdestudio/** | Multiple Languages; KDE-oriented |
| ActiveState's Komodo | **http://www.ActiveState.com/ Products/Komodo/** | Multiple Languages |
| Lazarus | **http://www.lazarus.freepascal.org/** | for Object Pascal/Delphi |
| MetaCard Corp.'s MetaCard | **http://www.metacard.com/** | for MetaTalk |
| NetBeans | **http://www.netbeans.org/** | for Java |
| OpenAmulet | **http://www.openip.org/** | a GUI library/framework |
| PerlComposer | **http://perlcomposer.sourceforge.net/** | for Perl/GTK |
| PythonWare's PythonWorks Pro | **http://www.pythonware.com/ products/works/** | for Python |
| Runtime Revolution Ltd.'s Revolution | **http://www.runrev.com/** | for Transcript |
| RHIDE | **http://www.rhide.com/** | Multiple Languages |
| Scintilla | **http://www.scintilla.org/** | for GTK+/C++ |
| Data Representations's Simplicity and Simplicity Professional | **http://www.datarepresentations.com** | for Java |
| CYGNUS's Source Navigator with the Insight debugger | **http://sources.redhat.com/ sourcenav/**, **http://sources.redhat.com/insight/** | From Red Hat/Cygnus, a wrapper around open-source tools including the **GNUPro Toolkit**, Multiple Languages. |
| Sun Java Studio Standard 5 | **http://wwws.sun.com/software/ sundev/jde/** | for Java |
| Tcl Developer Studio | **http://kakunin.chat.ru/tcldev/** | for Tcl/Tix |
| Titano | **http://titano.sourceforge.net/** | MultipleLanguages; built on GTK+ |
| VDKBuilder | **http://vdkbuilder.sourceforge.net/** | for C/C++; building GTK GUI's |
| IST's Visaj | **http://www.ist.co.uk/visaj/** | for Java |
| IBM's VisualAge Smalltalk | **http://www.ibm.com/software/ad /smalltalk/** | for Smalltalk |
| MicroEdge's Visual SlickEdit | **http://www.slickedit.com/** | Multiple Languages |
| Visual Tcl | **http://vtcl.sourceforge.net/** | for Tcl/Tk |
| IBM's WebSphere Application Developer | **http://www.ibm.com/software/ad/ studioappdev/** | for Java J2EE |
| WideStudio | **http://www.widestudio.org/** | for C++ |
| Archeopteryx Software's Wing IDE | **http://archaeopteryx.com/wingide/** | for Python |
| wxDesigner | **http://www.roebling.de/** | for C++, Java, Python |
| wxPerl | **http://wxperl.sourceforge.net/** | for Perl |
| wxPython | **http://www.wxpython.org/** | for Python |

| wxStudio | http://wxStudio.sourceforge.net/ | for C++, Java |
|---|---|---|
| Xwpe-alpha | http://www.identicalsoftware.com/ xwpe/ | Multiple Languages; old-fashioned. |
| Zend IDE | http://www.zend.com/products/ zend_studio | for PHP |
| Digital Creations's Zope Studio | http://www.zope.org/Products/ ZopeStudio | For Zope; built on Mozilla |

## 2.6   Labs

### Lab 1: Compiling

Make a simple **hello world** program. Compile it and execute it. The purpose of this exercise is just to make sure your compilation environment is working.

### Lab 2: Compiling with headers

Using the previous hello program as a starting point, put some functions in a separate source file. Also use a header file. Compile and execute it.

# Chapter 3

# Libraries

We will learn how libraries are used under **Linux**. Construction of both static and shared libraries will be considered, as will linking applications to them. We will also consider how to use **libdl** to add libraries selectively at run time.

## 3.1 Static Libraries

Static libraries have the extension .a. When a program is compiled, full copies of any loaded library routines are make part of the executable.

The following tools are used for maintaining static libraries:

- **ar** creates, updates, lists and extracts files from the library. The command

  ```
  ar rv libsubs.a *.o
  ```

will create `libsubs.a` if it does not exist, and insert or update any object files in the current directory.

- **ranlib** generates, and stores within an archive, an index to its contents. It lists each symbol defined by the relocatable object files in the archive. This index speeds up linking to the library. The command

  ```
  ranlib libsubs.a
  ```

  is completely equivalent to running **ar -slibsubs.a**. While running **ranlib** is essential under some **Unix** implementations, under **Linux** it is not strictly necessary, but it is a good habit to get into.

- **nm** lists symbols from object files or libraries. The command

  ```
  nm -s libsubs.a
  ```

  gives useful information. **nm** has a lot of other options.

## 3.2  Shared Libraries

A single copy of a shared library can be used by many applications at once; thus executable sizes are reduced.

Shared libraries have the extension **.so**. Typically the full name is something like `libc.so.N` where N is a major version number.

Under **Linux** shared libraries are carefully versioned. For example, a shared library might have any of the following names:

Table 3.1: **Shared library names**

| | |
|---|---|
| `libmyfuncs.so.1.0` | The actual shared library |
| `libmyfuncs.so.1` | The name included in the **soname** field of the library. Used by the executable at run-time to find the latest revision of the **v. 1** myfuncs library. |
| `libmyfuncs.so` | Used by **gcc** to resolve symbol names in the library at link time when the executable is created. |

To create a shared library first one must compile all sources with the **-fPIC** option, which generates so-called **P**osition **I**ndependent **C**ode; don't use **-fpic**; it produces somewhat faster code on m68k, m88k, and Sparc chips, but imposes arbitrary size limits on shared libraries.

```
gcc -fPIC -c func1.c
gcc -fPIC -c func2.c
```

To create a shared library, the option **-shared** must be given during compilation, giving the **soname** of the library as well as the full library name as the output:

```
gcc -fPIC -shared -Wl,-soname=libmyfuncs.so.1 *.o -o libmyfuncs.so.1.0 -lc
```

where the -Wl tells **gcc** to pass the option to the linker. The -lc tells the linker that **libc** is also needed which is generally the case.

You can usually get away ignoring the -fPIC and -Wl,soname options, but it is not a good idea. This is because **gcc** normally emits such code anyway; in fact giving the option prevents the compiler from ever issuing position-dependent code.

Note that it is really the linker (ld) that is doing the work, and the above step could also have been written as:

```
ld -shared -soname=libmyfuncs.so.1 *.o -o libmyfuncs.so.1.0 -lc
```

To get the above to link and run properly, you will also have to do:

```
ln -s libmyfuncs.so.1.0 libmyfuncs.so
ln -s libmyfuncs.so.1.0 libmyfuncs.so.1
```

If you leave out the first symbolic link you won't be able to compile the program; if you leave out the second you won't be able to run it. It is at this point the version check is done, and if you don't use the soname option when compiling the library, no check will be done.

In many cases both a shared and a static version of the same library may exist on the system, and the linker will choose the shared version by default. This may be overridden with the **-static** option to the linker. However, if you do this **all** libraries will be linked in statically, including **libc**, so the resulting executable will be large; you have to be more careful than that.

The GNU **libtool** script can assist in providing shared library support, helping with compiling and linking libraries and executables, and is particularly useful for distributing applications and packages. Full documentation can be obtained by doing `info libtool`.

## Finding shared libraries

A program which uses shared libraries has to be able to find them at run time.

**ldd** can be used to ascertain what shared libraries an executable requires. It shows the **soname** of the library and what file it actually points to:

```
$ ldd /bin/dd
        linux-vdso.so.1 =>  (0x00007fffd77e2000)
        librt.so.1 => /lib64/librt.so.1 (0x0000003f16c00000)
        libc.so.6 => /lib64/libc.so.6 (0x0000003f14400000)
        libpthread.so.0 => /lib64/libpthread.so.0 (0x0000003f15000000)
        /lib64/ld-linux-x86-64.so.2 (0x0000003f14000000)
```

**ldconfig** is generally run at boot time (but can be run anytime), and uses the file **/etc/ld.so.conf**, which lists the directories that will be searched for shared libraries. **ldconfig** must be run as root and shared libraries should only be stored in system directories when they are stable and useful.

Besides searching the data base built up by **ldconfig**, the linker will first search any directories specified in the environmental variable LD_LIBRARY_PATH, a colon separated list of directories, as in the PATH variable. It is important to do

```
export LD_LIBRARY_PATH=$HOME/foo/lib
```

rather than

```
LD_LIBRARY_PATH=$HOME/foo/lib
```

Do you see why?

## 3.3    Linking To Libraries

Whether a library is static or fixed, executables are linked to the library with:

```
gcc -o foo foo.c -L/mypath/lib -lfoolib
```

which will link in /mypath/lib/libfoolib.so, if it exists, and /mypath/lib/libfoolib.a otherwise..

The name convention is such that -lwhat refers to library libwhat.so(.a) If both libwhat.so and libwhat.a exist, the shared library will be used, unless -static is used on the compile line.

It is possible to have circular library dependencies, and since the loader makes only one pass through the libraries requested, you can have something like:

```
gcc .... -lA -lB -lA ..
```

if libB refers to a symbol in libA which is not otherwise referred to. While there is an option to make the loader make multiple passes (see **info gcc** for details) it is very slow, and a proper, layered, library architecture should avoid this kind of going in circles.

The default library search path will always include /usr/lib and /lib. To see exactly what is being searched you can do gcc --print-search-dirs. User-specified library paths come *before* the default ones, although there are extended options to **gcc** to reverse this pattern.

### Getting Debug Information

Once can use the environmental variable LD_DEBUG to obtain useful debugging information. For instance, doing:

```
LD_DEBUG=help
```

and then typing any command gives:

```
Valid options for the LD_DEBUG environment variable are:

  libs        display library search paths
  reloc       display relocation processing
  files       display progress for input file
  symbols     display symbol table processing
  bindings    display information about symbol binding
  versions    display version dependencies
  all         all previous options combined
  statistics  display relocation statistics
  help        display this help message and exit

To direct the debugging output into a file instead of standard output
a filename can be specified using the LD_DEBUG_OUTPUT environment
variable.
```

You can show how symbols are resolved upon program execution, and help find things like linking to the wrong version of a library. Try:

```
LD_DEBUG=all  ls
```

to see a sample.

## Stripping executables

The command

```
strip foobar
```

where **foobar** is an executable program, object file, or library archive, can be used to reduce file size and save disk space. The symbol table is discarded. This step is generally done on production versions.

Don't use **strip** on either the **Linux** kernel or kernel modules, both of which need the symbol information!

# 3.4  Dynamic Linking Loader

It is possible to avoid choosing the dynamic library until run-time, in fact after execution of the binary begins.

While the choice of which shared library to run can be controlled by environmental variables, it is also possible to dynamically load, unload, and substitute during the program execution.

The functions which accomplish this are:

```
#include <dlfcn.h>
```

```
void *dlopen(const char *filename, int flag);
const char *dlerror(void);
void *dlsym(void *handle, char *symbol);
int dlclose(void *handle);
```

The function dlopen() opens the shared library pointed to by filename; if this begins with a / then this is understood to be an absolute path; otherwise it is relative, or is looked for in the usual library list for the system or in the LD_LIBRARY_PATH environmental variable.

The flag variable controls when symbols are resolved. If RTLD_LAZY is used, symbols are resolved only when needed; if RTLD_NOW is used, resolution is immediate. In addition these flags can be or'ed with RTLD_GLOBAL which makes the symbols available to all subsequently loaded libraries.

The function dlsym() looks in the shared library pointed to by handle (which is the return value of dlopen()), for the function or variable pointed to by symbol. It returns a pointer to the symbol which can then be used.

The function dlclose() unloads the dynamic library.

The function dlerror() returns NULL if no errors have occurred since the last of these functions has been called; otherwise it returns a pointer to an string describing the error.

A short example shows how this all hangs together:

```
#include <stdio.h>
#include <stdlib.h>
#include <dlfcn.h>

int main (int argc, char *argv[])
{
    void *handle;
    void (*function) (void);

    handle = dlopen ("./libshared.so", RTLD_LAZY);
    if (!handle) {
        fprintf (stderr, "error opening library is  %s\n", dlerror ());
        exit (-1);
    }

    function = dlsym (handle, "lib_function");
    function ();
    dlclose (handle);
    exit (0);
}
```

This assumes that the library ./libshared.so exists and has a function named lib_function() in it, and that the resulting executable has been linked to libdlb; i.e, we have something like

```
gcc -O2 -Wall -pedantic -fPIC -shared -o libshared.so libshared.c
gcc -O2 -Wall -pedantic -o testit testit.c -ldl
```

As a further refinement, if the shared library contains **constructor** and **destructor** functions, they will be called when the library is loaded and unloaded.

The constructor functions are executed before `dlopen()` returns, or before `main()` is started if the library is loaded at load time. The destructor functions are executed before `dlclose()` returns, or after `exit()` or completion of `main()` if the library is loaded at run time.

Here's an example showing how they are used:

```
/* prototype them with attributes */
void init_fun (void) __attribute__ ((constructor));
void exit_fun (void) __attribute__ ((destructor));
/* then define them */
void init_fun (void ) { ... whatever ... };
void exit_fun (void ) { ... whatever ... };
```

## 3.5   Labs

### Lab 1: Libraries

Use the simple **hello world** program from the previous lesson. Make a static library out of the functions, and compile and link to it.

Do the same with a shared library.

### Lab 2: Dynamical Loading

Make a simple shared library (`libhello_dl.so`) that has a "hello world" print function, and one or more constructor and destructor routines.

Make a test program that dynamically loads the library and executes the function in it.

# Chapter 4

# Make

We will learn how **make** is used under **Linux**. They will learn how to build **Makefiles**, starting with simple cases and progressing to more complicated scenarios, including large projects with many subdirectories.

## 4.1    Using make and Makefiles

**make** is an essential utility for managing all but the smallest of projects. Using **make** facilitates coherent distribution of software and eases compilation on new systems.

Through careful construction of **makefiles**, much tedious and repetitive work can be performed automatically, hopefully minimizing errors.

We will consider directly only the GNU version of **make** which contains considerable enhancements over other implementations and is now available on virtually every platform.

One should note, however, there are other versions of **make**, including pre-GNU vendor-supplied versions, and similarly named systems such as **imake** and **CMake** which are sometimes used in particular projects.

Upon invocation **make** looks for a file named `makefile`; if it fails it looks for `Makefile`. It scans the makefile for rules and dependencies and then adds its own built-in rules. (These names can be overridden with the `-f` option.)

The GNU version of **make** overrides these rules and will give the highest priority to a file named `GNUmakefile`, which is intended to be used only on systems which fully support all the GNU extensions to the conventional **make** program.

Suppose you have a program which has several source files which must be compiled and linked. A trivial Makefile might look like:

```
foobar: main.c sub1.c sub2.c
    gcc -O -o foobar main.c sub1.c sub2.c
```

Simply typing `make` will compile `foobar`. If typed again nothing will happen because `foobar` is up to date. If `main.c` is now modified, a subsequent invocation of make will cause re-compilation.

**NOTE:** The action lines must start with a **TAB** (also bound to Ctrl-I in **emacs** and **vi**) not blank space!

It is possible to use **make** even without a Makefile, as there are built-in implicit rules for creating files with certain extensions. For example if a directory contains `main.c` and `sub.c`, typing

```
make main sub.o
```

produces

```
cc -o main main.c
cc -c sub.c
```

The **automake** and **autoconf** utilities can be used to generate makefiles across a wide variety of platforms and compilers. You have been using these facilities every time you download an application in source form, and then run the command `./configure` to generate the makefile. If you need to prepare software for wide distribution, familiarity with how to use these utilities may be a worthwhile investment of your time.

## 4.2   Building large projects

A non-trivial project may have the following complications and others:

- The source may be in a number of different directories.

- The source may need to be compiled on different platforms.

- The source may need to be compiled with different options.

- There may be many targets.

We'll work this out in exercises, but some of the ways these matters might be addressed involve noting:

- **make** can be recursive (call itself) and do it in subdirectories.

- output files can be placed in other directories.

- macros and environmental variables can be overridden on the command line.

- more than one `Makefile` can be used; it can be selected based on command line specifications and environmental variables.

## 4.3   More complicated rules

Within **Makefiles** string variables can be set by simply using the `=` sign; assignment is **not sticky**; i.e., white space doesn't matter.

Within the **Makefile** these variables are used by preceding them with `$` and surrounding them with parenthesis, e.g.:

```
MYOBJS = a.o b.o c.o
...
    $(CC) -o foobar $(MYOBJS)
```

Certain of these variables are predefined, such as `$(CC)` and `$(CFLAGS)`, but their values can be replaced in the **Makefile** or given on the **make** command line. By default the precedence is: command line first, assignment in **Makefile** second, and assignment in the shell environment third. Thus if you have

```
export CFLAGS='-Wall'
make foobar CFLAGS="-pedantic"
```

the `-pedantic` flag will be the effective one.

There are many things you can do in **Makefiles**; by no means are we trying to tell you everything. Full documentation can be obtained by doing `info Make`.

A little more complicated example would be:

```
foobar: main.o sub1.o sub2.o
   gcc -O -o foobar main.o sub1.o sub2.o
main.o: main.c defs.h
   gcc -O -c -I. main.c
sub1.o: sub1.c sub1.h
   gcc -O -c -I. sub1.c
sub2.o: sub2.c sub2.h
   gcc -O -c -I. sub2.c
```

A little fancier example, which is easier to modify, would be:

```
OBJS= main.o sub1.o sub2.o
INCS= -I. -I/include
DEFS= -Ddef1 -Udef2 -DHaveLibs
CPPFLAGS = $(INCS) $(DEFS)
CFLAGS= -O -g -Wall -pedantic
LOADLIBES = -L $(HOME)/mylib
LDLIBS = -lfoobarrou
TARGET= foobar

$(TARGET): $(OBJS)
    $(CC) $(DEFS) $(CFLAGS) $(CPPFLAGS)  -o $(TARGET) $(OBJS) \
                  $(LOADLIBES) $(LDLIBS)
main.o: main.c defs.h
sub1.o: sub1.c sub1.h
sub2.o: sub2.c sub2.h
```

The .PHONY target can be used to indicate that a target should not be interpreted as a file name; e.g., make install will malfunction if there happens to be a file named install.

An example showing recursion, the use of .PHONY, and manipulation of variables (appending to them):

```
CFLAGS:= -O $(CFLAGS)
CFLAGS+= -O
CFLAGS?= -O2 -Wall -pedantic

all: dir1 dir2

.PHONY: dir1 dir2

dir1:
        cd dir1 ; make

dir2:
        make -C dir2
```

Note that each action line is run under its own shell. Thus these two fragments are not equivalent:

```
        cd dir1 ; ls

        cd dir1
        ls
```

In the second example, the **ls** command will be run in the root directory as the directory change is only effective for the first action line.

Note the use of := in place of = when appending the value of **CFLAGS**; using := implies simple assignment, while using = functions recursively. The latter method is powerful but can lead to infinite loops (which **make** will generally catch) and slower execution.

## 4.4 Built-in rules

**make** contains implicit rules for many common operations, generally for how to produce a file with a given extension given an input file with a specific extension. You may want new ones, or to override the built-in ones. An example would be:

```
.SUFFIXES: .cpp
.cpp.o:
   c++ $(CFLAGS) -c $<
```

Since the default rule for making `foo.o` from `foo.c` amounts to:

```
$(CC) $(CFLAGS) $(CPPFLAGS) $(TARGET_ARCH) -c $(OUTPUT_OPTION) -o foo.o foo.c
```

and the default rule for making `foo` from `foo.c` is similarly

```
$(CC) $(CFLAGS) $(CPPFLAGS) $(TARGET_ARCH) -o foo foo.c $(LOADLIBES) $(LDLIBS)
```

by setting environmental variables alone, you can use **make** even without a **Makefile**.

Some special macros can be used:

Table 4.1: **Builtin make macros**

| Macro | Meaning |
|-------|---------|
| \\$@ | Full name of the current target |
| \\$? | List of files newer than the current target on which the target is dependent |
| \\$< | Single file that is newer than the target on which the target is dependent |
| \\$* | Name of the target file, without a suffix |
| \\$^ | Names of all prerequisites for the target ($¡ is the first prerequisite.) |
| \\$% | Name of the target when part of a library. If the target is `libfoo.a(bar.o)` then $while $@ is `libfoo.a`. |
| \\$(@D) | Directory part of the target file name. |
| \\$(@F) | File name within the directory of the target. |

**NOTE:** Typing `make -p` will give a list of all the implicit rules and predefined variables.

## 4.5   Labs

### Lab 1: Make (Simple)

Construct a Makefile for the previous section's exercise. It should have several targets, including the application built using either a static or shared library.

### Lab 2: Make (Complicated)

Construct a program that has the following properties:

- There should be a number of different functions, or source files.

- They should require the use of a number of header files.

- The source files should be in more than one directory, say a main directory and one or more subdirectories.

- There should be at least one library with more than one subprogram in it.

The exercise (besides writing the code) is to construct the Makefile(s) necessary to accomplish this project. You will then compile and execute it. Along the way you'll gain experience with what happens when you change only one file, how dependencies are set up, etc. Note that because of the built-in Makefile rules, you may not need to specify (if you don't want to) exactly how to compile etc, or make libraries, etc.

# Chapter 5

# Source Control

We will learn about source control tools under **Linux**, focussing on **RCS**, **CVS** and **Subversion**. We'll also examine the **git** tool, used for source control for the **Linux** kernel.

## 5.1 Source Control

Software projects become more complex to manage as the size of the project increases, or as the number of developers working on them goes up.

In order to organize updates and facilitate cooperation, many different schemes are available for source control. Standard features of such programs included the ability to keep an accurate history, or log, of changes, be able to back up to earlier releases, coordinate possibly conflicting updates from more than one developer, etc.

There is no shortage of available products, both proprietary and open; a brief list of products released under a **GPL** license includes:

Table 5.1: **Available source control systems**

| Product | URL |
|---|---|
| RCS | **http://www.gnu.org/software/rcs/** |
| CVS | **http://ximbiot.com/cvs/wiki** |
| Subversion | **http://subversion.tigris.org** |
| git | **http://www.kernel.org/pub/software/scm/git/** |
| GNU Arch | **http://www.gnu.org/software/gnu-arch** |
| Monotone | **http://www.monotone.ca** |
| PRCS | **http://prcs.sourceforge.net** |

We will briefly discuss **RCS** and **CVS**, and then focus in more detail on **Subversion**, a next generation product.

We will also discuss **git**, a somewhat different product arising from the **Linux** kernel development community.

## 5.2   RCS and CVS

### RCS

One of the oldest methods of source code control is **RCS** (**R**evision **C**ontrol **S**ystem) from the Free Software Foundation. Full documentation can be found at **RCS** web site or by looking at **man** pages.

Another older system, **SCCS** (Source Code Control System) was widely available in most **Unix** systems and is easy to convert to use **RCS**.

Normally there will be a sub-directory named RCS (or rcs) placed under the directory containing the files under control.

**make** has built-in rules for **RCS** which makes it easy to use in development projects. In addition, **emacs** can be used tightly with **RCS** using the **vc** mode and related functions, .e.g., **vc-ediff**.

When a file is **unlocked** no one can commit changes to a file, but the lock is available to anyone with access to the **RCS** repository.

When a file is **locked**, only the holder of the lock can commit changes to the file.

## CVS

**CVS** is the **C**oncurrent **V**ersions **S**ystem.

It is more powerful than **RCS** and does a more thorough job of letting multiple developers work on the same source concurrently. However, it has a steeper learning curve, as it has many more commands and possible environmental customizations.

**CVS** stores all files in a centralized **repository**. One never works directly with the files in the repository; instead you get your own copies into your working directory, and when you are finished with changes you check (or **commit**) them back into the repository.

It is possible for the repository to be on a remote machine anywhere in the world. Its location may be specified either by setting the `CVSROOT` environmental variable, or with the `-d` option; i.e., the two following lines are equivalent:

```
cvs -d /home/coop/mycvs init

export CVSROOT=/home/coop/mycvs ; cvs init
```

A number of users can make changes to a given module at once. There are a number of commands to help with resolving differences and merging work.

As for **RCS**, **emacs** can be used tightly with **CVS** using the **vc** mode and related functions.

## 5.3  Subversion

The open-source **Subversion** project is designed to be the successor to **CVS** and is gradually replacing it in many arenas.

In order to keep the transition smooth the **Subversion** interface resembles that of its predecessor, and it is easy to migrate **CVS** repositories over to it.

Directories, copies and renames are versioned, not just files and their contents. Metadata associated with files (such as permissions) can also be versioned.

Revision numbering is in a a **per-commit** basis, not per-file, and atomicity of commits is complete; unless the entire commit is completed no part of it goes through.

A standalone **Subversion** server can be set up using a custom protocol, which runs as an **inetd** service or as a daemon, offering authentication and authorization. One can also use **Apache** to set up a **http**-based server.

There are many enhancements that improve efficiency and reduce storage size requirements. In particular, costs are proportional to the size of the change set, not that of the data set.

In particular, binary files can be handled, and there are built in tools for the mirroring of repositories.

## 5.4   git

The **Linux** kernel development system has special needs in that it is widely distributed throughout the world, with hundreds (even thousands) of developers. Furthermore it is all done very very publicly, under the **GPL**.

For a long time there was no real source revision control system. Then major kernel developers went over to the use of **BitKeeper** (see **http://www.bitkeeper.com**), which while a commercial project granted a restricted use license for **Linux** kernel development.

However in a very public dispute over licensing restrictions in the spring of 2005, the free use of **BitKeeper** became unavailable for **Linux** kernel development.

The response was the development of **git**, whose primary author is Linus Torvalds. The source code for **git** can be obtained from **http://www.kernel.org/pub/software/scm/git/**, and full documentation can be found at **http://www.kernel.org/pub/software/scm/git/docs/**.

An article explaining the internals of **git** can be found at **http://lwn.net/Articles/130865/**.

A look at the **Kernel Hackers' Guide to git**, which can be found at **http://linux.yyz.us/git-howto.html**, shows how the source code management system is used by many senior kernel developers.

Technically **git** is **not** a source control management system in the usual sense, and the basic units it works with are not files. It has two important data structures: an **object** database and a directory cache.

The object database contains objects of three varieties:

- **Blobs:** Chunks of binary data containing file contents.
- **Trees:** Sets of blobs including file names and attributes, giving the directory structure.
- **Commits:** Changesets describing tree snapshots.

The directory cache captures the state of the directory tree.

By liberating the controls system from a file by file based system, one is better able to handle changesets which involve many files.

**git** is under rapid development and graphical interfaces to it are also under speedy construction. For example, see **http://www.kernel.org/git/**. One can easily browse particular changes as well as source trees.

## 5.5 Labs

### Lab 1: Version Control with Subversion

First you'll need to create a central repository:

```
$ svnadmin create my_repos
```

putting in whatever path you want for the last argument. Take a look at the directory tree created under there. Note that one should never manually edit the contents of the repository, but really on the tools that are part of the **Subversion** package.

Now you have to create a **project**, consisting of files and directories which you will import into the **Subversion** repository. For example:

```
$ mkdir my_project
$ cp -a  [whatever files and dirs you want] my_project
```

Note that we are keeping things simple; the recommended route is to create three subdirectories (`branch, tags,trunk`) and to put your files in the `trunk` subdirectory because this convention is often followed; however, **Subversion** doesn't require it.

Now it is time to import data into the repository with:

```
$ svn import my_project file:///tmp/SVN/my_repos -m "Original Import"
```

where the last argument just gives an identifying string. This will tell you about all the files it added, and if you examine the repository you can see where things went and what some of the other files created and modified look like.

Now lets checkout a copy of the project so we can work on it and modify it. Do this with:

```
$ svn checkout file:///tmp/SVN/my_repos/ my_project_work
```

Compare the contents of the working copy with the original project. You'll notice each subdirectory has a `.svn` subdirectory with revision control information.

Now make some changes to the contents of the files in the working copy. Execute

```
$ svn diff
```

(in your main source directory) to see the changes. Run

```
$ svn commit -m "I made some changes"
```

to place your changes in the repository. If you want to update your copy to whatever the most recent version is in the repository, you do it with

```
$ svn update
```

We could do a lot more, but this should get you started.

## Lab 2: Version Control with git

Your system may already have **git** installed. Doing `which git` should show you if it is already present. If not, while you may obtain the source and compile and install it, it is usually easier to install the appropriate pre-compiled binary packages.

For **RHEL**-based systems (including **CentOS**) the easiest way is to use the **EPEL** repository. Obtain the **rpm** for installing the repository from **http://fedoraproject.org/wiki/EPEL**. Then `yum install git` will accomplish installation. For **Fedora**-based systems the same command will work and there is no need to use **EPEL**.

For **Debian**-based systems (including **Ubuntu**) it should be sufficient to do `apt-get install git-core`.

For **Suse**-based systems, one can do `zypper install git-core`.

Now we can proceed, First we'll have to make a directory to work in, and then initialize **git**:

```
$ mkdir git-test ; cd git-test
$ git init
```

Next we have to add some files to our project:

```
$ git update-index --add [whatever files you want]
```

Now we modify one of the files in the project; perhaps something like:

```
$ echo "An extra line" >> [one of the project files]
```

and see the difference with the original repository created with:

```
$ git diff
```

To finish setting up the repository we do:

```
$ tree=$(git write-tree)
$ commit=$(echo 'The Initial Commit' | git commit-tree $tree)
$ git update-ref HEAD $commit
```

Doing `git diff HEAD` will also show us the changes now.

To actually commit the changes to the repository we do:

```
$ git commit
```

If we now do `git diff` we"ll see no changes with the committed repository. To see the history we can do:

```
$ git log
```

and for a detailed history:

```
$ git whatchanged -p
```

# Chapter 6

# Debugging

We'll examine the debugging and profiling tools used in **Linux**.We will learn the use of the **gdb** debugger and its graphical front ends. We will discuss how to get the time and measure intervals. Tools for probing memory problems and methods of profiling applications will be covered. We'll discuss the use of the many-purpose tool, **valgrind**.

## 6.1  gdb (ddd, kdbg, Insight)

**gdb** is the GNU debugger. Upon launch, after processing all command line arguments and options, it loads commands from the file `.gdbinit` in the current working directory (if it exists).

**gdb** allows you to step through **C** and **C++** programs, setting breakpoints, displaying variables, etc. (Actually it will work with programs in native **Fortran** and other languages that use **gcc** as a back end as well.) In addition, **gdb** can properly debug multi-threaded programs.

Programs have to be compiled with the -g option for symbol and line number information to be available to **gdb**. Note, however, you can still use **gdb** to get some information even if this hasn't been done; for instance the **where** command often tells you exactly where the program bombed.

There are many graphical interfaces to **gdb** which make it much easier to use; we will mention three: **ddd**, **kdbg**, and **Insight**. Technically, while none of these provides a complete integrated development environment, they can easily provide most of the ingredients for building your own.

- The home site for **ddd** is: **http://www.gnu.org/software/ddd**. Your distribution may offer it as a standard package.

- The **kdbg** graphical front end to **gdb** is part of the **KDE** desktop system, but can be run under other desktop managers such as **Gnome**. If only the **kdbg** package is installed, the debugger will work without problem, but one must install at least the **kdebase** package to have the help system be operational.

- The **Insight** graphical front end to **gdb** is written in **Tcl/Tk**, and is provided under the **GPL** by **Red Hat** and its **Cygnus Solutions** subsidiary. Documentation, sources and binaries can be downloaded from **http://sources.redhat.com/insight/**.

---

- If `fork()` is called, the default behaviour of **gdb** is to continue following the parent process. This can be controlled with the command:

  ```
  set follow-fork-mode child
  ```

  to proceed with debugging the child instead, after the `fork()` call.

- One can restore the default behaviour with:

  ```
  set follow-fork-mode parent
  ```

---

## 6.2  Electric Fence

**Electric Fence** is a memory allocation debugger, written by Bruce Perens. It is a rather old project, but still has very useful capabilities. Documentation can be accessed by typing `man efence`, or looking at **http://perens.com/FreeSoftware**.

This tool detects either overruns of `malloc()` memory allocations or accesses of memory allocations that have been released by `free()`. It can do such detections on both reads and writes. In order to do this, **Electric Fence** substitutes specialized versions of the `malloc()` and `free()` functions (and their relatives) for the dynamic allocation and freeing of memory.

To use **Electric Fence** all you have to do is link to its library with `-lefence` during compilation.

A number of environmental variables can be set which influence how it operates. You'll have to read the man page (`man efence`) to get the details.

## 6.3  Getting the Time

One often needs to know the time, either absolutely, or relatively to measure intervals. One can obtain the current time with up to microsecond resolution with:

```
#include <sys/time.h>

int gettimeofday (struct timeval *tv, struct timezone *tz);

struct timeval {
    time_t      tv_sec;  /* seconds */
    suseconds_t tv_usec; /* microseconds */
};

struct timezone {
    int tz_minuteswest;      /* minutes west of Greenwich */
    int tz_dsttime;          /* type of DST correction */
};
```

The time returned by this function is measured in seconds since the **Epoch**, midnight on January 1, 1970. If you just want to know the time, you can pass NULL for the third argument.

Knowing the `timeval` structures that bracket a certain task, you could calculate the elapsed time with a macro like:

```
#define GET_ELAPSED_TIME(tv1,tv2) ( \
  (double)( (tv2.tv_sec - tv1.tv_sec) + .000001 * (tv2.tv_usec - tv1.tv_usec)))
```

Two related functions, `time()` and `ftime()` return the same information in different formats and are available for backward compatibility with other **Unix**-like operating systems.

In order to set up and use an **interval timer** the system calls `setitimer()` and `alarm()` are also available.

## 6.4  Profiling and Performance

**Linux** comes with many performance and profiling tools already installed. Many other tools are available, either from proprietary, often expensive commercial vendors, or from free open-source alternatives.

**gprof** can be used for execution profiling. Information will be gathered about the time spent in each function, the number of times everything is called, etc. You don't get line by line information.

Using **gprof** is trivial. All you have to do is:

- Compile your code with the **-pg** option. (You need only compile those routines you want to profile; for others no time will be available.)

- Then running it as you normally do will produce a file called **gmon.out**. This is a binary file, so you can't look at it directly.

- Type **gprof foo** to get a report on program **foo**. (Use the **-b** option to make it less verbose.)

Input options control exactly what is reported, and the locations of the profile data file and the binary program.

The open-source **oprofile** project (**http://oprofile.sourceforge.net**) doesn't even require a recompilation to regenerate profiling information. It should come installed on most major **Linux** distributions. Full documentation including installation instructions and examples can be found at the project web site.

Intel offers the **VTune** (**http://developer.intel.com/software/products/vtune**) performance analyzer. This can perform time-based and event-based sampling, gain all kinds of performance statistics, and gives source-level tuning. Using **VTune** for **Linux** requires (at present) the use of a **Windows** computer to run the user-interface, together with the target **Linux** system.

The **TAU** (**T**uning and **A**nalysis **U**tilities) project ( **http://www.cs.uoregon.edu/research/ paracomp/tau/** gives a complete performance analysis environment for a number of languages, including C, C++, Java, Fortran, etc. **TAU** uses the **PAPI** (**P**erformance **A**pplication **P**rogramming **I**nterface) (**http://icl.cs.utk.edu/projects/papi/**) which provides the hooks into the hardware counters used for monitoring.

A number of small utilities should be found on your **Linux** distribution, which together form a quite robust suite of performance monitoring capabilities. Some of the main ones are:

Table 6.2: **Performance monitoring utilties**

| Utility | Package | Use |
|---------|---------|-----|
| **ps** | procps | Information about processes. |
| **top** | procps | Dynamic view of running tasks and system. |
| **vmstat** | procps | Information about memory paging, I/O, swapping, etc. |
| **free** | procps | Memory statistics. |
| **netstat** | net-tools | Network connections, routing, statistics, etc. |
| **iostat** | sysstat | Monitor I/O load. |
| **mpstat** | sysstat | Processor related statistics. |
| **sar** | sysstat | Collect, report, save system activity information. |

You can view the **man** pages for these utilities for more information, and note that the ones which are purely text-based can be accessed from GUI's under your desktop environment. You can find out about other such utilities that are on your system by looking at the various packages. For example, on an **RPM**-based system:

```
rpm -qil procps sysstat net-tools | grep bin
```

All of these utilities gain their information from reading entries in the **/proc** pseudo-filesystem. You can directly examine entries there without using special programs once you become familiar with the formats of the various entries.

## 6.5 valgrind

**valgrind** is an integrated set of tools useful for profiling and debugging under **Linux**. The three main tools involve memory error detection, cache profiling, and heap profiling. Complete documentation and the latest versions can be obtained from **http://valgrind.org**.

To invoke **valgrind** on an executable named **foobar**, just do:

```
valgrind --tool=<toolname> [options] foobar [arguments]
```

where `toolname` can be one of:

```
lackey
memcheck
corecheck
helgrind
addrcheck
massif
callgrind
cachegrind
none
```

By default `memcheck` should be chosen, but it depends on how **valgrind** is installed, so one should not assume this. In order to get the most information, programs should be compiled with the **-g** flag.

It is possible to divert **valgrind**'s output from the default **stderr**. For example, if one uses the helper program :

```
valgrind-listener [--exit-at-zero|-e] [port-number]
```

on a host with an address of `ipaddr`, and invokes valgrind as in

```
valgrind --log-socket=ipaddr[:port-number] --tool=memcheck foobar
```

output will appear on a socket being monitored by **valgrind-listener**. Note that the address must be given in numerical form, not by name (and could be the current host), and the default port number is 1500.

Programs run under **valgrind** are slowed down by a factor that can range from 5 to 100. Programs are instrumented and run under a simulated CPU; the amount of slowdown depends on which tool is being used. For example, **memcheck** increases code size by an order of magnitude and slows things down by a factor of 25 to 50.

Besides your application, **valgrind** will debug and profile whatever shared libraries it uses, and thus output can be quite noisy. It is possible to selectively **suppress** the output from the shared libraries.

There are general options (such as -v for verbose) and then specific options for each tool.  Usage
messages can be generated by typing variations on:

```
/usr/local/coop>valgrind --help --tool=memcheck
usage: valgrind --tool=<toolname> [options] prog-and-args

  common user options for all Valgrind tools, with defaults in [ ]:
    --tool=<name>              use the Valgrind tool named <name> [memcheck]
    -h --help                  show this message
    --help-debug               show this message, plus debugging options
    --version                  show version
    -q --quiet                 run silently; only print error msgs
    -v --verbose               be more verbose, incl counts of errors
    --trace-children=no|yes    Valgrind-ise child processes? [no]
    --track-fds=no|yes         track open file descriptors? [no]
    --time-stamp=no|yes        add timestamps to log messages? [no]
    --log-fd=<number>          log messages to file descriptor [2=stderr]
    --log-file=<file>          log messages to <file>.pid<pid>
    --log-file-exactly=<file>  log messages to <file>
    --log-file-qualifier=<VAR> incorporate $VAR in logfile name [none]
    --log-socket=ipaddr:port   log messages to socket ipaddr:port

  uncommon user options for all Valgrind tools:
    --run-libc-freeres=no|yes free up glibc memory at exit? [yes]
    --weird-hacks=hack1,hack2,...  recognised hacks: lax-ioctls,ioctl-mmap
                                                                    [none]
    --pointercheck=no|yes      enforce client address space limits [yes]
    --show-emwarns=no|yes      show warnings about emulation limits? [no]
    --smc-check=none|stack|all  checks for self-modifying code: none,
                                only for code found in stacks, or all [stack]

  user options for Valgrind tools that report errors:
    --xml=yes                  all output is in XML (Memcheck/Nulgrind only)
    --xml-user-comment=STR     copy STR verbatim to XML output
    --demangle=no|yes          automatically demangle C++ names? [yes]
    --num-callers=<number>     show <num> callers in stack traces [12]
    --error-limit=no|yes       stop showing new errors if too many? [yes]
    --show-below-main=no|yes   continue stack traces below main() [no]
    --suppressions=<filename>  suppress errors described in <filename>
    --gen-suppressions=no|yes|all    print suppressions for errors? [no]
    --db-attach=no|yes         start debugger when errors detected? [no]
    --db-command=<command>     command to start debugger [gdb -nw %f %p]
    --input-fd=<number>        file descriptor for input [0=stdin]
    --max-stackframe=<number>  assume stack switch for SP changes larger
                               than <number> bytes [2000000]

  user options for Memcheck:
    --leak-check=no|summary|full      search for memory leaks at exit? [summary]
    --leak-resolution=low|med|high    how much bt merging in leak check [low]
    --show-reachable=no|yes           show reachable blocks in leak check? [no]
    --partial-loads-ok=no|yes         too hard to explain here; see manual [yes]
    --freelist-vol=<number>           volume of freed blocks queue [1000000]
    --workaround-gcc296-bugs=no|yes   self explanatory [no]
    --alignment=<number>       set minimum alignment of allocations [8]
    --avoid-strlen-errors=no|yes  suppress errs from inlined strlen [yes]
```

```
Extra options read from ~/.valgrindrc, $VALGRIND_OPTS, ./.valgrindrc

Valgrind is Copyright (C) 2000-2005 Julian Seward et al.
and licensed under the GNU General Public License, version 2.
Bug reports, feedback, admiration, abuse, etc, to: www.valgrind.org.

Tools are copyright and licensed by their authors.  See each
tool's start-up message for more information.
```

Use of **valgrind** is best learned through experimentation with the different tools, but let's just survey the main ones:

## memcheck

Detect use of uninitialized memory.

Detect accessing memory past the end of **malloc**'ed regions, or accessing memory which has been freed.

Detect use of inappropriate stack areas,

Detect memory leaks (allocated buffers which are never re-used or freed.)

Pinpoint other memory access related errors.

## addrcheck

Same as **memcheck** but doesn't check for use of uninitialized memory; runs much faster as a result.

## cachegrind

Profiles the use of cache.

Simulates L1, L2, D1 CPU caches and logs the number of cache hits and misses, memory references and instructions for each line of program code.

Can slow programs down up to 100 times.

The helper program **callgrind** is a wrapper which gives even more information. The **KDE** application **kcachegrind** gives an advanced graphical interface.

## helgrind

Thread debugger which looks for multi-threaded race conditions.

Identifies memory locations used by more than one thread without mutual exclusion primitives.

**massiv**

Heap profiler which produces a graph of heap usage over time.

## 6.6   Labs

### Lab 1: Debugging Memory Overruns

Consider the following test program, which has a memory overrun error:

```
#include <stdio.h>
#include <stdlib.h>
#include <unistd.h>
#include <malloc.h>

int main (int argc, char *argv[])
{
    char *buf;
    int size = 800, index = 801;
    if (argc > 1)
        index = atoi (argv[1]);
    if (argc > 2)
        size = atoi (argv[2]);
    buf = malloc (size);

    printf ("I allocated  %d bytes, I'm going to use the %d element\n",
            size, index);
    buf[index] = 1;
    printf ("buf[index] = %d\n", buf[index]);
    exit (0);
}
```

If run with no arguments it tries to write 1 byte over the edge of an allocated array; if run with arguments you can specify the byte to write to and the size of the array.

Compile it with the **-g** option, and run it under **gdb** (You'll probably want to use **kdbg** or **ddd** as a graphical front end.)

You can familiarize yourself with using the debugger, trying basic navigation, like stepping through, using next, introducing breakpoints, examining source, etc.

If compiled with the standard **malloc()** function, you probably won't get any errors for slight overruns.

Do the same thing but compile using **ElectricFence** (**-lefence**).

Now run under **valgrind** and see what information can be obtained.

# Lab 2: Debugging Memory Leaks

Consider the following application, which introduces memory leaks (in this case, allocated arrays which are never freed once they are no longer needed.)

```
#include <stdio.h>
#include <stdlib.h>
#include <unistd.h>
#include <malloc.h>

void doit (void)
{
    char *buf;
    buf = malloc (1000);
}

int main (int argc, char *argv[])
{
    int j;
    for (j = 0; j < 10; j++) {
        doit ();
        printf ("I allocated the %3d buffer\n", j);
    }
    exit (0);
}
```

Fire up **valgrind** and trace the memory leaks.

# Chapter 7

# System Calls

We'll consider how **system calls** are made under **Linux**, and the different between higher level library function calls and lower level systems calls.

## 7.1   System Calls vs. Library Functions

Programs may request actions, or services, from the **Linux** kernel through a well defined set of **system calls**. This is done because all interaction with hardware (including memory) requires kernel privileges.

There are many other functions readily accessed from user programs which are not system calls, but which may make system calls on their own. An example would be `fopen()`. In principle, an application doesn't know whether it is making a system call, or a call to a library that can be satisfied without recourse to a system call.

Technically, all arguments to system calls (as they are presented to the kernel, not as they appear to the application) are **unsigned longs**, which may be interpreted as pointers. The library or application making the system call will take care of any casting required.

Usually, the maximum number of arguments to the system call as it is presented to the kernel is 6, including the system call number.

On line documentation can be found by doing `man 2 intro` or `man syscalls`. Since chapter 2 of the on line manual contains system call documentation, the command `ls /usr/share/man/man2` will give a list of relevant **man** pages. Note this documentation may not be up to date.

## 7.2   How System Calls are Made

In version 2.6.31 of the 32-bit **x86 Linux** kernel there are 336 system calls, and for 2.4.30 there are 252; the number has been gradually growing. For other architectures, the numbers can be quite different. Note that the precise number depends on the minor kernel version number.

Some calls have not been implemented (or are ancient relics) although space has been reserved for them. Calling any one of these system calls returns the error `-ENOSYS`.

These function calls are listed in **/usr/include/asm/unistd.h**. The head of this file includes:

```
#define __NR_exit        1
#define __NR_fork        2
#define __NR_read        3
#define __NR_write       4
#define __NR_open        5
#define __NR_close       6
#define __NR_waitpid     7
#define __NR_creat       8
#define __NR_link        9
#define __NR_unlink     10
....
```

The kernel level function usually has `sys_` prepended to the user level function name.

The arguments at the user level may be different than at the kernel level; the library takes care of any massage necessary.

When the user makes a system call (like **open()**) the library (**glibc** in this case) determines the number associated with that system call and then passes that to the kernel while making an **int 0x80** instruction, which generates an **exception**, which causes the CPU to enter **kernel mode** (on 32-bit **x86**).

Together with the routine number, the library passes any arguments to the kernel which then executes the call; when it is finished it returns an exit code to user-space.

## 7.3   Return Values and Error Numbers

Most (but not all) system calls return 0 on success and -1 on failure. To get more specific information use the function **perror()**. For example:

```
.....
#include <stdio.h>
#include <errno.h>
.....

if ( system_call_foobar(args) == -1 ) {
   perror("system_call_foobar failed");
   exit(errno);
}
```

The actual error codes can be found by working through **/usr/include/asm/errno.h**. The first few are:

```
#define EPERM     1   /* Operation not permitted */
#define ENOENT    2   /* No such file or directory */
#define ESRCH     3   /* No such process */
#define EINTR     4   /* Interrupted system call */
#define EIO       5   /* I/O error */
#define ENXIO     6   /* No such device or address */
#define E2BIG     7   /* Arg list too long */
#define ENOEXEC   8   /* Exec format error */
#define EBADF     9   /* Bad file number */
#define ECHILD   10   /* No child processes */
#define EAGAIN   11   /* Try again */
....
```

## 7.4 Labs

### Lab 1: Using strace.

**strace** is used to trace system calls and signals. In the simplest case you would do:

```
strace [options] command [arguments]
```

Each system call, its arguments and return value are printed. According to the man page:

*"Arguments are printed in symbolic form with a passion."*

and indeed they are. There are a lot of options; read the man page!

As an example, try

```
strace ls -lRF / 2>&1 | less
```

You need the complicated redirection because **strace** puts its output on `stderr` unless you use the `-o` option to redirect it to a file.

While this is running (paused under **less**), you can examine more details about the **ls** process, by examining the **/proc** filesystem. Do

```
ps aux | grep ls
```

to find out the process ID associated with the process. Then you can look at the pseudo-files

```
/proc/<pid>/fd/*
```

to see how the file descriptors are mapped to the underlying files (or pipes), etc.

## Lab 2: Using syscall().

The indirect system call function:

```
#include <unistd.h>
#include <sys/syscall.h>

int syscall (int call_number, .... );
```

can be used to invoke any system call known to the system. The first argument `call_number` can be read from the list in **/usr/include/bits/syscall.h**:

```
....
#define SYS__sysctl __NR__sysctl
#define SYS_access __NR_access
#define SYS_acct __NR_acct
#define SYS_add_key __NR_add_key
#define SYS_adjtimex __NR_adjtimex
#define SYS_afs_syscall __NR_afs_syscall
#define SYS_alarm __NR_alarm
#define SYS_brk __NR_brk
#define SYS_capget __NR_capget
....
```

The remaining variable number of arguments (indicated by ....) are the arguments to the actual system call.

This function is not meant to be widely used; it is there for the use of library writers, so don't use it in normal programs unless absolutely necessary.

Write a program that invokes `syscall()` to run some common system calls. For example you might do:

```
pid = syscall(_SYS_getpid);
```

# Chapter 8

# Memory Management and Allocation

We'll examine how memory can be is managed and allocacated in
**Linux**. We'll see how to tune the allocation methods and how to take into account alignment
considerations.

## 8.1   Memory Management

The **Linux** kernel manages the memory it directly uses for its own purposes as well as the memory
used by user processes. Processes have more limited privileges with respect to memory, and are given
a lower urgency when they request memory.

Each process lives in its own **address space**, which consists of a list of **virtual memory areas**,
each one of which is a range of contiguous **virtual** addresses. The addresses are virtual because they

do not directly correspond to the physical addresses used by the hardware; the kernel maintains the connection between these two types of addresses.

In fact the physical memory referred to by a given virtual address can change with time as memory is swapped in and out according to system needs.

The basic unit of memory is called a **page** whose size depends on the architecture. For most architectures a page is 4 KB in length, although it varies and some architectures can actually use more than one size. Access rights, permissions, swapping, sharing, etc. are done at the page level. Obtaining the page size is simply done with the function:

```
#include <unistd.h>
int getpagesize(void);
```

which is often a good size to use for various buffers since it is page aligned.

Memory management is quite different on 32-bit and 64-bit architectures, with 32-bit architectures requiring more complexity when significant amounts of memory are used.

Because a 32-bit address space can handle at most 4 GB of memory, it becomes complicated to deal with more than this. Even though the **x86** platform uses **PAE** (the **P**hysical **A**ddress **E**xtension mechanism) to enable 36-bit addresses and thus up to 64 GB of memory, processes are still limited to using 32-bits (or 4 GB) at a time.

Furthermore, 32-bit **Linux** architectures divide this 4 GB of address space into a portion used by the kernel, and a portion used by user space. Usually this division gives the lower 3 GB to applications and the upper 1 GB to the kernel. Thus without acrobatic maneuvers, **Linux** can not give an application more than 3 GB of memory to use on 32-bit systems.

This does not mean the kernel can only use 1 GB of memory and that applications can only use 3 GB in total; what it means is that the kernel has to do more complicated maneuvers to use more than this (to use the so-called **high memory**) and that **each** application is limited to 3 GB.

On 64-bit systems there is no concept of high memory and all memory access is **flat**. There is no direct limit on how much memory an application or the kernel can use.

Since memory prices continue to drop and 64-bit CPU's are becoming the norm the extra work involved in making 32-bit platforms work with really large amounts of memory is really no longer worth it.

## 8.2   Dynamical Allocation

Variables can be allocated either statically (in main memory, persisting through the life of the program) or automatically (off the stack, persisting only through the life of the code block they are contained in.)

Both these approaches are efficient and fast, but in both methods the size of the allocated object must be known at compile time. Furthermore the long lifetime of static variables can be wasteful. Also, automatic variables can overflow the stack both because the size of the stack is not necessarily known in advance.

The size of the stack can be controlled from the command line with

```
ulimit -s 1024
```

which would limit the stack to 1 MB, or from within a program with:

```
struct rlimit rl = {1024,1024};
setrlimit (RLIMIT_STACK, &rl);
```

(Consult the man page for `setrlimit()`.) Normal users can only decrease the stack size which by default is 8 MB on most **Linux** systems.

Thus **dynamical memory allocation** is extremely useful in that objects of arbitrary size (limited only by the total memory available in the system and even more) can be allocated and de-allocated when no longer necessary. The memory comes from the **heap**, the size of which can be elastically modified according to needs.

When using dynamical allocation it is important to free memory when it is no longer needed to avoid the generation of memory leaks. However, many programs rely on program termination to take care of freeing.

The standard functions are:

```
#include <stdlib.h>

void *malloc (size_t size);
void *calloc (size_t nmemb, size_t size);
void *realloc (void *ptr, size_t size);
void free (void *ptr);
```

where `size` is the number of bytes to be allocated. The `calloc()` function is equivalent to `malloc()` followed by clearing the memory. (Note it only cares about the product `nmemb*size`, the number of elements times the size of each one, so the parameter `size` is used somewhat differently in this case.)

The function `realloc()` will permit resizing the allocated buffer; if it can be done in place it will, but if necessary the new memory will be allocated and the contents of the original buffer copied over.

Old versions of **libc** required explicit casting of the pointers returned by `malloc()`, but using `void *` in the prototype eliminates that need. Such casting should not be used. (Note however, **C++** requires it.)

How memory allocation works depends explicitly on both **libc** and on the operating system kernel. In particular, a strategy which is both non-urgent and optimistic is followed.

By non-urgent one means that while a legal address may be given as a return value from `malloc()` there may not actually be physical memory yet associated with the address. For instance, not all of the memory may actually be used, so the kernel may tie physical memory to virtual memory addresses one page at a time (4 KB on **x86**) by using **demand page faulting**. It is also possible that the page may have been swapped out and needs to be swapped back in which also induces a normal page fault.

By optimistic, one means that the system is allowed to **overcommit** memory (like an airline overbooking a flight.) This can lead to invocation of the dreaded **OOM killer** (**O**ut **O**f **M**emory) which tries to select candidates to throw overboard. This can be turned off by:

```
$ echo 2 > /proc/sys/vm/overcommit_memory
```

There are many implementations of **malloc()** and depending on how a program is linked, different ones can be chosen at runtime by forcing certain shared library choices; this is often done for debugging purposes for example. It is also possible to tune the allocation routine's behaviour as we will discuss shortly.

## 8.3　Tuning malloc()

The `malloc()` implementation in libc permits a significant amount of tuning as well as the ability to gather information about ongoing allocations.

For small allocations `malloc()` uses the underlying `brk()` and `sbrk()` system calls, which reset and resize the data segment used by a process. For larger allocations, `malloc()` uses the `mmap()` system call, which always provides multiples of the page size (4 KB on **x86**).

The competition between `sbrk()` and `mmap()` can be influenced through the use of:

```
int mallopt (int param, int value);
```

The meaning of parameters and values passed to `mallopt()` are:

Table 8.1: **mallopt() parameters**

| Parameter | Value |
|---|---|
| M_MMAP_THRESHOLD | Any memory request greater than the value supplied are allocated using `mmap()` rather than `sbrk()`. Smaller chunks may still be allocated with `mmap()`. |
| M_MMAP_MAX | The value is the maximum number of chunks to allocate with `mmap()`; setting to 0 disables all use of `mmap()`. |
| M_TRIM_THRESHOLD | The value is the minimum bytes that will cause `sbrk()` to be called with a negative argument, thereby returning memory to the system. |
| M_TOP_PAD | The value is the amount of extra memory to obtain when calling `sbrk()`, and is the number of extra bytes to keep when shrinking the heap. This provides hysteresis in heap size to avoid overly frequent system calls. |

Statistics about the current allocations can be obtained using the functions:

```
struct mallinfo mallinfo (void)
void malloc_stats (void);

struct mallinfo {
  int arena;    /* non-mmapped space allocated from system */
  int ordblks;  /* number of free chunks */
```

```
    int smblks;    /* number of fastbin blocks */
    int hblks;     /* number of mmapped regions */
    int hblkhd;    /* space in mmapped regions */
    int usmblks;   /* maximum total allocated space */
    int fsmblks;   /* space available in freed fastbin blocks */
    int uordblks;  /* total allocated space */
    int fordblks;  /* total free space */
    int keepcost;  /* top-most, releasable (via malloc_trim) space */
};
```

The function `mallinfo()` returns a `mallinfo` structure containing the information. (Note the `smblks`, `usmblks`, `fsmblks` are unused in **Linux**.) The easy to use function `malloc_stats()` returns the main information in a form easily read by humans.

Sometimes it is necessary to force **alignment** of allocated memory. The function for allocating such aligned memory is:

```
#include <malloc.h>

int posix_memalign (void **memptr, size_t alignment, size_t size);
```

The allocated memory will be `size` bytes in length, and the address returned to `*memptr` will be a multiple of `alignment`. The value of `alignment` must be a power of two and a multiple of the pointer size (.e.g., `sizeof(void *)`.)

The older functions `memalign()` and `valloc()` should not be used as they do not properly check whether the supplied values make sense.

# 8.4   Labs

## Lab 1: Examining malloc() Behaviour

Write a program that uses `mallinfo()` and/or `malloc_stats()` to examine the system's allocation behaviour.

Try allocating a small, medium, and large amount of memory and see how much is allocated by resizing the data segment as compared to memory mapping.

Try using `mallopt()` to either turn off memory mapping altogether or to change the threshold between the two techniques.

## Lab 2: Running Out of Memory

Write a short program that allocates memory in chunks until the system can no longer obtain any more.

Eventually the **OOM** killer should be invoked. Look at `/var/log/messages` to see what decisions it made about what to processes to exterminate.

Try this with **swap** turned off and on, which you can do (as root) with `swapoff -a` and `swapon -a`.

# Chapter 9

# Files and Filesystems in Linux

We will consider how files, directories and devices are managed under **Linux**. We'll learn about the Virtual File System (**VFS**), how the **ext2/ext3** filesystem is structured, and about journalling filesystems. We'll examine the new **ext4** filesystem.

## 9.1 Files, Directories and Devices

It is often said that In **Unix everything is a file** (or is represented as a file):

Table 9.1: **Everything is a file**

| Executables: | /bin/ls |
|---|---|

| Directories: | `/usr/local` |
|---|---|
| Software or pseudo-devices: | `/dev/kmem` |
| Hardware devices: | `/dev/fd0` |

This isn't quite true as some important interfaces (such as networks) are not accessed through the filesystem, although they can use file-like I/O through sockets.

A file is a symbolic reference to an inode:

```
$ ls -li
total 32
809228 -rw-rw-r--  1 coop coop 5919 May 28 17:09 ext2.html
809240 -rw-rw-r--  1 coop coop 3608 May 28 17:09 files.html
809204 -rw-rw-r--  2 coop coop 1566 May 28 17:09 index.html
809204 -rw-rw-r--  2 coop coop 1566 May 28 17:09 index_ln.html
809877 lrwxrwxrwx  1 coop coop   10 May 28 17:12 index_ln-s.html -> index.html
809238 -rw-rw-r--  1 coop coop 2888 May 28 17:09 journal.html
809244 -rw-rw-r--  1 coop coop 1057 May 28 17:09 summary.html
809202 -rw-rw-r--  1 coop coop  217 May 28 17:09 TOC
```

The two links were made with:

```
ln    index.html index_ln.html
ln -s index.html index_ln-s.html
```

Note that hard link `index_ln.html` has the same inode as `index.html`, while the soft link `index_ln-s.html` has its own unique inode.

Device (special) files: `/dev/floppy`, `/dev/hdc`, `/dev/tty`, etc. are special files or device files representing hardware devices and pseudo-devices. They are created using the **mknod** command.

```
$ ls -l /dev
...
lrwxrwxrwx  1 root root          3 May 25 01:56 cdwriter -> hda
...
brw-rw----  1 coop floppy   2,   0 May 25 01:56 fd0
brw-rw----  1 coop floppy   2,   4 May 25 01:56 fd0d360
...
brw-rw----  1 root disk     8,   0 May 25 01:56 sda
brw-rw----  1 root disk     8,   1 May 25 01:56 sda1
brw-rw----  1 root disk     8,  10 May 25 01:56 sda10
...
crw-rw----  1 root lp       6,   0 May 25 01:56 lp0
crw-rw----  1 root lp       6,   1 May 25 01:56 lp1
...
crw-rw-rw-  1 root root     1,   5 May 25 01:56 zero
```

# 9.2 The Virtual File System

**Linux** implements a Virtual File System (VFS), as do all modern operating systems. For the most part neither the specific filesystem or actual physical media and hardware need be addressed by filesystem operations. Furthermore, network filesystems (such as NFS) can be handled transparently.

This permits **Linux** to work with more filesystem varieties than any other operating system. This democratic attribute has been a large factor in its success.

Most filesystems have full read/write access while a few have only read access and perhaps experimental write access.

A (partial) list of currently supported filesystem types:

Table 9.2: **Available filesystems**

| Name | Description |
|------|-------------|
| ext2 | Native **Linux** filesystem |
| minix | predecessor to ext2 |
| proc | Used for `/proc/` |
| msdos | MSDOS |
| umsdos | extensions to MSDOS |
| vfat | Windows VFAT (includes FAT32, FAT, etc) |
| ntfs | Windows NT NTFS (read-only) |
| sysv | SystemV/Xenix/Coherent FS |
| hpfs | OS/2 HPFS |
| affs | Amiga FFS Filesystem |
| ufs | Sun |
| udf | CD R/W, DVD |
| hfs | Apple MacIntosh Filesystem (HFS) |
| hfs+ | Apple MacIntosh Extended HFS. |
| befs | BeOS filesystem. |
| bfs | SCO Unixware Boot filesystem. |
| jffs, jffs2 | Journalling Flash File Systems |
| vxfs | Veritas VxFS, used on SCO Unixware |
| iso9660 | cdrom etc., including Joliet extensions |
| cramfs | Compressed read only file system. |
| romfs | Small read-only file system. |
| tmpfs | Ram disk that is swappable. |
| ramfs | Ram disk, for example of a file system. |
| gfs2 | Clustering filesystem from **Red Hat**. |
| nfs | Network File System (through version 4) |
| smb | Samba networking |
| ncp | Novell Netware FS using NCP Protocol |
| coda | Experimental distributed filesystem |
| afs | *Andrew* distributed filesystem, from Carnegie Mellon. |
| ocfs2 | Extent-based, disk cluster filesystem from **Oracle**. |

Some filesystem types, especially non-**Unix** based ones, may require more manipulation in order to be represented in the **VFS**.

For instance variants such as **vfat** do not have distinct read/write/execute permissions for the owner/group/world fields; the **VFS** has to make an assumption about how to specify distinct permissions for the three types of user, and such behaviour can be influenced by mounting operations.

Even more drastically, such filesystems store information about files in a File Allocation Table (FAT) at the beginning of the disk, rather than in the directories themselves, a basically different architectural method.

## 9.3    The ext2/ext3 Filesystem

The native filesystems for **Linux** are **ext2** and its **journalling** descendants, **ext3** and **ext4**.

Note that the **ext3** filesystem has the same **on-disk** layout as the **ext2** filesystem, the only important difference between the presence of a log file. Thus **ext3** filesystems can be mounted as **ext2** when convenient, such as when running a kernel which does not have **ext3** support.

The **ext3** filesystem has the following limits:

Table 9.3: **ext3 filesystem limits**

| Parameter | Value |
|---|---|
| Maximum Filesystem Size | 2TB |
| Maximum File Size | 2TB |
| Maximum Filename Length | 255 characters |

### Basic Filesystem Concepts

**Inodes:** Each file is represented by a structure called an inode, containing file type, access rights, owners, timestamps, size, and pointers to data blocks. Addresses of data blocks are stored in the inode. Each inode is indexed by a number which is unique per filesystem.

**Blocks:** A file's contents are kept in a linked list of **blocks**, whose size can be set when the filesystem is formatted. The block size can not be bigger than a page of memory, 4 KB on most architectures. For large filesystems, 4 KB is used by default, and for small filesystems, 1 KB. This is different from the hardware sector size, which is usually 512 bytes.

**Directories:** These are maintained in a hierarchical tree with files and subdirectories. A directory is actually a file containing a list of inodes and file names.

**Links:** Several names can be associated with an **inode**. (The inode contains a counter of the links to a inode.) This is called a **hard** link, and cannot be used for directories. **Symbolic** or **soft** links are files which contain a filename, can be used across filesystems, and for directories. Extremely useful.

**Device special files:** special file, uses no space, is only an access point to a device driver, generally under /dev. Block and character special files. Special files have both a major number (device type) and a minor number (unit). Note that a device node requires a small amount of disk space for the inode, but occupies no data blocks.

**Reserved Space:** Usually, 5 percent of the blocks (usually 4 KB in size) are reserved for **root**, to help with screw-ups where filesystem gets filled by a user. (This allocation can be changed with the **tune2fs** utility, without reformatting the filesystem.)

**State:** A field in the superblock indicates "Clean," "Not Clean" or "Erroneous." Used to see if **fsck** should be run at boot.

**Physical Structure:** Details of the disk structure can be viewed with the **dumpe2fs** utility. The structure looks like:

— Boot Sector — Block Group 1 — Block Group 2 — ... — Block Group N —

Each block group looks like:

| Super Block | Group Descriptors | Data Block Bitmap | Inode Bitmap | Inode Table (n blocks) | Data Blocks (n blocks) |
|---|---|---|---|---|---|

Figure 9.1: **ext3 filesystem layout**

The superblock and and filesystem descriptors are redundant in multiple block groups, which is great for safety. (Note block groups may not be tied to physical layout of the disk.)

**mkfs.ext2, mkfs.ext3** makes the filesystem. Checking the filesystem is done with **fsck.ext2, fsck.ext3**. **De-fragmentation** is generally neither necessary nor recommended. **fdisk** is the partitioning program; use with great care!

You can shrink or expand a partition with **resize2fs**, but be careful as it does not change the actual partition table; see the **man** page for details about how to do this in concert with **fdisk**. There are good graphical utilities, such as **gparted** which can reliably take care of the complications. Additionally many parameters can be reset or tuned after filesystem creation with the program **tune2fs**.

# 9.4 Journalling Filesystems

**Journalling** filesystems recover from system crashes or ungraceful shutdowns with little or no corruption, and they do so very rapidly. While this comes at the price of having some more operations to do, additional enhancements can more than offset the price.

In a journalling filesystem operations are grouped into **transactions**. A transaction must be completed without error, **atomically**; otherwise the filesystem is not changed. A log file is maintained of transactions. When an error occurs usually only the last transaction needs to be examined.

The following five journalling filesystems are freely available under **Linux**:

- The **ext3** filesystem is an extension of the **ext2** filesystem.

- The **ext4** filesystem is an extension of the **ext3** filesystem, and was included in the mainline kernel first as an experimental branch, and then as a stable production feature in kernel 2.6.28. Features include extents, 48-bit block numbers, and up to 16 TB size.

- The **Reiser** filesystem was the first journalling implementation in **Linux**, but has lost its leadership and development has stalled.

- The **JFS** filesystem is a product of **IBM** and has been ported from **IBM**'s **AIX** operating system.

- The **XFS** filesystem is a product of **SGI** and has ported from **SGI**'s **IRIX** operating systems. The main home page is **http://oss.sgi.com/projects/xfs**.

## 9.5   The ext4/ Filesystem

The **ext4** filesystem had its experimental designation removed with the 2.6.28 kernel release. Pre-existing **ext3** partitions can be migrated in place to **ext4** without risk; the new features will only be used in subsequent file system operations. However, one can not safely go back to **ext3** at a later time.

Maximum filesytem size has been increased to 1 EB from 16 TB, and maximum file size goes up to 16 TB from 2 TB. These limits arise from the 48-bit addressing that is used; full 64-bit addressing is probably in the future but not really needed at this point. The number of subdirectories, which was limited to 32 K, now has no limit.

Large files are now split into **extents** as large as possible, instead of using indirect block mapping. In addition, **multiblock** allocation can allocate space all at once instead of one block at a time. **Delayed allocation** can also increase performance.

One immediately obvious improvement is **fast fsck**. The speed of a filesystem check can easily go up by an order of magnitude or more.

There are some other new features for which introductory documentation can be found at: **http://kernelnewbies.org/Ext4**.

In order to use **ext4** you need a kernel for which it is compiled, and the newer version of the **e2fsprogs** utilities in order to have utilities including **mkfs.ext4, fsck.ext4, e4label, tune4fs, dumpe4s,** etc. Most recent **Linux** distributions have already taken this step. Depending on the distribution one may have to install **e4fsprogs**, or the **e2fsprogs** package may have been updated to handle **ext4**.

# 9.6   Labs

## Lab 1: Using the loopback Filesystem

The **loopback** filesystem driver can be used to mount a file to be used as a hard disk image. This can be very useful for mounting **CD** or **DVD** images as filesystems as well as for simulating or learning about various types of filesystems.

First you'll have to create a file to use for the image and it is best to fill it with zeros by doing:

```
# create a 200 MB loopback file

$ dd if=/dev/zero of=/tmp/fsimage bs=1024 count=204800
```

We can then create an **ext3** filesystem on it with:

```
$ mkfs.ext3 /tmp/fsimage
```

and mount it (as **root**) with:

```
$ mkdir /tmp/mnt
$ mount -o loop /tmp/fsimage /tmp/mnt
```

and one can verify its mounting and check capacity with:

```
$ df /tmp/mnt

Filesystem    Type    1K-blocks       Used Available Use% Mounted on
/tmp/fsimage  ext3       198337       5664    182433  4% /tmp/mnt
```

You may now go ahead and create files, read and write them etc. Such files will survive unmounting (with **umount  /tmp/mnt**) and remounting in any location.

You can do this with other filesystem types as long as you have both kernel support for them (examine **/proc/filesystems**) and the appropriate tool for formatting, such as **mkfs.ext4** or **mkfs.vfat**, etc.

# Chapter 10

# File I/O

We'll learn how to open, close, read, write and reposition a file using low-level systems calls. We will discuss the positional I/O calls (**pread(), pwrite()** and vector I/O calls (**readv(), writev()**.) We will then learn how to do the same operations using high-level standard library functions.

## 10.1  Unix File I/O

The basic file operations are opening and closing, reading and writing, and positioning within a file. Only a few functions are needed to perform these basic I/O operations under **Linux**: open(), close(), read(), write(), and lseek(). These basic file operations are **unbuffered**, unlike the *standard I/O* functions we will discuss later.

**Unix** I/O is **not** part of the ANSI **C** specification, and sometimes elementary textbooks either neglect it or recommend not using it. However, it is basic to programming on any **Unix**-like operating system, and such advice should be ignored.

Files are referenced using **file descriptors**, which are simple non-negative integers, not the *FILE stream type used in the standard I/O library.

Three file descriptors are connected by default and do not have to be opened and closed explicitly:

Table 10.1: **Predefined Unix I/O descriptors**

| Name | Symbolic Name | Value |
|------|---------------|-------|
| standard input | STDIN_FILENO | 0 |
| standard output | STDOUT_FILENO | 1 |
| standard error | STDERR_FILENO | 2 |

Full **POSIX** conformance requires the use of the symbolic names, but many programs use the actual values which are always used.

## 10.2   Opening and Closing

The following functions open and close files for **Unix** I/O:

```
#include <unistd.h>
#include <fcntl.h>
#include <sys/types.h>
#include <sys/stat.h>

int open  (const char *pathname, int flags, mode_t mode);
int creat (const char *pathname, mode_t mode);
int close (int fd);
```

When successful, `open()` returns a file descriptor for the file (or device) referenced by `pathname`. The third argument, `mode`, is needed only when a new file is created.

The `flags` argument must have one of the mandatory values:

Table 10.2: **Main open() flags**

| Flag | Meaning |
|------|---------|
| O_RDONLY | Read-only access. |
| O_WRONLY | Write-only access. |
| O_RDWR | Read/write access. |

which may be bitwise-OR'ed with one or more of the following optional values:

Table 10.3: **Additional open() flags**

| Flag | Meaning |
|---|---|
| O_CREAT | Create the file if it doesn't exist. |
| O_EXCL | If used with O_CREAT fail if the file already exists. |
| O_NOCTTY | If pathname is a terminal device, it will not become the processes' controlling terminal. |
| O_TRUNC | Truncate the file to 0 length if it already exists. |
| O_APPEND | Append to the end on each write. |
| O_NONBLOCK | Calling process won't wait. |
| O_SYNC | Each write() will wait for the physical I/O to finish. |
| O_NOFOLLOW | Fail if the file is a symbolic link. |
| O_DIRECTORY | Fail if the file is not a directory. |

In addition, there are additional non-standard flags (such as O_DIRECT) that can also be applied.

The older function call creat() is the same as calling open() with flags set equal to O_CREAT | O_WRONLY | O_TRUNC.

When a file is created, permissions are set by the mode argument. (Permissions may be modified by the process's umask; i.e., the permissions will be mode & ~umask.) The following values may be used:

Table 10.4: **File permissions for open()**

| Mode | Value | Meaning |
|---|---|---|
| S_IRWXU | 00700 | Owner can read/write, execute. |
| S_IRUSR (S_IREAD) | 00400 | Owner can read. |
| S_IWUSR (S_IWRITE) | 00200 | Owner can write. |
| S_IXUSR (S_IEXEC) | 00100 | Owner can execute. |
| S_IRWXG | 00070 | Group can read/write, execute. |
| S_IRGRP | 00040 | Group can read. |
| S_IWGRP | 00020 | Group can write. |
| S_IXGRP | 00010 | Group can execute. |
| S_IRWXO | 00007 | Others can read/write, execute. |
| S_IROTH | 00004 | Others can read. |
| S_IWOTH | 00002 | Others can write. |
| S_IXOTH | 00001 | Others can execute. |

open() returns the new file descriptor on success, and -1 on error (errno is set). The possible error returns are:

Table 10.5: **open() error return values**

| Value | Meaning |
|---|---|
| EEXIST | pathname already exists; O_CREAT and O_EXCL were used. |
| EISDIR | pathname is a directory and write access is requested. |
| EACCES | Access permission denied. |
| ENAMETOOLONG | pathname was too long. |
| ENOENT | Part of pathname does not exist, or is a dangling symbolic link. |
| ENOTDIR | Part of pathname is not a directory or O_DIRECTORY was requested and it is not a directory. |
| ENXIO | O_NONBLOCK \| O_WRONLY set, the file is a FIFO, but is not open for reading. Or the special device file doesn't exist. |
| ENODEV | pathname is a device file that doesn't exist. |
| ENOFS | pathname is on a read only filesystem and write access was requested. |
| ETXTBSY | pathname is an executable image to which write permission was requested. |
| EFAULT | pathname points to an illegal address. |
| ELOOP | Too many symbolic links, or hit O_NOFOLLOW flag. |
| ENOSPC | No room to create pathname. |
| ENOMEM | Not enough kernel memory available. |
| EMFILE | Maximum number of files already open. |
| ENFILE | System has reached its total file number limit. |

close() releases a file descriptor so it loses association with any file and may be reused. All file locks are released. If unlink() has been used on the file and this is the last file descriptor currently in use that references it, the file will be deleted.

On success close() returns 0; on failure it returns -1, with errno set to EBADF, which means fd was not a valid file descriptor. Terminating processes implicitly call close() on all open file descriptors.

# 10.3   Reading, Writing and Seeking

These three functions access a file descriptor already obtained through open():

```
#include <unistd.h>
#include <sys/types.h>

ssize_t read  (int fd, void *buf, size_t count);
ssize_t write (int fd, const void *buf, size_t count);
off_t   lseek (int fd, off_t offset, int whence);
```

read() gets count bytes from file descriptor fd and places them into buf.

On success, read() returns the number of bytes read and the file position is advanced appropriately. If this is non-negative, but less than count, it means fewer bytes are presently available due either to an end-of-file, no more data present on a read from a pipe or a terminal, or interruption by a signal.

On error, `read()` returns -1, the file position is indeterminate, and `errno` is set. The possible error returns are:

Table 10.6: **read() error return values**

| Value | Meaning |
| --- | --- |
| EINTR | Interrupted by a signal before any data read. |
| EAGAIN | O_NONBLOCK specified and data not immediately available for reading. |
| EIO | I/O error: a background process tries to read a `tty` or a low level error from a disk or tape. |
| EISDIR | `fd` is a directory. |
| EBADF | invalid file descriptor or not open for reading. |
| EINVAL | `fd` is not an object suitable for reading. |
| EFAULT | `buf` is not in the process's address space. |

`write()` writes `count` bytes to file descriptor `fd` from `buf`.

On success, `write()` returns the number of bytes written and the file position is advanced appropriately. On error, `write()` returns -1, the file position is indeterminate, and `errno` is set. The possible error returns are:

Table 10.7: **write() error return values**

| Value | Meaning |
| --- | --- |
| EINTR | Interrupted by a signal before any data written. |
| EAGAIN | O_NONBLOCK specified and no room immediately available in the pipe or socket `fd` is connected to. |
| EIO | a low level error occurred while modifying the inode. |
| EBADF | invalid file descriptor or not open for writing. |
| EINVAL | `fd` is not an object suitable for writing. |
| EFAULT | `buf` is not in the process's address space. |
| EPIPE | `fd` is connected to a pipe or socket whose reading end is closed. |

Note both `read()` and `write()` may produce other errors, depending on exactly what kind of object is connected to `fd`.

`lseek()` repositions the offset of `fd` to `offset` relative to the `whence` parameter, which can have the following values:

Table 10.8: **Values for whence in lseek()**

| Value | Meaning |
|-------|---------|
| SEEK_SET | From the beginning of the file. |
| SEEK_CUR | From the current location. |
| SEEK_END | From the end of the file. |

In general `lseek()` can be used only on regular files, not on streams like pipes, sockets, or FIFO's.

On success `lseek()` returns the resulting offset from the beginning of the file. Otherwise it returns `(off_t) -1` and `errno` is set. The possible error returns are:

Table 10.9: **lseek() error return values**

| Value | Meaning |
|-------|---------|
| EBADF | Invalid file descriptor. |
| ESPIPE | File descriptor associated with a pipe, socket or FIFO. |
| EINVAL | `whence` has an improper value. |

## 10.4   Positional and Vector I/O

We have by no means exhausted the entire list of I/O related functions in the unbuffered **Unix** I/O **API**. In particular we call attention to what we will term as **positional** and **vector** I/O.:

The positional I/O functions are:

```
#define _XOPEN_SOURCE 500

#include <unistd.h>

ssize_t pread  (int fd, void *buf, size_t count, off_t offset);
ssize_t pwrite (int fd, const void *buf, size_t count, off_t offset);
```

In additional to the usual I/O arguments, the `pread()` and `pwrite()` functions require one more, the offset from which the I/O should begin. They do not advance the offset, unlike normal reads and writes. They are useful, for instance, in multi-threaded programs where the file position may not be well known since it is shared in all threads.

The vector I/O functions are:

```
#include <sys/uio.h>
ssize_t readv  (int fd, const struct iovec *vector, int count);
ssize_t writev (int fd, const struct iovec *vector, int count);
```

```
struct iovec {
   void *iov_base;    /* Starting address */
   size_t iov_len;    /* Number of bytes */
};
```

These functions perform a gather/scatter I/O operation on a chain of buffers in one system call, instead of a series of system calls for each buffer, and can lead to enhanced efficiency.

## 10.5  Standard I/O Library

The standard I/O library is part of the ANSI **C** standard and allows for formatted I/O. We won't discuss these functions in detail as they are easily documented as part of ANSI C.

A file is represented as an I/O **stream**. Three streams are pre-opened and pre-defined to correspond to file descriptors:

Table 10.10: **Predefined standard I/O streams**

| Name | Symbolic Name | File Descriptor |
|------|---------------|-----------------|
| standard input | stdin | 0 |
| standard output | stdout | 1 |
| standard error | stderr | 2 |

The basic functions are:

```
#include <stdio.h>

FILE *fopen (char *path, char *mode);
FILE *fdopen (int fildes,char *mode);
FILE *freopen (char *path, char *mode, FILE *stream);
int fileno (FILE *stream);

int fclose (FILE *stream);

int fseek (FILE *stream, long offset, int whence);
long ftell (FILE *stream);

int fprintf (FILE *stream, const char *format, ...);
int printf (const char *format, ...);
int scanf (const char *format, ...);
int fscanf (FILE *stream, const char *format, ...);

size_t fread ( void *ptr, size_t size, size_t nmemb, FILE *stream);
size_t fwrite (void *ptr, size_t size, size_t nmemb, FILE *stream);

int  fflush   (FILE *stream);
```

```
int  feof    (FILE *stream);
int  ferror  (FILE *stream);
void clearerr (FILE *stream);
```

The FILE structure is not meant to be poked into.

All I/O is buffered; the size of the buffer depends on the implementation of **glibc** and the file utilities. On recent **Linux** systems the buffer size is 512 bytes; on older systems it was equal to the page size (4 KB on **x86**).

Note that you **can mix** Unix and standard I/O functions. The function fdopen() gives you a pointer to a **file** stream given an integer file descriptor, while the function fileno() performs the inverse operation.

## 10.6   Large File Support (LFS)

Normally 32-bit systems can not handle files greater than 2 GB in size (64-bit systems are not so limited.)

**Linux** permits this through use of the **LFS** system (**L**arge **F**ile **S**upport), which requires cooperation from the kernel, in particular for each kind of filesystem, and from **libc**. All major modern filesystems under use in **Linux** now support this.

There is more than one way to use **LFS**:

- If you compile your program with:

  `gcc -D_FILE_OFFSET_BITS=64 -D_LARGEFILE_SOURCE ....`

  **all** file access is 64-bit. You need to be careful with this as all the standard system calls are migrated to their 64-bit variants (e.g., open() becomes open64()). In addition types change; e.g., off_t becomes off64_t. Thus one had better not use an **int** instead of an off_t type anywhere.

- You can compile your program with:

  `gcc -D_LARGEFILE_SOURCE -D_LARGEFILE64_SOURCE ....`

  Then you can use **LFS** functions directly, like open64 on a file-by-file basis.

- You can open your files with the O_LARGEFILE flag on a file-by-file basis. This approach is not preferred as it is less portable.

Note that the first approach requires no change in the program source.

While larger then 2 GB file offsets are allowed, note that the ssize_t data type returned by the I/O functions is still just a 32-bit quantity. Thus you can't accomplish a humongous read or write with just one system call, but of course there is no need to do so.

Detailed documentation can be gotten by doing **info libc**.

## 10.7   Labs

### Lab 1: Files

Write a program that opens an existing file for read-only and displays it in hex.

Use the **Unix** API (not ANSI C) for file I/O.

You can check your results with **hexdump**, but be careful about byte-swapping; try `hexdump -C`.

### Lab 2: Files With Offset

Modify Lab 1 to start that hex display at a file offset specified as a parameter.

### Lab 3: Using the Standard I/O Library

Implement the previous lab using the standard I/O library instead of Unix I/O to see the differences.

### Lab 4: Using pread() and pwrite()

Write a program that uses `pread()` and `pwrite()`. Obtain the offset within the file using `lseek()` after each I/O operation and verify that it does not change.

Using `pwrite()` fill up a file with distinguishable values depending on position. Then read them back and verify their contents.

### Lab 5: Using readv() and writev()

Write a program that uses `readv()` and `writev()`.

Fill up a series of buffers with distinguishable values and write them to a file. Then read them back and verify their contents.

# Chapter 11

# Advanced File Operations

We'll learn to use a variety of advanced file operation functions, including how to get detailed information about a file, directory reading and manipulation and monitoring file changes with **inotify**. We'll also discuss file locking, using the **fcntl()** and **ioctl()** functions, and the **dup()** functions, and creating and inquiring about symbolic links. We'll also discuss using temporary files.

## 11.1 Stat Functions

Several related functions are available for gathering information about specified files:

```
#include <sys/stat.h>
#include <unistd.h>

int stat  (const char *file, struct stat *buf);
int lstat (const char *file, struct stat *buf);
int fstat (int fd, struct stat *buf);
```

stat() fills in the structure pointed to by the buf argument with information about file.

lstat() is identical to stat(), except only the **link** is looked at, not the file obtained by tracing links.

fstat() is identical to stat(), except it uses the file descriptor fd, instead of the file name.

While access rights are not needed to get a file's status, search rights must exist for the directories in the path leading to the file.

The **stat** structure contains the following fields:

```
struct stat
  {
        dev_t          st_dev;       /* device */
        ino_t          st_ino;       /* inode */
        mode_t         st_mode;      /* protection */
        nlink_t        st_nlink;     /* number of hard links */
        uid_t          st_uid;       /* user ID of owner */
        gid_t          st_gid;       /* group ID of owner */
        dev_t          st_rdev;      /* device type (if inode device) */
        off_t          st_size;      /* total size, in bytes */
        unsigned long  st_blksize;   /* blocksize for filesystem I/O */
        unsigned long  st_blocks;    /* number of blocks allocated */
        time_t         st_atime;     /* time of last access */
        time_t         st_mtime;     /* time of last modification */
        time_t         st_ctime;     /* time of last change */
  };
```

Some fields in this structure may not be implemented for some supported filesystems; e.g., **DOS** filesystems have only limited permission fields.

Note that the st_mtime field gives the time when the file's contents were last modified, while the st_ctime field gives the time the inode information was changed, such as owner, group, mode, etc.

Strangely enough, **stat**'ing the file does not change the stored access time.

The file type can be checking with the following (**POSIX**) macros:

Table 11.1: **stat() file type macros**

| Macro | Meaning |
|---|---|
| S_ISLNK(st_mode) | Symbolic link? |
| S_ISREG(st_mode) | Regular file? |
| S_ISDIR(st_mode) | Directory? |
| S_ISCHR(st_mode) | Character device? |

| `S_ISBLK(st_mode)` | Block device? |
| `S_ISFIFO(st_mode)` | FIFO? |
| `S_ISSOCK(st_mode)` | Socket? |

For example, you may want to do certain operations only if the object is a directory:

```
#include <sys/stat.h>
#include <unistd.h>
...
struct stat filestat;
...
 rc = stat (argv[1], &filestat)
 if ( S_ISDIR(filestat.st_mode) ) {
     / * Do directory operations */
}
...
```

The following flags are defined for the **st_mode** field in the **stat** structure:

Table 11.2: **stat() st_mode macros**

| Symbolic name | Value | Meaning |
|---|---|---|
| `S_IFMT` | 00170000 | Bit-mask for the file type bit-fields (not POSIX) |
| `S_IFSOCK` | 0140000 | Socket (not POSIX) |
| `S_IFLNK` | 0120000 | Symbolic link (not POSIX) |
| `S_IFREG` | 0100000 | Regular file (not POSIX) |
| `S_IFBLK` | 0060000 | Block device (not POSIX) |
| `S_IFDIR` | 0040000 | Directory (not POSIX) |
| `S_IFCHR` | 0020000 | Character device (not POSIX) |
| `S_IFIFO` | 0010000 | FIFO (not POSIX) |
| `S_ISUID` | 0004000 | Set UID bit |
| `S_ISGID` | 0002000 | Set GID bit |
| `S_ISVTX` | 0001000 | Sticky bit (not POSIX) |
| `S_IRWXU` | 00700 | User (file owner) has read, write and execute permission |
| `S_IRUSR` | 00400 | User has read permission (same as `S_IREAD`, which is not POSIX) |
| `S_IWUSR` | 00200 | User has write permission (same as `S_IWRITE`, which is not POSIX) |
| `S_IXUSR` | 00100 | User has execute permission (same as `S_IEXEC`, which is not POSIX) |
| `S_IRWXG` | 00070 | Group has read, write and execute permission |
| `S_IRGRP` | 00040 | Group has read permission |
| `S_IWGRP` | 00020 | Group has write permission |
| `S_IXGRP` | 00010 | Group has execute permission |
| `S_IRWXO` | 00007 | Others have read, write and execute permission |

| S_IROTH | 00004 | Others have read permission |
| S_IWOTH | 00002 | Others have write permission |
| S_IXOTH | 00001 | Others have execute permission |

On success these functions return 0. On error, they return -1 and **errno** is set. The possible error returns are:

Table 11.3: **stat() error return values**

| Value | Meaning |
|---|---|
| EBADF | Bad file descriptor **fd**. |
| ENOENT | Defective file name. |
| ENOTDIR | Part of the path is not a directory. |
| ELOOP | Too many symbolic links encountered. |
| EFAULT | Bad address. |
| EACCES | Permission denied. |
| ENAMETOOLONG | File name too long. |

## 11.2   Directory Functions

The following functions operate on directories:

```
#include <unistd.h>
#include <sys/stat.h>
#include <sys/types.h>
#include <dirent.h>
#include <fcntl.h>

DIR *opendir (const char *name);
int closedir (DIR *dir);
struct dirent *readdir (DIR *dir);
void rewinddir (DIR *dir);

int  mkdir   (const char *pathname, mode_t mode);
int  rmdir   (const char *pathname);
int  chdir   (const char *path);
char *getcwd (char *buf, size_t size);

struct dirent
   {
     long           d_ino;    /* inode number */
     off_t          d_off;    /* offset to this dirent */
     unsigned short d_reclen; /* length of this d_name */
```

```
    char                d_name[NAME_MAX+1];/*file name (null-terminated)*/
  }
```

where NAME_MAX=255.

The dirent structure varies a lot among different **Unix** implementations. The only element you can depend on is **d_name**; you are best advised not to use the others.

opendir() opens a directory and establishes a directory stream, returning a pointer to it. The stream is positioned at the first entry in the directory.

closedir() closes a directory stream and frees up resources associated with it.

readdir() returns a pointer to the next directory entry in the directory stream. Successive calls return further entries. Note that there is no ordering and that NULL is returned when there are no more entries in the directory.

rewinddir() resets the directory stream to the beginning.

mkdir() creates a directory and specifies permission through the mode argument.

rmdir() deletes a directory, which must be empty.

chdir() changes the working directory. A related function is fchdir(int fd), which is the same except the directory is given as an open file descriptor.

getcwd() gets the current working directory, and puts it in buf, which is of length size. The alternate function char *get_current_dir_name(void) is prototyped only if __USE_GNU is defined. The alternate function char *getwd(char *buf) is prototyped only if __USE_BSD is defined. These functions differ in how they malloc() the name buffer.

See the **man** pages for the returns and possible errors for these functions, which are quite straightforward.

## 11.3   Inotify

**Inotify** provides an easy way to monitor changes in files and directories. It is a kernel subsystem that issues notifications of events.

With **inotify** interested programs can take note when a file or directory is created or removed, read or written, has its attributions changed, etc., without having to resort to actually interrogating directories and files through some kind of polling mechanism.

The API is simple and includes the functions:

```
#include <sys/inotify.h>

int inotify_init (void);
int inotify_add_watch (int fd, const char *pathname, uint32_t mask);
int inotify_rm_watch (intfd, uint32_t wd);
```

First one calls inotify_init() which returns an integer file descriptor, which is then passed as the first argument to inotify_add_watch(). The pathname points to either a directory or file name; if it is a directory the **inotify** system will monitor all entries in the directory.

The `mask` argument specifies which kinds of events are to be monitored. Some of the main bits that can be set are:

Table 11.4: **inotify() mask bits**

| Bit | Meaning |
| --- | --- |
| IN_ACCESS | File was accessed. |
| IN_ATTRIB | File metadata was changed (attributes, timestamps, etc.). |
| IN_CLOSE_WRITE | File open for writing was closed. |
| IN_CLOSE_NOWRITE | File not open for writing was closed. |
| IN_CREATE | File/directory was created. |
| IN_DELETE | File/directory was deleted. |
| IN_OPEN | File was opened. |
| IN_MOVE | File/directory was moved. |

In addition the value `IN_ALL_EVENTS` can be used to turn on all the event bits.

The return value of `intoify_add_watch` is a non-negative **watch descriptor**, which labels the entry being watched.

The `inotify_rm_watch()` function removes the watch for the watch descriptor returned by `inotify_add_watch()`.

To get access to events as they occur one has to read from the file descriptor returned by `inotify_init()`. This can be done through various **polling** mechanisms such as `select()`, `poll()` and `epoll()` or through a simple `read()`, which will block until one or more events are registered.

Such a read returns a buffer containing an array of structures (one for each event) of type:

```
struct inotify_event {
    int      wd;       /* Watch descriptor */
    uint32_t mask;     /* Mask of events */
    uint32_t cookie;   /* Unique cookie associating related
                          events (for rename(2)) */
    uint32_t len;      /* Size of "name" field */
    char     name[];   /* Optional null-terminated name */
};
```

The actual length of the read for each event is given by:

```
sizeof (struct inotify_event) + len;
```

The kind of event is returned in `mask`.

The **inotify** mechanism is unique to **Linux** and is not portable to other operating systems.

## 11.4   Memory Mapping

Through use of the `mmap()` function regions of a file may be mapped directly to memory.

Access may be done through memory references rather than read/write functions. If permissions are appropriate more than one process may share the mapping simultaneously.

Mapping and unmapping are done with:

```
#include <unistd.h>
#include <sys/mman.h>

void *mmap (void *start, size_t length, int prot, int flags, int fd, off_t offset);
int munmap (void *start, size_t length);
```

The `mmap()` function maps `length` bytes starting at `offset` bytes from the beginning of the file referred to by `fd`. (The offset must be an integral number of **pages**, or an error occurs.)  Success yields a pointer to the memory mapped region, and `MAP_FAILED` on failure.

You use `mmap()` like you would a call to `malloc()`: i.e.,

```
char *buf, *buf2;
int nbytes;
...
buf  = mmap (NULL, nbytes, ...);
buf2 = malloc(nbytes)
....
memcpy (buf,buf2,nbytes);
....
munmap (buf, nbytes);
free (buf2);
```

The argument `start` gives a preferred address; usually 0 (or `NULL`) should be given and the system will furnish the address where the mapping occurs as a return value. If this argument is given, it must be page aligned and not already in use.

The `prot` argument can be:

### Table 11.5: mmap() protection values

| Value | Meaning |
|---|---|
| PROT_READ | Mapped pages may be read. |
| PROT_WRITE | Mapped pages may be written. |
| PROT_EXEC | Mapped pages may be executed. |
| PROT_NONE | Mapped pages may not be accessed. |

The protection must agree with the access flags used when the file was opened; e.g., you can't write to a file opened with `O_RDONLY`.

The `flags` argument can have the following values:

Table 11.6: mmap() flags

| Flag | Meaning |
|---|---|
| MAP_FIXED | If the specified address can not be used, fail. |
| MAP_SHARED | Share with other processes. Writes are written back to the file. |
| MAP_PRIVATE | Create a private copy-on-write mapping. |

Either `MAP_SHARED` or `MAP_PRIVATE` must be specified.

Note that a **private** mapping does not change the file on disk. Whatever changes are made will be lost when the process terminates.

Other non-POSIX flags can be specified (see **man mmap.**) In particular, the `MAP_ANONYMOUS` flag permits a mapping only in memory, without a file association.

`munmap()` releases the mapping and causes further references to the mapped address to fail. When the process terminates or begins a new program through an `exec()` call, unmapping is done automatically.

To find out how a given process is using memory mapping, you can do

```
cat /proc/<pid>/maps
```

where you substitute the process ID of any running process. Note a `p` indicates a **private** memory mapping and an `s` indicated a shared one.

This information can be filtered through the **pmap** utility to make it more readable: e.g.,

```
$ pmap -d <pid>
```

## 11.5   flock() and fcntl()

These two functions, `flock()` and `fcntl()` can be used to apply **locking** mechanisms to a file, or a region of a file. In addition `fcntl()` can be used for other purposes as well.

Locking can be **mandatory** or **advisory**; the first blocks all read and write access to a file or an area of a file, except to the owner of the lock. The second kind of lock is effective only when the user bothers to examine the lock on the file, and then permits read and write operations as long as the appropriate lock is set up and then released when done. Mandatory file locking is less efficient because of the extra checks that must be made on all I/O operations, and is not usually done.

By default, locks are advisory. One way to change a lock to mandatory to setting a file's set-group (**sgid**) bit while clearing its group-execute bit. Since this combination makes no sense, the kernel uses the combination as an indication to use mandatory locks.

If one wants to make all locks on a given filesystem mandatory, the filesystem can be mounted (or remounted) with the `MS_MANDLOCK` flag. This, however, requires super-user access `flock()` can apply or remove an advisory lock:

```
#include <sys/file.h>

int flock (int fd, int operation)
```

The file specified by `fd` must be open and `operation` may be:

Table 11.7: **fcntl() flock operations**

| Value | Meaning |
|-------|---------|
| LOCK_SH | More than one process may share the lock. |
| LOCK_EX | Only one process can hold the lock. |
| LOCK_UN | Unlock the file. |
| LOCK_NB | Don't block when locking. Can be OR'ed with other operations. |

On success, 0 is returned; on error −1, with `errno` set. Currently the only error is `EWOULDBLOCK` which means the file is locked and `LOCK_NB` was specified.

`fcntl()` can be used a number of ways to influence or modify the way a file descriptor is used:

```
#include <unistd.h>
#include <fcntl.h>

int fcntl (int fd, int cmd);
int fcntl (int fd, int cmd, long arg);
int fcntl (int fd, int cmd, struct flock * lock);
```

What `fcntl()` does depends on the value of `cmd`:

Table 11.8: **fcntl() commands**

| Value | Meaning |
|-------|---------|
| F_DUPFD | `arg` will be a copy of `fd`, which may be closed first if necessary (equivalent to `dup2()`). The new file descriptor is returned on success. |
| F_GETFD | Obtain the close-on-exec flag; if low order bit is 0 remain open across `exec()`; otherwise close. |
| F_SETFD | Set close-on-exec flag to `arg`'s lowest bit. |
| F_GETFL | Read all the flags of the file descriptor. |
| F_SETFL | Set the file descriptor's flags to `arg`; only `O_APPEND`, `O_NONBLOCK`, `O_ASYNC` may be set. |
| File Locking | |
| F_GETLK | If the file is unlocked set the `l_type` field of the `flock` structure to `F_UNLCK`. If the file is locked fill in the entire `flock` structure with values, not just the `l_type` element. |

| F_SETLK | Set the lock if l_type is F_RDLCK or F_WRLCK, or clear it (F_UNLCK). If somebody already has the lock return immediately with **errno** set to EACCES or EAGAIN. |
|---|---|
| F_SETLKW | Blocking version of F_SETLK. Calling process is put to sleep until the lock is available, or a signal is caught. |

In addition, the commands F_GETOWN, F_SETOWN, F_GETSIG and F_SETSIG can be used to control signals controlling whether input or output is possible; see the man page for details on this and the many error codes.

The flock structure is:

```
struct flock {
    short l_type;   /* type of lock requested */
    short l_whence; /* SEEK_SET, SEEK_CUR, or SEEK_END */
    off_t l_start;  /* off set in bytes, relative to l_whence */
    off_t l_len;    /* length of region to lock; 0 means to EOF */
    pid_t l_pid;    /* with F_GETLK, returns pid of lock owner */
};
```

l_type is F_RDLCK (a shared read lock), F_WRLCK (an exclusive write lock), or F_UNLCK (unlock a region.)

The trio of elements, l_whence, l_start, and l_len, work like the arguments of the lseek() function.

If a file (or region of one) has no locks, it is ok to request a read or a write lock. If a file has any read locks, no write locks can be requested. If a file has any write locks, no locks of any kind can be requested.

**Mandatory** locking is enforced on a file by file basis using a trick; one sets the sgid bit but not the execute bit, as in chmod g+s,g-x foofile. Once this is done:

- If a process has taken out a **read** lock (using fcntl()/lockf()), other processes can read from the region, but none can write to it.

- If a process has taken out a **write** lock other processes can neither read nor write from the region.

Note the other processes do not have to request locks to be affected.

To examine all current file locks on your system you can examine **/proc/locks** noting the first number printed is the process ID.

## 11.6 Making Temporary Files

Often one has a need to generate a temporary file to be used by an application. It is very important that the name of this file be unique so that collisions do not occur.

Another consideration may be that the filename not be easily predictable, so that anyone snooping around the system can compromise its integrity or security. The ancient practice of basing the filename on the process ID (which is unique) suffers from this security hole.

**Linux** provides a variety of functions to accomplish this. They differ in how seriously they take security, how safe they are with regard to race conditions, and historical compatibility with older **Unix**-type operating systems:

```
#include stdlib.h

int mkstemp (char *template);
char *mkdtemp (char *template);
FILE *tmpfile (void);
```

mkstemp() constructs a unique filename from `template`, which must contain XXXXXX for the last six characters. The value of `template` is modified in the filename construction. Thus it can't be a constant string.

This function actually will open the file with the O_EXCL flag, guaranteeing being the only user. It's return value is the file descriptor for the temporary file.

To make a directory use mkdtemp(); the `template` argument is used exactly the same way as in mkstemp().

The above functions do not remove the temporary file when the program completes, either normally or abnormally. Thus you must do an unlink() on the filename, or a rmdir() on the directory name.

The tmpfile() function names an opens a unique file without ever telling you the name. It differs from mkstemp() in that you don't supply a template for the name, and when you are done it is automatically deleted; no unlink() is required.

According to the standard, the temporary file appears in the directory P_tmpdir defined in **/usr/include/stdlib.h**; if that is not defined it goes into **/tmp**, which matches the actual definition in the header file anyway. However, under **Linux** the library substitutes an anonymous memory mapping for a file, and you'll be hard pressed to find the file.

The following functions are considered obsolete but you may find them in legacy code:

```
char *mktemp (char *template);
char *tempnam (const char *dir, const char *pfx);
char *tmpnam (char *s);
```

These functions do not actually create and open the file. This creates a race condition between testing whether a file already exists and opening it that can be a security risk, particularly because old **BSD** versions of some of these functions constructed a filename by simply replacing XXXXXX by a single letter and the process identifier in a predictable way. Thus one should not use these functions and should replace them in legacy code.

---

- The **tmpfs** filesystem (mounted on `/dev/shm`) provides an easy way to generate temporary files that leave no record on the permanent file system.

- This filesystem exists purely in memory (i.e., it is a ramdisk) and creating temporary files in this location can lead to significant performance boosts, since no actual disk operations are required. No special permissions are needed to create, use and remove files under `/dev/shm` and they can be easily removed after use and disappear automatically on reboot.

---

## 11.7   Other System Calls

### ioctl()

This function (whose name stands for Input/Output Control) is a multi-purpose system call which can be used to control a particular device or class of device:

```
#include <sys/ioctl.h>

int ioctl (int fd, int command, char *argp...);
```

The `command` parameter controls what the `ioctl()` will do and has to be known to the hardware or software device which has already been opened and is connected to file descriptor `fd`.

The third argument is really a pointer whose meaning depends on the `command`. For many commands it is unused.

On success 0 is returned, and on error -1 is returned with **errno** set. The possible error returns are:

Table 11.10: **ioctl() error return values**

| Value | Meaning |
|--------|------------------------------------------------------------------|
| EBADF | Bad file descriptor `fd`. |
| ENOTTYF | File descriptor `fd` not associated with a character special device. |
| EINVAL | Invalid `command` or `argp`. |

### dup(), dup2()

These functions duplicate file descriptors:

```
#include <unistd.h>
```

```
int dup  (int oldfd);
int dup2 (int oldfd, int newfd);
```

File descriptor `oldfd` is duplicated and the old and new descriptors may be used interchangeably, and share locks, pointers and flags.

**dup()** uses the lowest-numbered unused descriptor for the new descriptor, while **dup2()** makes `newfd` be the copy of `oldfd`, closing `newfd` first if necessary.

On success the new descriptor is returned, and on error `-1` is returned with `errno` set. The possible error returns are:

Table 11.11: **dup(), dup2() error return values**

| Value | Meaning |
|-------|---------|
| EBADF | `oldfd` is not an open file descriptor, or `newfd` is out of the allowed range. |
| ENFILE | Maximum number of file descriptors would be exceeded. |

An example in the use of `dup()` would be:

```
fd = open (.....);
close (STDOUT_FILENO);
dup (fd);
```

This redirects standard output to file descriptor `fd`.

## link(), symlink(), unlink(), readlink()

These functions deal with symbolic links and with deleting files.

```
int link    (const char *oldpath, const char *newpath);
int symlink  (const char *oldpath, const char *newpath);
int readlink (const char *path, char *buf, size_t bufsiz);
int unlink  (const char *pathname);
```

`link()` creates a hard link (a new name) to an existing file. If `newpath` exists it won't be overwritten. The new name and the old name may be used interchangeably.

`symlink()` creates a symbolic link. If `newpath` exists it won't be overwritten. Permissions are irrelevant; the link may also be *dangling*.

These functions return `0` on success and `-1` on failure with `errno` set. The possible error returns are:

Table 11.12: **symlink(), link() error return values**

| Value | Meaning |
|-------|---------|
| EPERM | The filesystem containing newpath does not support symbolic links. (symlink() only.) |
| EFAULT | One of the paths is an invalid memory reference. |
| EACCES | No write access for newpath directory. |
| ENAMETOOLONG | Name too long. |
| ENOENT | newpath directory improper of dangling, or oldpath is an empty string. |
| ENOTDIR | newpath is not a directory. |
| ENOMEM | Insufficient memory available. |
| EROFS | newpath is on a read-only filesystem. |
| EEXIST | newpath already exists. |
| ELOOP | Too many symbolic links. |
| ENOSPC | No room for the directory entry on the device. |
| EIO | I/O error occurred. |
| EXDEV | oldpath and newpath are not on the same filesystem. (link() only.) |
| EMLINK | File referred to by oldpath already has too many links. (link() only.) |

readlink() places the contents of the symbolic link path in buf, returning the number of characters placed in buf. Error returns are similar to those of symlink().

unlink() removes a file. If the name is a symbolic link, the link is removed but not the underlying file. If the name is a link to a file being used, the file will not be deleted until the last file descriptor referring to it is released. On success 0 is returned, on error -1 with errno set. Error returns are similar to those for link().

## chmod(), chown()

These functions change the ownership and permission of filesystem entries.

```
#include <sys/types.h>
#include <sys/stat.h>
#include <unistd.h>

int chmod (const char *path, mode_t mode);
int chown (const char *path, uid_t owner, gid_t group);
```

chmod() changes the permissions on path, according to mode, which carries the possible values we discussed in reference to the stat() functions.

chown() changes the ownership on path. Only the superuser can change the owner; any user can change the group on a file they own to another group they belong to. Using -1 for either the owner or group ID makes no change for that component.

One can also use int fchmod (int fd, mode_t mode) and fchown (int fd, uid_t owner, gid_t group), which differ only in that a file descriptor is used instead of a path name. lchown() differs only in that it does not follow symbolic links.

## 11.8 Labs

### Lab 1: Directories

Write a program to search a directory and print out the contents. (In other words, write an **ls** program.)

**Optional**: Enhance your code to display file permissions in octal, user/group information in decimal, and the size of the file; i.e., mimic the **-l** option to **ls**. You'll have to play with **stat()** to accomplish this.

### Lab 2: Memory Mapping

Write a program that uses **mmap** to access a file.

Have the program both read and write to the file using memory access rather than read/write functions. (Make sure you work on a file you don't care about!)

### Lab 3: Symbolic links

Write a program to search a directory for symbolic links.

If it finds any, check to see if the link is valid or broken.

### Lab 4: File locking

Write a program to examine file locking.

Arguments may be specified on the command line or from an input file, which say whether the lock should be exclusive or not, whether it should be read or write, and what region of the file (or the whole file) it should apply to.

Run more than one instance of the program simultaneously to examine what happens.

### Lab 5: Making Temporary Files

Write a program that uses **mkstemp()** and **tmpfile()** to create and open temporary files, and **mkdtemp()** for a directory.

While the program is running (you can use **sleep()** do induce a delay) verify the files are created and check their names against the template for **mkstemp()**, **mkdtemp()**. For **tmpnam()** you may want to run your program under **strace** to see what is really happening.

### Lab 6: Using inotify to Monitor a Directory

Use **inotify** to monitory changes to the **/tmp** directory.

When reading events check the bits in the returned mask to see what kinds of events have occurred, when you create files, remove them, read them, change their attributes, etc.

You man want to consult the **man** page for **inotify** to get a complete list of event bits.

# Chapter 12

# Processes - I

We'll learn what **processes** are and what and how limits may be imposed on them. We'll understand the relationship between parent and child processes, and about process groups. We'll examine the **proc** pseudo-filesystem. Finally we'll survey the available methods of inter-process communication.

## 12.1   What is a Process?

A process is an instance of a program in execution. It may be in a number of different states, such as running, sleeping, etc.

Every process has a **pid** (Process ID), a **ppid** (Parent Process ID), and a **pgid** (Process Group ID). In addition every process has program code, data, variables, file descriptors, and an environment.

**init** is usually the first user process run on a system, and thus becomes the ancestor of all subsequent processes running on the system, except for those initiated directly from the kernel, (which show up with [] around their name in a **ps** listing.)

If the parent process dies before the child, the **ppid** of the child is set to 1; i.e., the process is adopted by **init**.

A child process which terminates (either normally or abnormally) before its parent, which has not waited for it and examined its exit code is known as a **zombie** (or defunct) process. Zombies have released almost all resources and remain only to convey their exit status. One function of the **init** process is to check on its adopted children and let those who have terminated die gracefully. Hence it is sometimes knows as the **zombie killer**, or more grimly, the **child reaper**.

We will discuss how to **wait** for a process and interpret its exit status.

Processes are controlled by **scheduling**, which is completely preemptive. Only the kernel has the right to preempt a process; they can't do it to each other.

The following functions are used to obtain **pid**'s, **ppid**'s and **pgid**'s:

```
#include <unistd.h>

pid_t getpid  (void);
pid_t getppid (void);
pid_t getpgid (void);
```

For historical reasons, the largest PID has been limited to a 16-bit number, or 32768. It is possible to alter this value by changing **/proc/sys/kernel/pid_max**, since it may be inadequate for larger servers. As processes are created eventually they will reach `pid_max`, at which point they will start again at `pid = 300`.

On many **Unix**-like operating systems, there may be more than one **thread** per process, each of which shares the same **pid**, but has a unique thread identifier. These threads differ in some characteristics from normal full-weight processes. We will discuss such **light-weight processes** (LWP's) when we discuss multi-threading.

## 12.2   Process Limits

Per-process usage, or resource, limits are described by an array of **rlimit** structures:

```
struct rlimit rlim[RLIM_NLIMITS];
```

This is an array of size `RLIM_NLIMITS=15` of `rlimit` data structures of the form:

```
struct rlimit {
        unsigned long   rlim_cur;
        unsigned long   rlim_max;
};
```

defined in **/usr/src/linux/include/linux/resource.h**.

The `rlim_cur` field is the current usage limit for the resource, and the `rlim_max` field is the maximum value to which it can be set.

Only the superuser can change `rlim_cur` to a value greater than `rlim_max`, or change the `rlim_max` field.

Most of these usage limits are initialized to `RLIM_INFINITY=~0UL` which means no effective limit is imposed.

For **x86** the following resource limits are defined in **/usr/src/linux/include/linux/ resource.h**:

Table 12.1: **Resource limits**

| Limit | Default `rlim_cur` | Default `rlim_max` | Meaning |
|---|---|---|---|
| RLIMIT_CPU | RLIM_INFINITY | RLIM_INFINITY | Maximum CPU time in msecs. If a process exceeds this limit it gets a **SIGXCPU** signal, and then a **SIGKILL** if it doesn't terminate. |
| RLIMIT_FSIZE | RLIM_INFINITY | RLIM_INFINITY | Maximum file size. Attempts to exceed this generate a **SIGXFSZ** signal.. |
| RLIMIT_DATA | RLIM_INFINITY | RLIM_INFINITY | Maximum (heap) data size. This limit is checked whenever the kernel expands the heap of a process. |
| RLIMIT_STACK | _STK_LIM=8M | RLIM_INFINITY | Maximum stack size. This limit is checked whenever the kernel expands the user mode stack of a process. |
| RLIMIT_CORE | 0 | RLIM_INFINITY | Maximum core dump file size. If set to 0 no core dumps are produced. |
| RLIMIT_RSS | RLIM_INFINITY | RLIM_INFINITY | Maximum resident set size (number of page frames owned by a process) |
| RLIMIT_NPROC | 0 | 0 | Maximum number of processes a user can own. Both values reset during initialization to half the maximum number of threads. |
| RLIMIT_NOFILE | INR_OPEN=1024 | INR_OPEN=1024 | Maximum number of open files. |
| RLIMIT_MEMLOCK | RLIM_INFINITY | RLIM_INFINITY | Maximum locked-in-memory (non-swappable) address space. |
| RLIMIT_AS | RLIM_INFINITY | RLIM_INFINITY | Maximum size of process address space. Checked whenever a `malloc()`-like function is used. |

| RLIMIT_LOCKS | RLIM_INFINITY | RLIM_INFINITY | Maximum number of file locks held by a process. |
|---|---|---|---|
| RLIMIT_SIGPENDING | 0 | 0 | Maximum number of signals that may be queued. |
| RLIMIT_MSGQUEU | MQ_BYTES_MAX=819200 | MQ_BYTES_MAX | Maximum number of bytes that can be allocated for **POSIX** message queues. |
| RLIMIT_NICE | 0 | 0 | Ceiling to which a process's nice value can be raised. |
| RLIMIT_RTPRIO | 0 | 0 | Ceiling on the real time priority a process can have. |

The following functions can be accessed from user-space to get and set usage limits and report on current usage totals:

```
#include <sys/time.h>
#include <sys/resource.h>

int getrlimit (int resource, struct rlimit *rlim);
int setrlimit (int resource, const struct rlimit *rlim);
```

The getrlimit() and setrlimit functions are used in a pretty obvious way to get or set the particular limit referenced by the **resource argument**; e.g., a statement like

```
struct rlimit rlim = {8*1024*1024, RLIM_INFINITY};
....
setrlimit(RLMIT_CORE, &rlim);
....
```

will set the maximum core dump size to 8 MB.

One can also examine and adjust values from the **bash** shell using the ulimit command:

```
$ ulimit -a

core file size          (blocks, -c) 0
data seg size           (kbytes, -d) unlimited
scheduling priority             (-e) 0
file size               (blocks, -f) unlimited
pending signals                 (-i) 38912
max locked memory       (kbytes, -l) 64
max memory size         (kbytes, -m) unlimited
open files                      (-n) 1024
pipe size            (512 bytes, -p) 8
POSIX message queues      (bytes, -q) 819200
real-time priority              (-r) 0
stack size              (kbytes, -s) 8192
```

```
cpu time                  (seconds, -t) unlimited
max user processes                 (-u) 38912
virtual memory            (kbytes, -v) unlimited
file locks                         (-x) unlimited
```

(Note the pipe size given by `ulimit -p` cannot be changed and is not part of the `RLIMIT` set.)

One can also examine **/proc/[pid]/limits** to read the values set for a particular process ID.

Values for individual users and groups, as well as system defaults can be set by editing the file **/etc/security/limits.conf**.

It is important to note that child processes inherit the `rlim` field of the parent task structure, and thus begin with the same limits.

It is also possible to use the system call:

```
int getrusage (int who, struct rusage *usage);
```

The `getrusage()` function uses an additional data structure

```
struct  rusage {
    struct timeval ru_utime;    /* user time used */
    struct timeval ru_stime;    /* system time used */
    long    ru_maxrss;          /* maximum resident set size */
    long    ru_ixrss;           /* integral shared memory size */
    long    ru_idrss;           /* integral unshared data size */
    long    ru_isrss;           /* integral unshared stack size */
    long    ru_minflt;          /* page reclaims */
    long    ru_majflt;          /* page faults */
    long    ru_nswap;           /* swaps */
    long    ru_inblock;         /* block input operations */
    long    ru_oublock;         /* block output operations */
    long    ru_msgsnd;          /* messages sent */
    long    ru_msgrcv;          /* messages received */
    long    ru_nsignals;        /* signals received */
    long    ru_nvcsw;           /* voluntary context switches */
    long    ru_nivcsw;          /* involuntary  */
};
```

and obtains some detailed information about current usage totals. The `who` argument can be either `RUSAGE_SELF` or `RUSAGE_CHILDREN`.

Not all the fields are properly maintained in **Linux**. In particular, the documentation indicates that only

```
ru_utime,  ru_stime
ru_minflt, ru_majflt
ru_nvcsw,  ru_nivcsw
```

can be assumed to be meaningful under **Linux**.

# 12.3   Process Groups

Besides having a **pid**, every process is also a member of a **process group**. The Process Group ID
(**pgid**) is also a positive integer, expressed in the `pid_t` type. Processes can join or leave process
groups.

A process group has a leader which has `pid = pgid`. The group continues even if the group leader
terminates, ending only when all of its members terminate.

The following functions are used to manipulate process groups:

```
#include <unistd.h>

int    setpgid (pid_t pid, pid_t pgid);
pid_t getpgid (pid_t pid);
int    setpgrp (void);
pid_t getpgrp (void);
```

The function `setpgid()` sets the **pgid** of process pid to pgid. If `pid = 0`, the current process **pid**
is used. If `pgid = 0` the **pgid** of process pid is used.

The function `getpgid()` returns the **pgid** of process pid. If `pid = 0`, the current process **pid** is used.

The function `setpgrp()` is equivalent to `setpgid(0,0)`.

The function `getpgrp()` is equivalent to `getpgid(0)`.

On success, these functions return 0. On failure, they return −1 with **errno** set. The possible error
returns are:

Table 12.2: **Process group function error return values**

| Value | Meaning |
|-------|---------|
| EINVAL | pgid < 0. |
| EPERM | Permission violation. |
| ESRCH | pid doesn't match any process. |

# 12.4   The proc Filesystem

The **proc** filesystem is a pseudo-filesystem which; exists only in memory; i.e., the `/proc` directory is
empty when the system is not running. Information in the **proc** filesystem is generated only when
examined; it is not continually updated.

Entries in `/proc` can be used to obtain system information when read. Writing to entries can set
various system parameters.

The name **proc** is short for process and thus it should be no surprise that it contains abundant
information about each process running on the system, in addition to global information. For each

process on the system there is a subdirectory named with the process ID. For example:

```
$ ls -lF /proc/28448

/total 0
-r--------    1 coop coop 0 Oct 23 16:33 auxv
--w-------    1 coop coop 0 Oct 23 16:33 clear_refs
-r--r--r--    1 coop coop 0 Oct 23 16:33 cmdline
-rw-r--r--    1 coop coop 0 Oct 23 16:33 coredump_filter
lrwxrwxrwx    1 coop coop 0 Oct 23 16:33 cwd -> /tmp
-r--------    1 coop coop 0 Oct 23 16:33 environ
lrwxrwxrwx    1 coop coop 0 Oct 23 16:33 exe -> /usr/bin/emacs-x*
dr-x------    2 coop coop 0 Oct 23 16:33 fd/
dr-x------    2 coop coop 0 Oct 23 16:33 fdinfo/
-r--------    1 coop coop 0 Oct 23 16:33 limits
-r--r--r--    1 coop coop 0 Oct 23 16:33 maps
-rw-------    1 coop coop 0 Oct 23 16:33 mem
-r--r--r--    1 coop coop 0 Oct 23 16:33 mountinfo
-r--r--r--    1 coop coop 0 Oct 23 16:33 mounts
-r--------    1 coop coop 0 Oct 23 16:33 mountstats
dr-xr-xr-x    5 coop coop 0 Oct 23 16:33 net/
-rw-r--r--    1 coop coop 0 Oct 23 16:33 oom_adj
-r--r--r--    1 coop coop 0 Oct 23 16:33 oom_score
-r--------    1 coop coop 0 Oct 23 16:33 pagemap
-r--------    1 coop coop 0 Oct 23 16:33 personality
lrwxrwxrwx    1 coop coop 0 Oct 23 16:33 root -> //
-r--r--r--    1 coop coop 0 Oct 23 16:33 schedstat
-r--r--r--    1 coop coop 0 Oct 23 16:33 smaps
-r--------    1 coop coop 0 Oct 23 16:33 stack
-r--r--r--    1 coop coop 0 Oct 23 16:33 stat
-r--r--r--    1 coop coop 0 Oct 23 16:33 statm
-r--r--r--    1 coop coop 0 Oct 23 16:33 status
-r--------    1 coop coop 0 Oct 23 16:33 syscall
dr-xr-xr-x    3 coop coop 0 Oct 23 16:33 task/
-r--r--r--    1 coop coop 0 Oct 23 16:33 wchan
```

Some of these entries are very useful. For example, the **maps** entry shows the memory mappings associated with the process, **schedstat** gives scheduling information, and the **fd** subdirectory gives information about all open file descriptors.

Typing **man proc** will give information about many of the entries, both the process-oriented ones and the global ones. However, one should be forewarned that the exact contents of the **proc** filesystem tend to vary with kernel version as new information is added and deprecated entries are removed. The best way to learn about it is to take some time and explore it.

## 12.5   Inter-Process Communication Methods

There are many inter-process communication techniques and we are going to discuss them in detail. Here is a brief overview.

## Signals

**Signals** can be used to send short messages between any two processes, regardless of their relationship, as long as privileges are appropriate. This is one of the oldest methods of **IPC**.

Normally only a signal number is delivered, but with the **siginfo** interface, more information including the identity of the sending process can be supplied.

Upon receiving a signal, a process suspends its normal operation, invokes a handling routine, and then returns to its instruction flow or exits.

## Pipes

**Pipes** (created by the `popen()` or `pipe()` functions), create a data flow between two processes which may or may not have an ancestral relationship.

Data flow proceeds only when both a reader and a writer are present.

## Named Pipes (Fifos)

**Named Pipes** (fifos) create a data flow between two processes which may or may not have an ancestral relationship.

A filesystem entry is setup and flow through the pipe is accomplished through normal I/O calls through the **fifo**.

Data flow proceeds only when both a reader and a writer are present. There can be more than one reader and more than one writer.

## Unix Domain Sockets

**Unix Domain Sockets** create a data flow between two processes which may or may not have an ancestral relationship.

A filesystem entry is set up and flow through the socket is accomplished by opening up socket descriptors and reading and writing through them.

Unlike **fifos** communication is truly multiplex and bidirectional. There can be more than one reader and more than one writer.

## Internet Sockets

**Internet Sockets** create a data flow between two processes which may be on different machines. There is no filesystem entry associated with them.

Flow through the socket is accomplished by opening up socket descriptors and reading and writing through them, just as with Unix Domain Sockets.

Once again communication is truly multiplex and bidirectional.

## System V IPC

**System V IPC** consists of three methods: shared memory, semaphores, and message queues.

Any processes which have access to the appropriate **identifier** can use these methods whether or not there is an ancestral relationship.

These methods are prone to leaks and have an interface which shows its age. They are used abundantly in legacy code, but can be avoided in new programs.

## POSIX IPC

**POSIX IPC** consists of the same three methods as **System V IPC**, but has a vastly improved interface and implementation.

Shared resources show up as special filesystem entries.

These methods are not prone to leaks and are a better choice than **System V IPC**.

### Multi-threading

**Multi-threaded** applications have more than one thread of execution. They communicate among each other through shared resources such as memory and file descriptors.

Careful coordination is required to preserve the integrity and sequencing of shared resources.

### Advanced Modern Techniques

Desktop applications often communicate through various **IPC** protocols closely connected to their windowing environment.

**DCOP** is closely integrated into the **KDE** desktop environment, and the **QT** object-oriented libraries.

**Bonobo**, based on **CORBA**, is heavily used in the **Gnome** desktop, and the **GTK** graphic toolkit..

**SOAP** and **XML-RPC** are designed for Web services, and use **http** as the transport protocol.

**D-BUS** is an up and coming, lightweight protocol, with low overhead.

These methods are generally tied to an underlying framework, and are best studied as part of those environments. They can work together for unified "drag and drop" protocols etc.

## 12.6 Labs

### Lab 1: Getting and Setting Limits

Write a user-space program that examines and sets usage limits, and reports statistics on total usage.

The program should first obtain and print out the current usage limits.

It should then modify one or more of them, and then print out the new limits.

The program should give birth to several children using `fork()`, each of which should print out their usage limits, compare to those of the parent and then sleep for a while. The parent should **wait** for the children using `wait()` or `waitpid()`.

Have the parent use the `getrusage()` function to obtain statistics both for itself and for the children.

## Lab 2: Process Groups

Write a program that first prints out its process group using both `getpgid()` and `getpgrp()`.

Then feeding as an argument to the program the process ID of a currently running process (you could simply do `cat &` and use the echoed process ID as an argument) print out the **pgid** of the process.

Now try to change it with `setpgid()` to be the same as that of your program. Read the **man** page to understand your results.

## Lab 3: The proc filesystem

Find a process on your system that uses multiple threads. A good candidate would be **firefox**. To gain information about the process you can do:

```
$ ps -eLF  | grep -e PID -e firef
UID     PID  PPID    LWP  C NLWP     SZ    RSS PSR STIME TTY       TIME CMD
coop   4889     1   4889  0    1  15970   1228   1 07:16 ?     00:00:00 /bin/sh /usr/lib64/
                                                                        firefox-3.0.15/run-moz
coop   4914  4889   4914  2    7 185029 257084   0 07:16 ?     00:11:38 /usr/lib64/firefox-
coop   4914  4889   4948  0    7 185029 257084   0 07:16 ?     00:00:02 /usr/lib64/firefox-
coop   4914  4889   4949  0    7 185029 257084   0 07:16 ?     00:00:17 /usr/lib64/firefox-
coop   4914  4889   4963  0    7 185029 257084   3 07:16 ?     00:00:00 /usr/lib64/firefox-
coop   4914  4889   4964  0    7 185029 257084   3 07:16 ?     00:00:00 /usr/lib64/firefox-
coop   4914  4889   4965  0    7 185029 257084   3 07:16 ?     00:00:00 /usr/lib64/firefox-
coop   4914  4889  16800  0    7 185029 257084   2 09:42 ?     00:00:00 /usr/lib64/firefox-
coop  25769  4567  25769  0    1  15302    808   3 16:27 pts/1 00:00:00 grep -e PID -e firef
```

Note the second process listed has 7 **LWP**'s (light weight processes, or threads) associated with it. If you examine the associated subdirectory in the **proc** filesystem (`/proc/4914` in the above example) you will find a subdirectory under the `tasks` subdirectory for each process.

While you are there take a good look at the entries in the subdirectories, some of which we will discuss later.

# Chapter 13

# Processes - II

We'll show how to create processes with **system()**, **fork()**, **exec()**, and **clone()** and how to exit them. We'll also learn how to use the **wait()** functions. We'll show how to setup background **daemons**.

## 13.1   Using system() to Create a Process

The system() call runs a process from inside another program:

```
#include <stdlib.h>

int system (const char *cmd);
```

In effect, `system()` invokes `/bin/sh -c cmd` and sends the output of `cmd` to standard output. (This differs from what will happen when we use the `popen()` function in our discussion of **pipes**, which actually re-directs standard input and/or output onto file descriptors.)

For example:

```
  printf("exit status = %d\n", system("ps aul"));
```

On success `system()` returns the exit code for `cmd`; if it fails because it can't start a shell it returns 127 with any other error returning -1.

The calling program will block, waiting for `system()` to complete its actions. One can use `&` to run `cmd` as a background process but results can be unpredictable.

The `system()` call is not very efficient, but it is very easy to use. For more critical tasks one should use one of the `exec()` functions.

**Never** use `system()` from within a program with super-user privileges; this can be a wide open security hole because behaviour can be influenced by environmental variables set by the normal user.

## 13.2   Using fork() to Create a Process

Creating a new (**child**) process without terminating the old one can be done with:

```
#include <unistd.h>
#include <sys/types.h>

pid_t fork (void);
```

After a `fork()` two processes are running. The child inherits the parent's resources. Only the `pid, ppid,` file locks and pending signals are not carried forth. File descriptors, memory, etc., are inherited. However, **Linux** uses a **copy-on-write** implementation, so memory is not duplicated until it is actually altered.

An additional process creation call, `vfork()` creates a child that shares the memory address space of the parent. To prevent the parent from stepping on the child's use of the memory, the parent's execution is blocked until the child exits or issues an `execve()` call. Note that the child cannot **write** to this address space and thus there is no need to copy page table entries.

`vfork()` is primarily a vestige of earlier **Unix** implementations which did not have a `copy-on-write` technique. It can be dangerous and/or inefficient and should generally be avoided.

`fork()` returns 0 to the child process and the child's **pid** to the parent process, on success. On failure it returns -1 and `errno` is set. The possible error returns are:

Table 13.1: **fork() error return values**

| Value | Meaning |
|---|---|
| EAGAIN | Cannot allocate sufficient memory to copy the parent's page tables and allocate necessary data structures. |
| ENOMEM | Cannot allocate the necessary kernel structures. |

For example:

```
main ()
{
  if ((pid = fork ()) == 0)
    {
      /* this is the child */
    }
  else if (pid > 0)
    {
      /* this is the parent */
    }
  else
    {
      perror ("Call to fork failed!!");
    }
}
```

## 13.3   Using exec() to Create a Process

The exec() family of functions is another way to launch a new process:

```
#include <unistd.h>

extern char **environ;

int execl  (const char *path, const char *arg, ...);
int execlp (const char *file, const char *arg, ...);
int execle (const char *path, const char *arg , ...,
                       char *const envp[]);
int execv  (const char *path, char *const argv[]);
int execvp (const char *file, char *const argv[]);
int execve (const char *path, char *const argv[], char *const envp[]);
```

These functions replace the current process with a new one. The new process has the same **pid** as the creating process. In addition, it inherits all open file descriptors (unless the file has the FD_CLOEXEC flag set, perhaps by fcntl().)

The exec() functions don't return unless an error occurs, in which case they return -1 and errno is set. There are many possible error conditions; see the man page for execve() to get a listing.

The various functions differ in how they represent the program to be executed, hand over arguments, and environmental variables.

`path` is a full pathname, while using `file` implies the current `PATH` variable will be used. If `file` contains a slash it is interpreted as a full path name; i.e, the same as `path`.

The argument list must be terminated with a `NULL` pointer, whether it is strung out in a list or the `argv` array is used.

`**environ` can be played with directly to modify the environment.

Note that the first argument has to be the command name, which may seem repetitious.

Some examples:

```
const char *ps_argv[] = {"ps", "-ax", NULL};
const char *ps_envp[] = {"PATH=/bin:/usr/bin", "TERM=console", NULL};

execl ("/bin/ps", "ps", "-ax", NULL);
execlp("ps",      "ps", "-ax", NULL);
execle("/bin/ps", "ps", "-ax", NULL, ps_envp);
execv ("/bin/ps", ps_argv);
execvp("ps",      ps_argv);
execve("/bin/ps", ps_argv, ps_envp);
```

## 13.4   Using clone()

In addition to the traditional `fork()` call that generates a child that is a full peer to the parent, a so-called **heavyweight process**, **Linux** permits the creation of so-called **lightweight** processes that share many kernel data structures (including memory areas) between parents and children; this is the basis of the **multi-threaded** programming implementation under **Linux**.

All these methods of process creation invoke the same basic function under **Linux**, with the different behaviours being influenced by the arguments passed and flags chosen. From user-space, there is a system call (unique to **Linux**) named `clone()`, for which you can get documentation by doing `man clone`:

```
#include <sched.h>

int clone (int (*fn) (void *arg), void *child_stack, int flags, void *arg);
```

There is a corresponding `sys_clone()` function in the **Linux** kernel.

The first argument, `fn` points to the function that will be executed by the process when it begins. Anything pointed to by the last argument, `arg` will be passed to this function. The integer return value of the function should contain the exit code for the child process.

The `child_stack` argument points to the stack used by the child process. If a value of 0 is given, the child gets the same stack pointer as the parent. However, as soon as either of them modifies the stack the **copy-on-write** technique ensures they get their own copies.

However, if the child and parent are sharing the same memory area (i.e., they are lightweight processes, or threads), then this value must be non-null. The parent process must set up memory for the child stack and pass this pointer. (Note that stacks grown **downward** so the pointer should point to the topmost address of the child stack in this case.)

The `flags` argument has more than one purpose. Its low byte should contain the number of the signal sent to the parent when the child dies (e.g., `SIGCHLD`). This is bitwise-or'ed with any combination of the following values, in order to control what is shared between parent and child:

Table 13.2: **clone() flags**

| Flag | Set | Not Set |
| --- | --- | --- |
| CLONE_VM | Parent and child process share memory space; writes to memory by one process are seen by the other and any memory mapping is seen by both processes. | Each process gets its own memory space, subject to the `fork()` copy-on-write behaviour. |
| CLONE_FS | Parent and child share filesystem information, including the filesystem root, current working directory, `umask`, etc. Note this means if the child does a call like `chdir()` it affects the parent too! | None of this information is shared. |
| CLONE_FILES | Parent and child share the same table of file descriptors, which thus refer to the same files in each process. If either process opens or closes a file descriptor, the other is affected. | They begin with the same table, but then can diverge as open and closing occurs. |
| CLONE_SIGHAND | Parent and child share the same set of signal handlers. A call to `sigaction()` by either process affects the other one. On the other hand, each process has its own signal mask and pending signal set, and one can block or unblock a signal and not affect the other. | The child gets the parent's signal handlers but subsequent changes do not effect the other process. |
| CLONE_PID | The child process has the same process ID as the parent. This is only allowed in the boot thread. | The child gets a new process ID |
| CLONE_PTRACE | If the parent process is being traced with the `ptrace()` system call, the child will be traced as well. | No tracing of the child, even if the parent is being traced. |
| CLONE_VFORK | Is used by the `vfork()` system call. If set the parent is asking the child to wake it up when it releases its memory region. | |
| CLONE_PARENT | The cloned process will have the same parent process as the cloner. | |
| CLONE_THREAD | The cloned process will have the same thread group as the cloner. | |

There are some other specialized flags that can be used: consult the **man** page for clone().

Thus, the fork() system call has flags = SIGCHLD and vfork() has flags = SIGCHLD | CLONE_VM | CLONE_VFORK.

## 13.5   Exiting

The following functions result in process termination, which may be normal or abnormal:

```
#include <unistd.h>

void _exit (int status);

#include <stdlib.h>

void exit (int status);
void abort (void);
```

Normal termination can occur in three ways:

- Calling return() from main(); this is the same as calling exit().

- Calling exit(). All open streams are flushed and closed. All handlers registered with atexit() and on_exit() (to be discussed shortly) are called (in reverse order of registration.)

- Calling _exit() (which is also called by exit()). All open file descriptors are closed, all child processes are inherited by process 1 (init) and SIGCHLD is sent to the parent process.

Abnormal termination can occur two ways:

- An abort() generates SIGABRT and causes a core dump to be generated. All open streams are closed and flushed. If SIGABRT is blocked or ignored, abort() will still terminate and core dump, but if the signal is caught it may be avoided.

- Any signal whose default behaviour is termination and for which a non-terminating signal handler is not installed kills the process.

Exit handling functions may be registered with the functions:

```
#include <stdlib.h>

int atexit  (void (*function)(void));
int on_exit (void (*function)(int, void *), void *arg);
```

The on_exit() is similar to atexit() except that the function is passed the argument to exit() and the **arg** argument. These functions return 0 on success; -1 on failure. (**errno** is not set.)

Note that these functions are **not** called in the case of an abnormal termination.

It is also possible to use **destructor** methods as we describe next.

## 13.6 Constructors and Destructors

The **gcc** compiler permits the use of special **constructor** and **destructor** functions.

The constructor functions are called **before** the `main()` routine is called.

The destructor functions are called **after** the `exit()` function is called from `main()`; if `exit()` or `return()` is not explicitly called, the destructor routines will still be called.

We already saw the use of these methods in our discussion of libraries, and repeat the example of how they are used:

```
/* prototype them with attributes */
void init_fun (void) __attribute__ ((constructor));
void exit_fun (void) __attribute__ ((destructor));
/* then define them */
void init_fun (void ) { ... whatever ... };
void exit_fun (void ) { ... whatever ... };
```

## 13.7 Waiting

The parent process can **wait** (suspend execution) until one of its child processes dies or is stopped, or a signal interrupts it.

```
#include <sys/types.h>
#include <sys/wait.h>

pid_t wait (int *status);
pid_t waitpid (pid_t pid, int *status, int options);
```

`wait()` returns on any child process; `waitpid()` on a particular process or set of processes.

`status` contains the exit status of the process, unless it is set to `NULL`. The following interrogation macros can be used:

Table 13.3: **Wait status interrogation macros**

| Macro | Meaning |
|-------|---------|
| WIFEXITED(status) | Non-zero if the child exited normally. |
| WEXITSTATUS(status) | If WIFEXITED is non-zero, returns child exit code. |
| WIFSIGNALED(status) | Non-zero if child terminated on uncaught signal. |
| WTERMSIG(status) | If WIFSIGNALED is non-zero, returns signal number. |
| WIFSTOPPED(status) | Non-zero if the child has stopped on a signal. |
| WSTOPSIG(status) | If WIFSTOPPED is non-zero, returns signal number. |

The macros `WIFSTOPPED()` and `WSTOPSIG()` are meaningful only if the flag `WUNTRACED` is given.

`pid` can have the following values:

Table 13.4: **pid value and who is waited on**

| Value | Meaning |
|---|---|
| `pid < -1` | Wait for any child process with a process group ID = - `pid` |
| `pid = -1` | Wait for any child process. (Same as using `wait()`.) |
| `pid = 0` | Wait for any child process whose process group ID is the same as the calling process. |
| `pid > 0` | Wait for the child process with ID = `pid` . |

The `options` flag can be used to modify behaviour, and is an OR of zero and either or both of the following:

Table 13.5: **Waiting option flags**

| Flag | Meaning |
|---|---|
| `WNOHANG` | Return immediately if no child has exited. |
| `WUNTRACED` | Return for stopped children whose status has not been reported. |

These functions return the **pid** of the child which exits, on success, and -1 on error (**errno** is set). The possible error returns are:

Table 13.6: **Wait functions error return values**

| Value | Meaning |
|---|---|
| `EINVAL` | `options` argument is invalid. |
| `ECHILD` | `pid` doesn't exist or it is not a child of the calling process. |
| `ERESTARTSYS` | `WNOHANG` was not set and an unblocked signal or `SIGCHLD` was caught. `EINTR` may actually be returned in this case. |

## 13.8   Daemon Processes

A **daemon** process runs in the background, not directly controlled by a user. By convention the names of daemon processes usually end with the letter **d**; examples include **klogd, cupsd, nfsd, xinetd** etc.

The basic prescription for creating a daemon process is to fork off a child and then terminate the parent; the child is then adopted by the **init** process with process ID = 1.

Other steps are taken including:

- Closing all open file descriptors and then redirecting **stdin, stdout** and **stderr** to `/dev/null`, thereby breaking any association from the controlling terminal.

- Becoming the session and process group leader.

- Setting the root directory to /. This lets one potentially unmount the file system the process was started from, and also avoids security and other errors that would depend on where the process was started.

One can construct this all by hand, but to make things easy one can use the function:

```
#include <unistd.h>

int daemon (int nochdir, int noclose);
```

If `nochdir` is not zero, the root directory is not reset to /.

If `noclose` is not zero, standard input, output and error are not redirected to `/dev/null`.

## 13.9   Labs

### Lab 1: Forking

Write a simple forking example:

Parent and child must be able to identify themselves as to which is which.

The parent should **wait** for the child to terminate.

### Lab 2: Zombie Limescale

Modify the previous forking program so that the child terminates quickly, while the parent hibernates for a period of time with `sleep()`.

Run the program in one terminal window (or in background with **&**) while monitoring your active processes with **ps ux**, noting the state of the child. The child should disappear when the parent exits.

### Lab 3: More Forking and Waiting

Modify your **ls** program from the previous section so that, for every subdirectory found (you can use `stat()` and `S_ISDIR()` to detect directories), it forks a child to process that subdirectory (you probably want to skip processing . and ..).

If the output gets too muddled, you can have the parent `wait()` for each child to finish.

It is possible to create too many processes and hang your machine. See `help ulimit` and type `ulimit -a` to get the current limits. Set the maximum number of processes to a reasonable value.

## Lab 4: Cloning

Write a short program that uses the `clone()` system call to create master and slave threads that share all memory resources.

Have a global variable and show that either thread can modify it and the value can be seen by the other.

Be careful with creation of the slave thread's stack pointer, to point to the top of the stack since it grows down.

What happens if the slave thread dies before the master thread?

Note you can use this as a nucleus of your own multi-threaded programming method that does not use the standard threading libraries. You can also play with sharing file descriptors or not etc.

## Lab 5: Exiting

Have a program use `atexit()` (or `on_exit()`), or the constructor/destructor methods for exit handling..

Register at least two handlers to be processed during exiting.

Can you make what happens depend on the exit code from your main routine?

## Lab 6: Memory Mapping

Write a program that uses **anonymous** memory mapping for parent/child communication.

Have the child write to the memory mapped region and have the parent read from it.

## Lab 7: Daemons

Write a simple program that starts a daemon process. It can be as simple as just calling **pause()** to go to sleep until a signal is received.

Once the program is running, type **ps lx** to verify it is running in background and that its parent process is **init**

Send a signal to the daemon to interrupt the sleep; for instance one could do `kill -SIGUSR1 <pid>`. The process should disappear.

# Chapter 14

# Pipes and Fifos

We'll learn about how to make and use pipes for parent/child communication, and about how to used named pipes (FIFO's) more generally. We'll also learn about the new system calls **splice()**, **vmsplice()** and **tee()**.

## 14.1 Pipes and Inter-Process Communication

**Pipes** permit processes to exchange **data**, not just short **signals**. These processes may either be independent or have a parent-child relationship.

A process may also use a pipe to receive input from or direct output to a command.

One often invokes piping from the command line through use of the | symbol; e.g., if one does:

```
$ ls -l | sort | tail -20
```

three separate processes will run **simultaneously** (**ls, sort** and **tail**) feeding through the pipeline as they go, without use of temporary or intermediate files.

In what follows we will be concerned with the programming interface for accomplishing this within programs in an efficient way.

## 14.2   popen() and pclose()

These functions are used to open and close a pipe using the standard I/O library:

```
#include <stdio.h>

FILE *popen (const char *command, const char *mode);
int  pclose (FILE *stream);
```

**popen()** initiates a process by creating a pipe, forking, and invoking the shell, using the **system()** call.

The **mode** argument is the same as that used in **fopen()**. However it can take only the values "r" or "w". Disallowed are "r+" or "w+" and append modes.

The **command** argument points to a null-terminated string which contains a shell command line which is passed to **/bin/sh** using the **-c** flag. (which reads commands from **command** and does any required interpretation..)

- Writing to a such a stream writes to the **stdin** of the command; the command's **stdout** is the same as that of the process that called **popen()**.

- Likewise, reading from such a stream reads the command's **stdout**, and the command's **stdin** is the same as that of the process that called **popen()**.

**popen()** returns a normal I/O stream except in all it must be closed with **pclose()** and not **fclose()**. If the underlying **pipe()** or **fork()** calls fail or memory cannot be allocated. **NULL** will be returned and **errno** is not reset. If **mode** is invalid **errno** will be set to **EINVAL**.

**pclose()** waits for the associated process to terminate and returns the exit status of the command. On error it return **-1** if an error is detected.

For example:

```
#include <stdio.h>
#include <stdlib.h>
#include <unistd.h>

int main ()
{
    FILE *fp;
    int nbytes, BSIZE=getpagesize();
```

```
        char *buffer = malloc(BSIZE);
        fp = popen ("finger", "r");
        while ((nbytes = fread (buffer, 1, BSIZE, fp)) > 0)
            fwrite (buffer, 1, nbytes, stdout);
        printf ("EOF = %d and Error = %d\n", feof (fp), ferror (fp));
        pclose (fp);
        exit (EXIT_SUCCESS);
}
```

## 14.3  pipe()

The lower-level `pipe()` function passes data between two processes without the overhead of invoking a shell and gives more control:

```
#include <unistd.h>

int pipe (int filedes[2]);
```

A parent and child process may be connected or a process may even connect to itself.

The pipe has a read end and a write end; Any data written to `filedes[1]` can be read back from `filedes[0]` Data is processed in a first-in, first-out (FIFO) basis.

`filedes` is a file descriptor; thus `read()` and `write()` must be used, not `fread()` and `fwrite()`.

Exactly how these pipes work differs somewhat from one **Unix** variant to another. In **System V**, the pipes are full-duplex; both descriptors can have reads and writes. In the **Posix** standard each process must close one end of the pipe before using the other. Under **Linux** while the communication in each pipe is only one way, no close operation is required. Keep these considerations in mind for writing portable code.

On success 0 is returned, and on error −1 is returned (`errno` is set.) The possible error returns are:

Table 14.1: **pipe() error return values**

| Value | Meaning |
|-------|---------|
| ENFILE | Process is using too many file descriptors, or the system file table is full.. |
| EFAULT | `filedes` is not valid. |

A simple `pipe()` example:

```
#include <unistd.h>
#include <stdio.h>
#include <stdlib.h>
#include <string.h>
```

```
int main ()
{
    int rc, filep[2], length;
    char *in_data = "pdat";
    char *out_data;
    length = strlen (in_data) + 1;
    out_data = malloc (length);
    memset (out_data, 0, length);

    if (pipe (filep) == 0) {
        rc = write (filep[1], in_data, 4);
        printf ("wrote %d bytes\n", rc);
        rc = read (filep[0], out_data, 4);
        printf ("read %d bytes which were %s\n", rc, out_data);
        exit (EXIT_SUCCESS);
    }
    exit (EXIT_FAILURE);
}
```

A simple pipe example between child and parent:

```
#include <unistd.h>
#include <stdio.h>
#include <stdlib.h>
#include <string.h>
#include <errno.h>
#include <sys/wait.h>

#define SIZE 1024
int main ()
{
    int rc, status, filedes[2];
    pid_t pid;
    char buffer[SIZE];
    if (pipe (filedes) != 0)
        exit (EXIT_FAILURE);

    memset (buffer, 0, SIZE);
    pid = fork ();

    if (pid > 0) {                /* parent */
        memset (buffer, 'X', SIZE);
        close (filedes[0]);
        rc = write (filedes[1], buffer, SIZE);
        printf ("\nParent wrote %d bytes\n", rc);
        (void)wait (&status);
        printf ("\nParent now exiting\n");
        exit (EXIT_SUCCESS);
    }
    if (pid == 0) {               /* child */
        close (filedes[1]);
        rc = read (filedes[0], buffer, SIZE);
        printf ("\n     Child read %d bytes  \n", rc);
```

```
        write (STDOUT_FILENO, buffer, SIZE);
        exit (EXIT_SUCCESS);
    }
    printf ("fork failed");
    exit (EXIT_FAILURE);
}
```

## 14.4   Named Pipes (FIFOs)

Named pipes (or FIFO's) allow you to create a pipe between two processes which may or may not have a common ancestor. **FIFO** stands for **F**irst **I**n, **F**irst **O**ut.

You can create a named pipe and wait for another process to establish a communication link with it.

Unlike pipes, named pipes create an entry in the filesystem that can then be accessed by another process.

No data transfer can take place until both a reader and writer are present (i.e., a *rendezvous* takes place).

A FIFO may be created either from the command line or by using a system call. From the command line try:

```
cd /tmp
mkfifo afifo
cat < afifo &
ls -l > afifo
```

Note the use of &. Without it you couldn't type the next line, since **cat** blocks waiting for input.

As a system call:

```
#include <sys/types.h>
#include <sys/stat.h>

int mkfifo (const char *pathname, mode_t mode );
```

For example:

```
rc = mkfifo ("/tmp/afifo", 0666) ;
```

FIFO's may be opened for reading or writing but not for both; i.e., in `mode`, `O_RDWR` is not allowed, but `O_RDONLY` and `O_WRONLY` may be used in combination with `O_NONBLOCK`.

A read on a non-blocking FIFO with no data will return 0 bytes; a write on a non-blocking FIFO that can't accept all of the bytes being written will either fail or write only some of the bytes.

The amount of information that can be in the pipe at any one time is given by the size of a **page** of memory, (which is 4096 bytes on **x86**). Another limit, PIPE_BUF=4096 gives the limit for an **atomic** write to the pipe; on **x86** these numbers are the same but on other architectures with bigger page sizes, such as the **alpha**, they can be different.

On success 0 is returned, on error -1 is returned with **errno** being set. The possible error returns are:

Table 14.2: **fifo() error return values**

| Value | Meaning |
| --- | --- |
| EEXIST | pathname already exists. |
| EACCES | A directory in pathname does not allow search (execute) permission. |
| ENAMETOOLONG | Name is too long. |
| ENOENT | Part of pathname does not exist or is a dangling symbolic link. |
| ENOSPC | No room on filesystem. |
| ENOTDIR | Part of pathname is not a directory. |
| EROFS | pathname is on a read-only filesystem. |

A FIFO can also be created with **mknod()** either as a command line call, or a system library call:

```
#include <sys/types.h>
#include <sys/stat.h>
#include <fcntl.h>
#include <unistd.h>

int mknod (const char *pathname, mode_t mode, (dev_t )0 );
```

To create a FIFO entry in the filesystem, **mode** must be comprised of the desired permissions, bitwise OR'ed with S_IFIFO. mknod() is also used to create device special files; see its **man** page.

When a FIFO is no longer needed, it must be deleted from the command line with **rm**, or one must use **unlink()** from within the code.

Unix domain **sockets**, which we will discuss later, offer an alternative to named pipes and have additional capabilities, including bi-directionality, multiplexing, and network communication. However, they are somewhat more difficult to set up.

# 14.5   splice(), vmsplice() and tee()

The 2.6.17 **Linux** kernel introduced several new system calls that involve pipes (and/or normal file descriptors and socket descriptors). The first one,

```
#define _GNU_SOURCE
#include <fcntl.h>

long splice (int fd_in, off_t *off_in, int fd_out, off_t *off_out,
             size_t len, unsigned int flags);
```

transfers up to **len** bytes from **fd_in** to **fd_out**.

The input/output offset arguments, `off_in`, `off_out`, require some care. For file descriptors corresponding to a pipe they must be `NULL` or an error results. For normal file descriptors a `NULL` offset is just a normal read and the file position is advanced. If the offset is not `NULL` the read or write begins from the offset, but the file position is **not** advanced; i.e., the read/write calls function like `pread()`, `pwrite()`.

One or both of the file descriptors **must** be a pipe or an error is returned. On successful execution `splice()` returns the number of bytes transferred.

Before looking at the `flags` argument we should consider why this system call exists and what it does. One could always accomplish the same thing with normal reads followed by writes. However, this involves two significant overheads:

- One has to make two system calls, not one.

- One has to create a buffer to store the data from the read before doing the write.

Of course one could keep the buffer small by chunking the I/O but that just raises the number of system calls.

We will see later that the `sendfile()` system call has some of the same objectives when the output file descriptor is a socket, and indeed the goal is to eventually implement `sendfile()` in terms of the newer system call `splice()`.

These two considerations are not the whole picture. Essentially `splice()` makes a kernel buffer available to user-space. Whenever possible there is no movement of data, only passing of pointers. The kernel does this by implementing a pipe buffer as a set of pointers (which are reference-counted) to pages of memory. Copies do not involve copying the pages, just the pointers.

The second system call,

```
long tee (int fd_in, int fd_out, size_t len, unsigned int flags);
```

copies up to `len` bytes from pipe `fd_in` to pipe `fd_out` without consuming the data; i.e, a `splice()` call after a `tee()` will still see the data. Thus it functions like the command line **tee** utility and can be used to split an output stream to two different destinations.

The third system call,

```
#include <sys/uio.h>:

long vmsplice (int fd, const struct iovec *iov,
               unsigned long nr_segs, unsigned int flags);

struct iovec {
    void   *iov_base;          /* Starting address */
    size_t iov_len;            /* Number of bytes */
};
```

takes `nr_segs` of user memory, each described by an `iovec` structure, and maps them into `fd`, which must be a pipe descriptor. Doing I/O on the pipe thus works on the memory buffers.

The `flags` argument in these system calls is a combination of the following values:

Table 14.3: **splice() flags**

| Flag | Meaning |
|---|---|
| SPLICE_F_MOVE | Trying moving the pages, avoiding a copy. This is just a hint, and if the buffers don't refer to full pages of memory, or the kernel can't move the buffer for any other reason, copies still happen. For tee(), vmsplice() this flag has no effect. |
| SPLICE_F_NONBLOCK | Make the I/O non-blocking. However, blocking can still occur if the spliced file descriptors don't have O_NONBLOCK set and they block. |
| SPLICE_F_MORE | A hint that more data is coming. For tee(), vmsplice() this flag has no effect. |
| SPLICE_F_GIFT | Unused for splice(), tee(). For vmsplice(), the user pages are given to the kernel and the application may never modify them. |

These system calls are **Linux**-specific and can not be used in portable programs.

## 14.6   Labs

### Lab 1: pipe - parent/child with exec

Change the parent/child lab example have the child **exec()** a command (say an **ls -l /usr/bin**) and stuff it into the pipe, and have the parent read the output from the pipe and display it.

Do this using only the **pipe()**, call, and not the **popen()** call.

### Lab 2: popen/pclose

Modify the previous lab to have the child use **popen()/pclose()**.

### Lab 3: FIFO's

Have your program create a node using **mkfifo()** or **mknod()** function call. Fork and then have the child stuff a message in the FIFO and have the parent read it and print it out.

### Lab 4: Using splice()

Write a program that reads data from an input file and transfers it to an output pipe using **splice()**.

By default the program should do it all in one system call. As an optional argument give the number of bytes that should be done in one transfer and loop until the total is consumed.

Create a fifo as the output pipe and then run your program in one window, while doing **cat < afifo** in another. Try starting the **cat** before and after your program runs.

# Chapter 15

# Asynchronous I/O

We will discuss asynchronous I/O, the functional interface for it, and methods of implementation under **Linux**.

## 15.1   What is Asynchronous I/O?

Normally all I/O operations are performed **synchronously**; an application will block until the read or write is completed, successfully or unsuccessfully.

Note that this doesn't mean all pending writes will be flushed to disk immediately, only that interaction with the virtual file system has been completed.

But what if I/O requests could be queued up, and program execution continued in parallel with completion of the I/O request? This can be particularly useful on **SMP** systems and when using **DMA**, which does not involve the CPU. When this is done, it is called **asynchronous I/O**, or **AIO**.

In order for this to work properly, there has to be notification when the I/O request is complete and code must contain synchronization points, or completion barriers.

In addition, policies must be set as to whether queued requests are serialized, especially when they refer to the same file descriptors.

You can request asynchronous I/O by using the `ASYNC` flag when opening a file, or the `-o async` option to the **mount** command, but this won't give true asynchronous I/O.

## 15.2   The Posix Asynchronous I/O API

The POSIX 1.b standard defines a basic data structure, the `aiocb`, which stands for **AIO control block**, and a set of basic functions that can be performed on it. These are defined and prototyped in **/usr/include/aio.h** and are provided with **glibc**:

The data structure looks like:

```
struct aiocb
{
  int aio_fildes;             /* File desriptor.  */
  int aio_lio_opcode;         /* Operation to be performed.  */
  int aio_reqprio;            /* Request priority offset.  */
  volatile void *aio_buf;     /* Location of buffer.  */
  size_t aio_nbytes;          /* Length of transfer.  */
  struct sigevent aio_sigevent; /* Signal number and value.  */
  __off64_t aio_offset;       /* File offset
  ...
};
```

where we have omitted the purely internal members of the data structure.

`aio_fildes` can be any valid file descriptor, but it must permit use of the `lseek()` call.

`aio_lio_opcode` is used by the `lio_listio()` function and stores information about the type of operation to be performed.

`aio_reqprio` can be used to control scheduling priorities.

`aio_buf` points to the buffer where the data is to be written to or read from.

`aio_nbytes` is the length of the buffer.

`aio_sigevent` controls what if any signal is sent to the calling process when the operation completes.

`aio_offset` gives the offset into the file where the I/O should be performed; this is necessary because doing I/O operations in parallel voids the concept of a current position.

The basic functions are actually not part of **glibc** proper, but are part of another library, **librt**. These functions are:

```
#include <aio.h>

void aio_init (const struct aioinit *init);
int aio_read  (struct aiocb *cb);
```

```
int aio_write (struct aiocb *cb);
int iol_listio(int mode, struct aiocb *const cblist[], int nent, struct sigevent *sig);
int aio_error (const struct aiocb *cb);
ssize_t aio_return (const struct aiocb *cb);
int aio_fsync (int op, struct aiocb *cb);
int aio_suspend (const struct aiocb *cb, const cblist[], int nent,
                const struct timespec *timeout);
int aio_cancel (int fd, struct aiocb *cb);
```

A typical code fragment might have:

```
struct aiocb *cb = malloc (sizeof struct aiocb);
char *buf = malloc (nbytes);
....
fd = open (....);
cb->aio_filedes = fd;
cb->aio_nbytes = nbytes;
cb->aio_offset = offset;
cb->aio_buf = buf;
....
rc = aio_read (cb);
....
while (aio_error (cb) == EINPROGRESS){};
....
```

where we use the `aio_error()` function call to wait for completion of pending requests on the control block.

## 15.3  Linux Implementation

The original **AIO** implementation for **Linux** was done by **glibc** completely in user-space. A thread was launched for each file descriptor for which there were pending **AIO** requests.

This approach is costly, however, if there are large numbers, even thousands, of such requests; true support within the kernel can lead to far better performance. Thus **glibc** also permits the important parts of the implementation to be passed off to the kernel and done more efficiently in kernel-space.

The 2.6 kernel contains full kernel support for **AIO**; in fact **all** I/O is really be done through the asynchronous method, with normal I/O being the result if certain flags are not set.

A document describing the details of this implementation can be found at **http://lse.sourceforge.net /io/aionotes.txt**.

However, there is a native user-space **API** in **Linux** with new system calls that can be used efficiently; it just isn't portable. To use this you have to have the **libaio** package installed, and if you want to compile code using it you have to have the **libaio-devel** package installed. Your code will have to include the header file **/usr/include/libaio.h**. The basic functions are:

```
#include <libaio.h>
```

```
long io_setup (unsigned nr_events, aio_context_t *ctxp);
long io_submit (aio_context_t ctx_id, long nr, struct iocb **iocbpp);
long io_getevents (aio_context_t ctx_id, long min_nr, long nr, struct io_event *events,
                  struct timespec *timeout);
long io_destroy (aio_context_t ctx);
long io_cancel (aio_context_t ctx_id, struct iocb *iocb, struct io_event *result);
```

These functions all have **man** pages so we won't describe them completely.

Before any I/O work can be done, a **context** has to be set up to which any queued calls belong; otherwise the kernel may not know who they are associated with. This is done with the call to `io_setup()`, where the context **must** be initialized; e.g.,

```
io_context_t ctx = 0;
rc = io_setup (maxevents, &ctx);
```

where `maxevents` is the largest number of asynchronous events that can be received. The handle returned is then passed as an argument in the other functions. The function `io_destroy()` will wipe out the context when you are finished.

The `io_submit()` function is used to submit asynchronous requests, which have their **iocb** structures properly set up.

The `io_getevents()` function is used to check the status, and `io_cancel()` can be used to try and cancel a pending request. (**Note**; the `events` argument must point to an **array** of structures at least as large as the maximum number of events you are looking at. The documentation is not clear about this and missing it is a good way to get segmentation faults.)

The control block structure itself is given by:

```
struct iocb {
   void *data;   /* Return in the io completion event */
   unsigned key; /* For use in identifying io requests */

   short   aio_lio_opcode;
   short   aio_reqprio;
   int     aio_fildes;

   union {
      struct io_iocb_common    c;
      struct io_iocb_vector    v;
      struct io_iocb_poll      poll;
      struct io_iocb_sockaddr  saddr;
   } u;
};

struct io_iocb_poll {
   int events;
};   /* result code is the set of result flags or -'ve errno */

struct io_iocb_sockaddr {
   struct sockaddr *addr;
   int     len;
};   /* result code is the length of the sockaddr, or -'ve errno */
```

```
struct io_iocb_common {
    void         *buf;
    unsigned long nbytes;
    long long     offset;
};  /* result code is the amount read or -'ve errno */

struct io_iocb_vector {
    const struct iovec *vec;
    int                 nr;
    long long           offset;
};  /* result code is the amount read or -'ve errno */
```

While you can get by with just these functions and structures, it can be tedious to insert all the right values in the right places before submitting requests. There are a number of helper functions in the header file which will do most of the work for you. Unfortunately the **man** pages don't mention them. Two in particular you will definitely want to use are:

```
void io_prep_pread  (struct iocb *iocb, int fd, void *buf, size_t count, long long offset);
void io_prep_pwrite (struct iocb *iocb, int fd, void *buf, size_t count, long long offset);
```

After calling these functions in an obvious way, you can just call `io_submit()` to get your I/O going.

Eventually the **glibc** maintainers will get around to doing the wrapping necessary to permit the **Posix API** to be used. At that point, if portability is desired, the native **Linux** applications that use **AIO** should be portable in a straightforward way, if portability is required.

## 15.4   Labs

### Lab 1: Testing Asynchronous I/O with POSIX and Linux API's

Write a program that uses the native **Linux API**. Have it send out a number of write and read requests and synchronize properly. You can work with a disposable file.

We also present a solution using the **Posix API** for the application.

Make sure you compile by linking with the right libraries; use **-laio** for the **Linux API** and **-lrt** for the **Posix API**. (You can use both in either case as they don't conflict.)

# Chapter 16

# Signals - I

We'll learn how **Linux** uses signals, what the available signals are, and how to dispatch them and handle them. We'll learn about alarms, pausing, and sleeping. We'll discuss signal sets and the **sigaction()** interface.

## 16.1   What are Signals?

**Signals** are *software interrupts* and provide a way to handle asynchronous events. They provide a basic method of **inter-process communication**; the communicating processes may or may not be related and under most conditions the only information sent is the type of signal.

A process can send signals only to a process for which it has the appropriate permissions.

Signals may be used to alert a process to take certain actions or to die gracefully. For most signals, if a process receives it without first arranging to catch it the process will terminate.

If the process does not terminate execution will be resumed by going back to the instruction that was being executed when the signal was received.

However, it is possible using the functions `setjmp()`, `sigsetjmp()`, `longjmp()`, `siglongjmp()`, to resume execution at an alternative location. This requires some care to avoid stack corruption.

The earliest implementations of `signal()` were not *reliable*; i.e., it could not be assured that signals would not get lost. Under **Linux** the newer reliable `sigaction()` interface is used and the older `signal()` interface is a wrapper around it.

The signal API dates back to the early days of **Unix**, before some other methods of inter-process communication and alternatives were developed, in particular before multi-threading was a viable option. While the API is mature it also contains a lot of baggage, and is in some sense old-fashioned.

If you are developing a new application that makes extensive use of signals you should question whether your design model makes sense, and whether you would be better off using threading, memory mapping to share memory, etc.

## 16.2   Signals Available

The command `kill -1` will list available signals, and the command `man 7 signal` will give further documentation. The header file giving the actual definitions is **/usr/include/asm-x86_64/signal.h**.

Here is a list of signals for the **x86** platform; the available signals will differ on other architectures:

Table 16.1: **Available signals**

| Signal | Value | Default Action | Posix? | Meaning |
| --- | --- | --- | --- | --- |
| SIGHUP | 1 | Terminate | Yes | Hangup detected on controlling terminal or death of controlling process. |
| SIGINT | 2 | Terminate | Yes | Interrupt from keyboard. |
| SIGQUIT | 3 | Core dump | Yes | Quit from keyboard. |
| SIGILL | 4 | Core dump | Yes | Illegal Instruction. |
| SIGTRAP | 5 | Core dump | No | Trace/breakpoint trap for debugging. |
| SIGABRT SIGIOT | 6 | Core dump | Yes | Abnormal termination. |
| SIGBUS | 7 | Core dump | Yes | Bus error. |
| SIGFPE | 8 | Core dump | Yes | Floating point exception. |
| SIGKILL | 9 | Terminate | Yes | Kill signal (can not be caught or ignored). |
| SIGUSR1 | 10 | Terminate | Yes | User-defined signal 1. |
| SIGSEGV | 11 | Core dump | Yes | Invalid memory reference. |
| SIGUSR2 | 12 | Terminate | Yes | User-defined signal 2. |
| SIGPIPE | 13 | Terminate | Yes | Broken pipe: write to pipe with no readers. |
| SIGALRM | 14 | Terminate | Yes | Timer signal from alarm. |
| SIGTERM | 15 | Terminate | Yes | Process termination. |

| SIGSTKFLT | 16 | Terminate | No | Stack fault on math co-processor. |
|---|---|---|---|---|
| SIGCHLD | 17 | Ignore | Yes | Child stopped or terminated. |
| SIGCONT | 18 | Continue | Yes | Continue if stopped. |
| SIGSTOP | 19 | Stop | Yes | Stop process (can not be caught or ignored) |
| SIGTSTP | 20 | Stop | Yes | Stop typed at tty. |
| SIGTTIN | 21 | Stop | Yes | Background process requires tty input. |
| SIGTTOU | 22 | Stop | Yes | Background process requires tty output. |
| SIGURG | 23 | Ignore | No | Urgent condition on socket (4.2 BSD). |
| SIGXCPU | 24 | Core dump | Yes | CPU time limit exceeded (4.2 BSD). |
| SIGXFSZ | 25 | Core dump | Yes | File size limit exceeded (4.2 BSD). |
| SIGVTALRM | 26 | Terminate | No | Virtual alarm clock (4.2 BSD). |
| SIGPROF | 27 | Terminate | No | Profile alarm clock (4.2 BSD) |
| SIGWINCH | 28 | Ignore | No | Window resize signal (4.3 BSD, Sun) |
| SIGIO SIGPOLL | 29 | Terminate | No | I/O now possible (4.2 BSD) (System V) |
| SIGPWR | 30 | Terminate | No | Power failure (System V) |
| SIGSYS SIGUNUSED | 31 | Terminate | No | Bad System Called. Unused signal. |

# 16.3   Dispatching Signals

Dispatching (sending) signals is easy; handling (catching) them properly and avoiding race conditions is more difficult. There are two functions for raising signals:

```
#include <sys/types.h>
#include <signal.h>

int kill (pid_t pid, int sig);
int raise (int sig);
```

kill() can send any signal to any process group or process. Note that the sending process must have the proper permissions to send a signal to another process.

raise() is used for a process to send a signal to itself; raise(sig) is equivalent to kill(getpid(),sig) in the case of a single-threaded process. In a multi-threaded process it sends a signal only to the current thread.

The pid argument in kill() can be used in several ways:

Table 16.2: **kill() process selection**

| Value | Meaning |
|-------|---------|
| `pid > 0` | Signal sent to process with process ID `pid`. |
| `pid = 0` | Signal sent to all processes whose process group ID is the same as the sender for whom the sender has permission. |
| `pid < -1` | Signal is sent to all processes whose process group ID is the absolute value of `pid` and for whom the sender has permission. |
| `pid = -1` | Signal is sent to every process except for the first one, from higher numbers in the process table to lower. |

These functions return 0 on success, -1 on error (**errno** is set). The possible error returns are:

Table 16.3: **kill() error return values**

| Value | Meaning |
|-------|---------|
| `EINVAL` | Invalid signal number specified. |
| `ESRCH` | `pid` or process group doesn't exist. |
| `EPERM` | Permission denied |

## 16.4   Alarms, Pausing and Sleeping

The function:

```
#include <unistd.h>

unsigned int alarm (unsigned int seconds);
```

sets a timer to expire **seconds** later and raises the **SIGALRM** signal. If **seconds = 0** any outstanding request is canceled.

There can be only one alarm clock per process; if a previously registered alarm clock exists the number of seconds left is returned and the timer is reset to the new value. On success the return value is zero for a new alarm.

Pausing and sleeping are done with:

```
#include <unistd.h>

int pause (void);
unsigned int sleep (unsigned int seconds);
```

pause() causes a process to sleep until a signal is received. The function returns only if a signal handler is executed and that handler returns. In this case **pause()** returns -1 with **errno** set to EINTR.

sleep() makes the current process sleep until **seconds** have elapsed or a signal arrives which is not ignored. The function returns 0 if the requested time has elapsed, or the number of seconds left to sleep.

For finer control of the sleeping interval, one can use the functions:

```
#include <unistd.h>
void usleep (usec);

#include <time.h>
int nanosleep (const struct timespec *req, struct timespec *rem);

struct timespec{
    time_t tv_sec;
    long   tv_nsec;
}
```

where **usleep()** suspends execution for **usec** microseconds, and **nanosleep()** suspends sleep for a period of **tv_sec** seconds and **tv_nsec** nanoseconds. See the **man** page for a full description of its arguments and a discussion of the precision, which can be less than requested.

It is also possible to use the **select()** function with NULL file descriptor sets to request sleeping with microsecond resolution as in:

```
select (1, NULL, NULL, NULL,  struct timeval *timeout);
struct timeval {
    long tv_sec,
    long tv_usec
}
```

## 16.5 Setting up a Signal Handler

The **signal()** function is the simplest approach to dealing with signals; as we shall see, **sigaction()** is better and is actually under the hood for **signal()** under **Linux**.

```
#include <signal.h>

void (*signal(int signum, void (*handler)(int)))(int);
```

The **signal()** system call installs a new signal handler for the signal with number **signum**. The signal handler is set to **handler()** which may be a user specified function, or one of the following:

Table 16.4: **Default signal handlers**

| Value | Meaning |
|---|---|
| SIG_IGN | Ignore the signal. |
| SIG_DFL | Reset the signal to its default behavior |

The integer argument that is handed over to the signal handler routine is the signal number. This makes it possible to use one signal handler for several signals.

Signal handlers cannot be set for SIGKILL or SIGSTOP.

The prototype is confusing. In practice it looks like:

```
typedef void (*sighandler_t)(int);
sighandler_t signal (int signum, sighandler_t handler);
```

signal returns the previous value of the signal handler, or SIG_ERR on error.

According to the man page for **signal()**, under **Linux** signals are reset to their default behavior when raised. This is **not true**. An inspection of the **glibc** source shows this to be otherwise. The reason is that the **signal()** system call is actually never invoked; instead **sigaction()** is called with flags that give different behaviour.

Thus, if you want to be sure the default behaviour is reinstated you'll have to call **signal()** again with SIG_DFL. If you want to make sure the default is not restored (portably) you would have to make the signal handler reinstall itself after it deals with a signal.

The signal that activates the handler is blocked while the handler executes; however, the handler might be interrupted if another signal that it handles is raised.

An example:

```
#include <signal.h>
#include <stdio.h>
#include <unistd.h>

void ouch (int sig)
{
    printf ("OUCH! - I got a signal %d\n", sig);
    signal (sig, SIG_DFL);
}

int main ()
{
    signal (SIGINT, ouch);
    while (1) {
        printf ("Hello World!\n");
        sleep (1);
    }
}
```

# 16.6   Signal Sets

It is possible to create a data type to represent multiple signals, a so-called **signal set**. With such a set one can tell the kernel to block, not block, or change the effect of any of the signals in the set on a given process.

There are five elementary functions in the POSIX standard for manipulating signal sets:

```
#include <signal.h>

int sigemptyset (sigset_t *set);
int sigfillset  (sigset_t *set);
int sigaddset   (sigset_t *set, int signum);
int sigdelset   (sigset_t *set, int signum);
int sigismember (const sigset_t *set, int signum);
```

We don't need to consider how the `sigset_t` data type is defined.

- `sigemptyset()` initializes the signal set to empty; all signals excluded.

- `sigfillset()` initializes the signal set to full.

- `sigaddset()` adds `signum` to `set`.

- `sigdelset()` deletes `signum` from `set`.

- `sigissmember()` tests whether `signum` is a member of `set`.

The first four functions return 0 on success, −1 on error. `sigismember()` returns 1 if `signum` is a member, 0 if it is not, and −1 on error. On errors, `errno` is set to `EINVAL` if `sig` is not a valid signal.

The following three functions permit more elaborate manipulations of signal sets:

```
#include <signal.h>

int sigprocmask (int  how,  const  sigset_t *set, sigset_t *oldset);
int sigpending (sigset_t *set);
int sigsuspend (const sigset_t *mask);
```

`sigprocmask()` changes the list of currently blocked signals, according to value of `how`:

Table 16.5: **Signal mask selection**

| Value | Meaning |
|---|---|
| SIG_BLOCK | Set of blocked signals is the *union* of the current set and **set** argument; i.e., **set** contains the additional signals to block. |
| SIG_UNBLOCK | Set of blocked signals is the *intersection* of the current set and the complement of the **set** argument; i.e., the signals specified in **set** are removed from the current set. |
| SIG_SETMASK | The set of blocked signals is to set to the argument **set**. |

If `oldset` is not NULL, the previous value of the signal set is retrieved into it.

If `set` is NULL the value is unchanged, independent of `how`; i.e., one can just retrieve the signal set.

`sigpending()` allows examination of signals which have been raised while blocked, and the mask of pending signals is stored in `set`.

`sigsuspend()` temporarily replaces the signal mask with that given by its argument, and then suspends the process until a signal is received.

These functions return 0 on success, -1 on error (`errno` is set). The possible error returns are:

Table 16.6: **Signal mask function error return values**

| Value | Meaning |
|---|---|
| EINVAL | Invalid signal specified (including if one tries to change the action for SIGKILL or SIGSTOP). |
| EFAULT | Invalid memory reference for `set`, `oldset`. |
| EINTR | System call was interrupted. |

## Example:

The following code will block all signals for 5 seconds and then restore the default signal handlers.

```
#include <stdio.h>
#include <unistd.h>
#include <signal.h>
#include <stdlib.h>

int main (int argc, char *argv[])
{
    int rc;
    sigset_t sigsus, oldset;

    /* block all possible signals */
    rc = sigfillset (&sigsus);
    rc = sigprocmask (SIG_SETMASK, &sigsus, &oldset);

    printf (" going to sleep 5 seconds, try control-C!\n");
    sleep (5);
    printf (" going ahead\n");

    /* restore original mask */
    rc = sigprocmask (SIG_SETMASK, &oldset, NULL);

    /* Do something pointless, forever */
    for (;;) {
```

```
        printf ("This is a pointless message.\n");
        sleep (1);
    }
    return 0;
}
```

---

• You can examine the masks of pending, blocked, ignored and caught signals for all processes on your system with:

```
$ ps axs
  UID   PID        PENDING          BLOCKED         IGNORED
             CAUGHT STAT TTY      TIME COMMAND
    0     1 0000000000000000 0000000000000000 fffffffe57f0d8fc
      00000000280b2603 Ss    ?           0:00 init [5]
....
   68  3684 0000000000000000 0000000000000000 0000000000001000
      0000000180014000 Ss    ?           0:03 hald
....
  500  4250 0000000000000000 0000000000000000 0000000020384004
      000000004b813efb Ss+   pts/0       0:00 bash
....
  500  4427 0000000000000000 0000000000010000 0000000020000004
      0000000000010002 S     ?           0:00 /bin/sh /usr/lib64/firefox-3.
  500  9638 0000000000000000 0000000000000000 0000000000000000
      0000000051817efd S     pts/1       0:01 emacs -bg black -fg white -ge
  500  9663 0000000000000000 0000000000000000 0000000000000000
      0000000073d3fef9 R+    pts/1       0:00 ps axs
```

---

## 16.7   sigaction()

The `sigaction()` function can be used to change (or examine) the action a process takes upon receipt of a particular signal. It supersedes the **signal()** function call:

```
#include <signal.h>

int sigaction (int signum, const struct sigaction  *act, struct sigaction *oldact);
struct sigaction {
   void (*sa_handler)(int);
   void (*sa_sigaction)(int, siginfo_t *, void *);
   sigset_t sa_mask;
   int sa_flags;
   void (*sa_restorer)(void);
            }
```

Any valid signal can be used for **signum** (except, of course, SIGKILL and SIGSTOP.)

When `act` is not `NULL`, a new handler for `signum` is taken from `act`. When `oldact` is not `NULL`, the previous action is retrieved into it.

`sa_handler()` is either `SIG_DFL` for the default action, `SIG_IGN` to ignore the signal, or a pointer to a signal handler.

`sa_sigaction()` is an alternative signal handler, to be used instead of `sa_handler()`, with some other capabilities. We'll detail its use later when we discuss `siginfo`.

You can not use both `sa_sigaction()` and `sa_handler()` at the same time; there is a union involved and you have choose one or the other. If you choose both the second one will wipe out the first one.

`sa_mask` is a mask of signals to be **blocked** while the handler executes. (Note that the signal which invoked the handler will also be blocked unless `SA_NODEFER` or `SA_NOMASK` are used in `sa_flags`.)

`sa_restorer()` is an historical vestige and should not be used. It is not part of the POSIX standard. There has been discussion in the past about using this field for various other purposes but it seems to have dried up.

`sigaction()` has the same error codes as the other functions which operate on signal sets.

The `sa_flags` field modifies the signal handling behaviour. It is made up of the bitwise OR of any combination (or none) of the following:

Table 16.8: **Signal handler flags**

| Flag | Meaning |
| --- | --- |
| SA_NOCLDSTOP | If `signum` is SIGCHLD, no notification when child processes stop. |
| SA_ONESHOT or SA_RESETHAND | Restore the signal action to its default state once the handler is done. |
| SA_RESTART | System calls returning EINTR are restarted after the signal is handled. There are some exceptions such as `sleep()` and `pause()`, for which restarting could lead to an infinite loop. System calls which return -ERESTARTSYS always restart. |
| SA_NOMASK or SA_NODEFER | Don't prevent the signal from being received from inside its own signal handler. If SA_NOMASK is used, the signal mask field (`sa_mask`) is ignored completely; the list of blocked signals for the process remains unchanged while the handler executes. |
| SA_SIGINFO | Use the `sa_sigaction()` function as the handler instead of `sa_handler()`. Three arguments are specified, not one. |

# 16.8 Labs

## Lab 1: Signals

Using the `signal()` interface for installing signal handlers, write a simple program to do something pointless in an infinite loop. (Like printing out the same message after every second.)

Upon getting a CTRL-C (SIGINT) the program should print a message, but not die.

Upon getting a CTRL-\ (SIGQUIT) it should call `abort()` to dump core.

**Note:** Some **Linux** distributions set the maximum core dump size to 0. Type `ulimit -c` to find out what you actually have. If the maximum core dump size has to be set, do it with `ulimit -c {nbytes}`.

## Lab 2: sigaction()

Adapt the previous exercise (or start fresh) to use the `sigaction()` interface. Set up a signal set and mask to do this.

Have the SIGINT handler sleep for a couple of seconds; what happens if you send a SIGQUIT while it is sleeping?

## Lab 3: Blocking Signals

Adapt the previous exercise so that SIGQUIT is blocked while the handler for SIGINT is running.

## Lab 4: Examining Signal Priorities.

In the below, do not send or handle either of the signals SIGKILL or SIGSTOP.

Write a **C** program that includes a signal handler that can handle any signal. The handler should avoid making any system calls (such as those that might occur doing I/O).

The handler should simply store the sequence of signals as they come in, and update a counter array for each signal that indicates how many times the signal has been handled.

The program should begin by suspending processing of all signals (using `sigprocmask()`.

It should then install the new set of signal handlers (which can be the same for all signals, registering them with the `sigaction()` interface.

The program should send every possible signal to itself multiple times, using the `raise()` function.

Signal processing should be resumed, once again using `sigprocmask()`.

Before completing, the program should print out statistics including:

- The total number of times each signal was received.

- The order in which the signals were received, noting each time the total number of times that signal had been received up to that point.

Note the following items:

- If more than one of a given signal is raised while the process has blocked it, does the process receive it multiple times?

- Are all signals received by the process, or are some handled before they reach it?

- What order are the signals received in?

One signal, SIGCONT (18 on **x86**) may not get through; can you figure out why?

---

- It appears that in the 2.6 kernel signals 32 and 33 can not be blocked and will cause your program to fail. Even though header files indicate SIGRTMIN=32, the command kill -1 indicates SIGRTMIN=34.

- Note that one should always be using signal names, not numbers, which are allowed to be completely implementation dependent.

- Avoid sending these signals.

---

# Chapter 17

# Signals - II

We'll discuss the issue of reentrancy and signal handlers. We'll also learn more advanced signal operations involving jumping to alternate returns, and the **sigqueue** function. Finally we'll discuss **real time** signals.

## 17.1  Reentrancy and Signal Handlers

Exactly when a signal handler is going to be called is of course unpredictable. Thus one has to be particularly careful about the various resources that a signal handler uses. In practice this means one has to worry about reentrancy and thread-safety; these are not the same thing.

Being careful about reentrancy simply means being careful about functions which can call themselves, directly or indirectly.

Being thread-safe means that any data areas that can be touched in more than one thread must be protected by proper locking mechanisms.

For the moment we'll concentrate on reentrancy. For an excellent article on this problem in signal handlers, see **http://www.ibm.com/developerworks/linux/library/l-reent.html**.

A function is reentrant if it:

- Does not hold static data over successive calls.

- Does not return a pointer to static data; all data is provided by the caller of the function.

- Uses local data or ensures protection of global data by making a local copy of it.

- Does not call any non-reentrant functions.

In practice this means a function is **not** reentrant if it:

- Calls `malloc()` or `free()`.

- Uses static data structures.

- Uses the standard I/O library.

This doesn't mean you can't use non-reentrant functions in a signal handler. What it means is you had better be careful if you do that you understand your code well enough to ensure that the functions that can cause problems are never called in a context where the signal may be received and then called in the signal handler itself.

Note that code can be reentrant but not thread-safe. These are two independent concepts.

## 17.2   Jumping and Non-Local Returns

Normally after a non-fatal signal handler is executed, execution will resume from the point in the code where the signal was received.

The following functions permit alternative non-local goto's after a handler is invoked:

```
#include <setjmp.h>

int setjmp (jmp_buf env);
void longjmp (jmp_buf env, int val);

int sigsetjmp (sigjmp_buf env, int savesigs);
void siglongjmp (sigjmp_buf env, int val);
```

An initial call to `setjmp()` or `sigsetjmp()` saves the stack context and environment in the first argument, `env`, so that it can later be restored. (One need not look into the details of how the `jmp_buf` and `sigjmp_buf` buffers are defined.) The initial call will give a return value of 0.

A subsequent call to `longjmp()` or `siglongjmp()` will reposition the instruction flow at the place of the call to `setjmp()` or `sigsetjmp`, and the second argument, `val`, will provide the return value of the setting functions.

The difference between the two sets of functions is in how they deal with the signal environment. If the **savesigs** argument is non-zero the mask of block signals is saved when `sigsetjmp()` is called and is restored when `siglongjmp()` is called.

The simpler functions have signal behaviour that is not specified in the **Posix** standard and can vary in different **Unix** implementations. Therefore they should be avoided if signals are involved.

Here's an example of a program using these functions to have an alternative return from a signal handler:

```
#include <stdio.h>
#include <unistd.h>
#include <signal.h>
#include <stdlib.h>
#include <errno.h>
#include <string.h>
#include <setjmp.h>

#define DEATH(mess) { perror(mess); exit(errno); }

sigjmp_buf senv;

void sig_int (int what)
{
    static int counter = 0;
    printf ("We have received SIGINT\n");
    siglongjmp (senv, ++counter);
}
int main (int argc, char *argv[])
{
    int savesigs = 1;
    struct sigaction act;
    memset (&act, 0, sizeof (act));
    act.sa_handler = sig_int;
    if (sigaction (SIGINT, &act, NULL) < 0) /* for CTRL-C */
        DEATH ("sigaction");
    printf ("Successfully installed signal handler for SIGINT\n");
    printf ("returning from setjmp/longjmp, rc=%d\n",
            sigsetjmp (senv, savesigs));
    /* hit Ctl-C while the sleep is proceeding */
    sleep (10);
    DEATH ("returned to the wrong place!\n");
}
```

These methods can cause subtle problems and make programs difficult to maintain and comprehend. So they are not recommended for new code, but may be encountered when dealing with previously written programs.

# 17.3   siginfo and sigqueue()

When `SA_SIGINFO` is used the enhanced signal handler routine has the prototype:

```
void (*sa_sigaction)(int sig, siginfo_t *si, void *ctx);
```

the second argument of which is a pointer to a structure of type:

```
siginfo_t {
    int      si_signo;  /* Signal number */
    int      si_errno;  /* An errno value */
    int      si_code;   /* Signal code */
    pid_t    si_pid;    /* Sending process ID */
    uid_t    si_uid;    /* Real user ID of sending process */
    int      si_status; /* Exit value or signal */
    clock_t  si_utime;  /* User time consumed */
    clock_t  si_stime;  /* System time consumed */
    sigval_t si_value;  /* Signal value */
    int      si_int;    /* POSIX.1b signal */
    void *   si_ptr;    /* POSIX.1b signal */
    void *   si_addr;   /* Memory location which caused fault */
    int      si_band;   /* Band event */
    int      si_fd;     /* File descriptor */
}
```

The interpretation of most of these arguments is pretty self-evident. The **man** page for `sigaction()` gives detailed possibilities for the field `si_code`. Using this structure one can obtain information about why the signal was sent, and by what process, for example.

The third argument to the **sa_sigaction()** function points to an object of type `ucontext_t`, referring to the receiving process' context when it was interrupted.

One can make use these enhanced capabilities by dispatching signals with the **sigqueue()** function:

```
#include <signal.h>

int sigqueue (pid_t *pid, int *sig, const union sigval value);

union sigval {
    int   sival_int;
    void *sival_ptr;
};
```

The second argument will appear in the **siginfo** structure as the `si_value` field, but one can also directly use the fields `si_int` and `si_ptr` to point to the members of the union more directly.

Not all the other fields may be valid as the structure is laid out in a complicated way, and the contents depend on the type of signal.

Here's an example of a simple program that sends a signal to itself:

```
#include <stdio.h>
#include <unistd.h>
```

```c
#include <signal.h>
#include <stdlib.h>
#include <errno.h>
#include <string.h>

#define DEATH(mess) { perror(mess); exit(errno); }

/* our signal handlers */

void sig_act (int sig, siginfo_t * si, void *a)
{
    printf ("in handler pid=%d, SIGNAL = %d\n", getpid (), sig);

    printf ("si_signo = \t%d\n", si->si_signo);
    printf ("si_code = \t%d\n", si->si_code);
    printf ("si_pid = \t%d\n", si->si_pid);
    printf ("si_uid = \t%d\n", si->si_uid);
    printf ("si_value = \t%d\n", si->si_value.sival_int);
    printf ("si_int = \t%d\n", si->si_int);
}

int main (int argc, char *argv[])
{
    struct sigaction act;;
    int j;
    union sigval sv;

    memset (&act, 0, sizeof (act));
    act.sa_sigaction = sig_act;
    act.sa_flags = SA_SIGINFO;
    if (sigaction (SIGINT, &act, NULL) < 0) /* for CTRL-C */
        DEATH ("sigaction");

    printf ("pid=%d Successfully installed signal handler for SIGINT\n",
            getpid ());

    for (j = 0; j < 3; j++) {
        printf ("This is a pointless message\n");
        sv.sival_int = j * 100;
        printf ("sigqueue returns %d\n", sigqueue (getpid (), SIGINT, sv));
        sleep (1);
    }
    exit (0);
}
```

## 17.4  Real Time Signals

**Real time** signals differ from ordinary signals in that they can be queued up; i.e., if more than one signal of a given type is received, the signal handler can be called multiple times.

The command kill -l lists the available signals as:

1) SIGHUP       2) SIGINT       3) SIGQUIT       4) SIGILL

```
 5) SIGTRAP      6) SIGABRT      7) SIGBUS       8) SIGFPE
 9) SIGKILL     10) SIGUSR1     11) SIGSEGV     12) SIGUSR2
13) SIGPIPE     14) SIGALRM     15) SIGTERM     16) SIGSTKFLT
17) SIGCHLD     18) SIGCONT     19) SIGSTOP     20) SIGTSTP
21) SIGTTIN     22) SIGTTOU     23) SIGURG      24) SIGXCPU
25) SIGXFSZ     26) SIGVTALRM   27) SIGPROF     28) SIGWINCH
29) SIGIO       30) SIGPWR      31) SIGSYS      34) SIGRTMIN
35) SIGRTMIN+1  36) SIGRTMIN+2  37) SIGRTMIN+3  38) SIGRTMIN+4
39) SIGRTMIN+5  40) SIGRTMIN+6  41) SIGRTMIN+7  42) SIGRTMIN+8
43) SIGRTMIN+9  44) SIGRTMIN+10 45) SIGRTMIN+11 46) SIGRTMIN+12
47) SIGRTMIN+13 48) SIGRTMIN+14 49) SIGRTMIN+15 50) SIGRTMAX-14
51) SIGRTMAX-13 52) SIGRTMAX-12 53) SIGRTMAX-11 54) SIGRTMAX-10
55) SIGRTMAX-9  56) SIGRTMAX-8  57) SIGRTMAX-7  58) SIGRTMAX-6
59) SIGRTMAX-5  60) SIGRTMAX-4  61) SIGRTMAX-3  62) SIGRTMAX-2
63) SIGRTMAX-1  64) SIGRTMAX
```

Note that what you see may depend on exactly which kernel you are using.

The real time signals thus lie between SIGRTMIN and SIGRTMAX.

The maximum queue length for real time signals can be viewed and modified (per user) from the command line with the ulimit -i command, and from a program using getrlimit() and setrlimit(), with the usual restriction that only a superuser can increase their limit.

If multiple real time signals of the same number are pending, they are delivered in FIFO order.

The **POSIX** standard dictates that if more than one real time signal is pending, the lowered number signal should be delivered first. Further **Linux** gives priority to normal signals over real time signals, although **POSIX** is mum on this issue.

# 17.5   Labs

## Lab 1: Using siginfo and sigqueue().

Take the simple example using sigqueue() and expand it to pass a structure into the enhanced signal handler.

Do this a number of times and print out values of interest.

## Lab 2: Using sigsetjmp() and siglongjmp().

Write a simple program with a signal handler for SIGINT (Control-C). Have the signal handler return with a call to siglongjmp() to a point in your main program where sigsetjmp() is invoked.

For the first four times the signal handler is hit have the program continue; the fifth time have it terminate.

# Chapter 18

# POSIX Threads - I

We'll learn how **Linux** implements the POSIX threads (**pthreads**) standard for multi-threaded programming. We'll learn the basic program structure, how to create, destroy and join threads. We'll see how multi-threaded programs handle signals. We'll then discuss the relative merits of forking and threading.

## 18.1   Multi-threading under Linux

**Threads** are so-called **light-weight** processes that share access to a single memory space and environment, and are quite different from ordinary Unix processes.

A **multi-threaded** approach divides a process into a number of execution paths that can be executed in parallel; the threads may be spawned and then joined back together. Careful synchronization is required among the parallel processes.

On multiple processor (**SMP**) machines, multi-threading can be used to divide work up for parallel execution; doing so on a single processor is counterproductive. On any machine, multi-threading can be used to handle concurrent tasks, such as waiting for action on windows, server requests etc.

User programs gain access to multi-threading by compiling with the right options and linking to the **pthreads** library, included with the **glibc** distribution. This implements the "shared everything" approach; all data and all program code is available to all threads.

The **Linux** kernel implements multi-threading through use of the `clone()` system call, which creates a new process like `fork()` does. However, the child process shares the memory space, table of file descriptors, and table of signal handlers with the parent process,

Note that all sibling threads share the same process identifier, and return the same result from `getpid()`. However, they will each have a distinct **thread identifier**.

## 18.2   Basic Program Structure

In order to compile and link an application to the **pthreads** library one has to use the -pthread option as in:

```
gcc -o prog -O2 -Wall -pedantic -pthread  prog.c
```

Any locks that will be needed must be declared and initialized. They are declared as type `pthread_mutex_t` and are initialized with `pthread_mutex_init()`.

The program begins as a single process, and then new threads are spawned with `pthread_create()` with arguments denoting the new thread's function and any additional information to be passed. Each thread has an associated variable of type `pthread_t` for identification purposes.

The parallel threads now run. Synchronization involves using `pthread_mutex_lock()` and `pthread_mutex_unlock()`. One may also use **semaphores** and **condition variables** to control cooperation among threads.

When the threads complete their work they can be joined to with `pthread_join()`, unless they have been created in a **detached** state.

## 18.3   Creating and Destroying Threads

The following operations create and destroy POSIX threads:

```
#include <pthread.h>

int  pthread_create (pthread_t *thread, pthread_attr_t * attr,
         void * (*start_routine)(void *), void *arg);
int  pthread_join (pthread_t thread, void **thread_return);
int  pthread_detach (pthread_t thread);
int  pthread_cancel (pthread_t thread);
void pthread_exit (void *retval);
```

`pthread_create()` creates a new thread of control that runs in parallel with the calling thread. It starts `start_routine()` passing it `arg`.

A thread terminates either explicitly by calling `pthread_exit()`, or implicitly by returning from `start_routine()`.

The `attr` argument specifies thread attributes: see the man page for `pthread_attr_init()` for a complete list of attributes. If it is `NULL`, default attributes are used: the thread is join-able (not detached) and has the default scheduling policy.

One particular attribute that may need to be set is the **stack size**. By default on most **Linux** systems this is set to be 8 MB (per thread); if you start to create thousands of threads you might easily exceed memory requirements. To set the stack size the following code would do:

```
#define STACK_SIZE = 128 * 1024;
pthread_attr_t thread_attr;
rc = pthread_attr_init (&thread_attr);
rc = pthread_attr_setstacksize (&thread_attr, STACK_SIZE);
rc = pthread_create (&thread, &thread_attr, myfun, &myarg);
```

On success the location pointed to by `thread` receives the new thread's identifier and the return value is 0. On failure the possible errors are:

Table 18.1: **pthread_create() error return values**

| Value | Meaning |
|---|---|
| EAGAIN | Not enough system resources to create a thread, or more than `PTHREAD_THREADS_MAX` are already active. |

An example:

```
  if ( pthread_create (&thread0, NULL, process, "0") ||
       pthread_create (&thread1, NULL, process, "1") ) {
    fprintf (stderr, "%s: cannot make thread\n", argv[0]);
    exit(1);
  }
```

`pthread_join()` suspends execution of the calling thread until `thread` terminates (either by calling `pthread_exit()` or being canceled). If `thread_return` is not NULL, the return value of `thread` is stored in the location it points to.

The joined thread must not have been detached with `pthread_detach()`.

Memory resources are not de-allocated until another thread joins with it; thus `pthread_join()` must be called for all join-able threads to avoid memory leaks.

On success 0 is returned. On failure the possible errors are:

Table 18.2: **pthread_join() error return values**

| Value | Meaning |
|---|---|
| ESRCH | Thread `thread` could not be found. |
| EINVAL | `thread` has been detached or another thread is waiting on its termination. |
| EDEADLK | Thread `thread` refers to the calling thread. |

An example:

```
void *retval;
  if ( pthread_join (thread0, &retval) ||
      pthread_join (thread1, &retval) ) {
    fprintf (stderr, "%s: thread join failed\n", argv[0]);
    exit (1);
  }
```

`pthread_detach()` detaches `thread`, which means that memory resources will be freed immediately upon termination; i.e., no join is necessary. After detachment other threads can not synchronize with `thread` using `pthread_join()`.

It is also possible to create a thread in a detached state, using the `PTHREAD_CREATE_DETACHED` attribute.

On success `0` is returned. On failure the possible errors are:

Table 18.3: **pthread_detach() error return values**

| Value | Meaning |
|---|---|
| ESRCH | Thread `thread` could not be found. |
| EINVAL | `thread` has been detached. |

`pthread_cancel()` permits one thread to send a cancellation request to another thread. The target thread can ignore the request, honor it immediately, or defer until it reaches a cancellation point, such as `pthread_join()`.

Threads are always created as cancellation enabled and deferred. The auxiliary functions `pthread_setcancelstate()`, `pthread_setcanceltype()`, `pthread_testcancel()`, can be used to change (or interrogate) this behaviour.

On success 0 is returned. On failure the possible errors are:

Table 18.4: **pthread cancellation error return values**

| Value | Meaning |
|-------|---------|
| ESRCH | Thread `thread` could not be found. |

`pthread_exit()` terminates execution of the calling thread, and never returns.. `retval` is the return value of the thread.

Cleanup handlers, previously registered by the calling thread with `pthread_cleanup_push()`, are run in reverse order of registration.

Note there are a number of other related functions, which we won't discuss in detail, such as:

Table 18.5: **Additional pthread functions**

| Value | Meaning |
|-------|---------|
| `pthread_self()` | Return identifier of current thread. |
| `pthread_equal()` | Compare two thread identifiers. |

See `man -k pthread` for a list of all the available functions.

# 18.4   Signals and Threads

Signal handlers are shared among all threads of a multi-threaded application. However, each thread can have its own unique masks of pending and blocked signals.

A termination signal must terminate all threads; however the **Linux**-specific `tkill()` system call can send a signal to just one thread.

When a signal is sent using `kill()` **any** thread may receive it. The kernel will pick any thread which does not have the signal blocked and one cannot control the choice of which thread gets the assignment.

Note that for a multi-threaded process, it is **not** true that `raise(sig) = kill(getpid(),sig)`; in fact `raise()` will send a signal only to the current thread and not to any and all of them as `kill()` does.

It is therefore not uncommon to have an application block all blockable signals in all but one thread, which takes on the role of signal handler.

Two function calls which implement this are:

```
#include <signal.h>
```

```
int pthread_sigmask(int how, const sigset_t *set, sigset_t *oldset);
int sigwait(const sigset_t *set, int *sig);
```

The first function has the exact same arguments and use as `sigprocmask()`, except it affects only the current thread.

The second function, `sigwait()` takes as its first argument a mask describing which signals to wait for; upon return the second argument contains which signal caused the return, which also supplies the return value if successful.

Using these functions it is possible deal with signals without actually using signal handlers and `sigaction()`; one first blocks all possible signals in all threads with `sigprocmask()`. Then one has a signal-dealing thread use `sigwait()` to deal with the signals. This can help avoid some complexities in signal handlers.

## 18.5   Forking vs. Threading

There are at least three basic approaches one can take when developing applications under **Linux** which lend themselves to threading:

- Use the POSIX **pthreads** approach.
- Use the parent/child **fork** (and possibly **exec**) approach.
- Use the **clone** call directly.

Some of the advantages and disadvantages are:

- The **pthreads** approach is POSIX compliant, and recent improvements have improved both compliance and conformance.
- The parent/child model is straightforward and very portable. However, creating new processes is expensive, and why not use the more modern multi-threaded approach?
- The **clone** call is used (under **Linux**) to implement both of the other approaches. However it is very non-portable.
- For short-lived tasks one should probably avoid forking; the overhead for creating a whole new process is expensive, while threads are much cheaper. On the other hand, if the new task can be performed without much interaction with the parent, forking is a better solution because it is easier and more portable.

Thus each application requires evaluation as to which is the proper programming framework; there is no "one size fits all" solution.

# 18.6   Labs

## Lab 1: Threads

Write a counting program, which should have two threads.

While one thread loops, incrementing a counter as fast as it can, the other one occasionally peeks at the counter and prints out its value.

## Lab 2: Signals and Threads

Write a program that launches multiple threads, which has one thread reserved for dealing with signals, using `sigwait()`, `pthread_sigmask()`.

Send one or more signals to the process either from the command line (you can use `SIGINT` which is `Control-C`), or using `kill()`.

Verify which thread deals with the signals using `pthread_self()` to print out the thread ID's.

## Lab 3: Signals, Threads and Handlers

Instead of dedicating one thread to signals, install a signal handler.

After launching a number of threads, block handling the signal in the master thread.

Send one or more signals to the process either from the command line (you can use `SIGINT` which is `Control-C`), or using `kill()`.

Verify which thread deals with the signals using `pthread_self()` to print out the thread ID's.

## Lab 4: Threads and Initialization and Exit Handlers

Extend the counter exercise to have constructor and destructor functions.

Are they run for each thread? Or for only the master thread?

# Chapter 19

# POSIX Threads - II

We'll continue our discussion of how **Linux** implements the **pthreads** standard for multi-threaded programming. We'll consider some common problems. We'll study the use of **mutual exclusion** (mutex) operations, semaphores, futexes, and conditional operations.

## 19.1   Deadlocks and Race Conditions

Multi-threaded programs are prone to **deadlocks** and **race conditions**. This is particularly, but not exclusively true, on multiple processor systems where threads can be running simultaneously on different CPUs.

Here's a code fragment that shows a canonical freeze up:

```
void *fun1 (void *arg){
```

```
    pthread_mutex_lock (&lockA);
    do_something ();
    pthread_mutex_lock (&lockB);
    do_something ();
    pthread_mutex_unlock (&lockB);
    pthread_mutex_unlock (&lockA);
}
void *fun2 (void *arg){
    pthread_mutex_lock (&lockB);
    do_something ();
    pthread_mutex_lock (&lockA);
    do_something ();
    pthread_mutex_unlock (&lockA);
    pthread_mutex_unlock (&lockB);
}
```

Such programs can be difficult to debug since they may "work" most of the time.

One has to be particularly careful when adapting non-threaded programs to a multi-threaded model. If care hasn't been put in the original design it is easy for problems to arise.

## 19.2   Mutex Operations

A **mutex** is a **MUT**ual **EX**clusion device, used to protect shared data structures from concurrent modifications and protecting critical sections of code.

A mutex can be *unlocked* (not owned by any thread); or *locked* (owned by a thread.) Normally a thread which tries to lock an already locked mutex is suspended.

```
#include <pthread.h>

int pthread_mutex_init (pthread_mutex_t *mutex, const pthread_mutexattr_t *mutexattr);
int pthread_mutex_lock    (pthread_mutex_t *mutex);
int pthread_mutex_trylock (pthread_mutex_t *mutex);
int pthread_mutex_unlock  (pthread_mutex_t *mutex);
int pthread_mutex_destroy (pthread_mutex_t *mutex);
```

- pthread_mutex_lock() does what is says. If the mutex is already locked the thread is suspended until it is unlocked (by default), but this can be modified by changing attributes.

- pthread_mutex_trylock() is the same as pthread_mutex_lock() except it does not block if the mutex is already locked by another thread.

- pthread_mutex_unlock() does what is says.

- pthread_mutex_destroy() destroys a mutex object, freeing any resources. It actually just checks the mutex is unlocked.

A mutex can be initialized in an unlocked state with the macro:

```
pthread_mutex_t my_mutex = PTHREAD_MUTEX_INITIALIZER;
```

For more control one can use the `pthread_mutex_init()` function, which initializes a mutex object with attributes pointed to by the `mutexattr` field. If it is `NULL` defaults are used. (The **man** pages contain an extended discussion on possible attributes.)

The mutex kind can be **fast**, **recursive**, or **error checking**; the default is **fast**. These describe what happens if a thread tries to lock a mutex it already owns with `pthread_mutex_lock()`:

Table 19.1: **Posix threads mutex types**

| Type | Symbolic Name | Meaning |
|---|---|---|
| fast | PTHREAD_MUTEX_FAST_NP | Suspend the calling thread forever. |
| recursive | PTHREAD_MUTEX_RECURSIVE_NP | Return immediately with a success return code. |
| error checking | PTHREAD_MUTEX_ERRORCHECK_NP | Return immediately with error code EDEADLK. |

The _NP suffix indicates these are non-portable extensions to the POSIX standard and shouldn't be used in portable code.

## 19.3   Semaphores

It is also possible to use POSIX **semaphore** operations to control access to resources. We will defer a full treatment until we discuss **POSIX IPC**, even though it properly belongs here.

The following functions are for POSIX 1003.1b semaphores (not System V) and are **counters** for resources shared between **threads**:

```
#include <pthread.h>
#include <semaphore.h>

int sem_init (sem_t *sem, int pshared, unsigned int value);
int sem_wait (sem_t *sem);
int sem_trywait (sem_t *sem);
int sem_post (sem_t *sem);
int sem_getvalue (sem_t *sem, int *sval);
int sem_destroy (sem_t *sem);
```

The structure `sem_t *sem` points to a semaphore object. One need not be concerned with the internal details of the structure.

`sem_init()` initializes the semaphore object pointed to by `sem`, setting it to **value**. If `pshared` is 0 the semaphore is local to the current process; otherwise it may be shared.

`sem_wait()` suspends the calling thread until the semaphore pointed to by `sem` has non-zero count and then atomically decreases the count.

`sem_trywait()` is a non-blocking version of `sem_wait()`. If the semaphore count is 0 it returns EAGAIN.

`sem_post()` atomically increases the semaphore count. It never blocks.

`sem_getvalue()` retrieves the current semaphore count and puts it in *`*sval`.

`sem_destroy()` destroys the semaphore object.

`sem_wait()` and `sem_getvalue()` always return 0; all other functions return 0 on success, `-1` on error and write an error code in `errno`.

It is also possible to use **named semaphores**, using the `sem_open()` and `sem_close()` calls. We'll review this when we discuss **POSIX IPC**.

If counting capability is not needed (i.e., you need only a binary semaphore), a **mutex** is a better choice. It is lighter in weight and since only one critical section at a time can possess the lock is easier to trace and debug.

## 19.4    Futexes

In **Linux** both mutexes and semaphores are built upon the same underlying mechanism: **futex**es (**F**ast **U**serspace mu**TEX**es.)

A **futex** is nothing more than a section of memory shareable between more than one task. This section of memory behaves like a semaphore in that it contains a counter that can be incremented and decremented, and tasks can wait upon a positive value.

The reason futexes are fast is that if there is no contention for the futex everything is done in user-space; i.e., no system call is required. The kernel need only be involved in the contented case. For locking mechanisms contention is generally the unlikely case so the savings in context switches, scheduling, etc., are considerable.

While it is possible to use the bare futex API in applications (see **man 2 futex**), the intended users are library implementers. In this case the futex constitutes the underlying infrastructure for locking primitives such as mutexes and semaphores. (See **man 7 futex**.)

## 19.5    Conditional Operations

It is possible to have **condition variables** that allow threads to suspend execution until some condition on shared data is satisfied.

The relevant functions (all of which return 0 on success and set **errno** on failure) are:

```
#include <pthread.h>

pthread_cond_t cond = PTHREAD_COND_INITIALIZER;

int pthread_cond_init (pthread_cond_t *cond, pthread_condattr_t *cond_attr);
int pthread_cond_wait (pthread_cond_t *cond, pthread_mutex_t *mutex);
int pthread_cond_timedwait (pthread_cond_t*cond, pthread_mutex_t *mutex,
                            const struct timespec *abstime);
int pthread_cond_signal (pthread_cond_t *cond);
int pthread_cond_broadcast (pthread_cond_t *cond);
int pthread_cond_destroy (pthread_cond_t *cond);
```

The basic operations are initialization, signalling, waiting, and destruction.

A condition variable can be initialized first with `pthread_cond_init()`; using `NULL` for the second argument gives default attributes. However, a static allocation using `PTHREAD_COND_INITIALIZER` is sufficient.

Condition variables are connected to a mutex to avoid race conditions that would arise when one thread signals a condition before another thread actually waits on it.

`pthread_cond_wait()` unlocks the mutex and waits for the condition variable to be signalled. The `_timedwait()` version gives a maximum waiting time.

`pthread_cond_signal()` restarts **one** of the threads waiting on `cond`; `pthread_cond_broadcast()` wakes up **all** waiting threads.

As an example from the man page (See `man pthread_cond_init`):

Consider two shared variables x and y, protected by the mutex `mut`, and a condition variable `cond` that is to be signaled whenever x becomes greater than y.

```
int x,y;
pthread_mutex_t mut = PTHREAD_MUTEX_INITIALIZER;
pthread_cond_t cond = PTHREAD_COND_INITIALIZER;
```

Waiting until x is greater than y is performed as follows:

```
pthread_mutex_lock(&mut);
  while (x <= y) {
      pthread_cond_wait(&cond, &mut);
  }
  /* operate on x and y */
  pthread_mutex_unlock(&mut);
```

Modifications on x and y that may cause x to become greater than y should signal the condition if needed:

```
pthread_mutex_lock(&mut);
/* modify x and y */
if (x > y) pthread_cond_broadcast(&cond);
pthread_mutex_unlock(&mut);
```

Note that `pthread_cond_wait()` also make use of the same mutex that is referred to in the `pthread_mutex_lock()` function.

One subtlety is that the function `pthread_cond_wait()` function releases the mutex upon entry and then reacquires it upon exit. Otherwise, it would be impossible to broadcast that the condition has been satisfied, since the mutex lock is taken out in order to do so.

# 19.6   Labs

## Lab 1: Threads with Mutexes

Extend the counter exercise from the previous section previous exercise to protect the counter variable with a mutex.

What happens if the counter thread exits while holding the mutex? Does it release the lock?

## Lab 2: POSIX Semaphores and Threads

Modify the **pthreads** exercise (which may have already been enhanced to use **mutexes**), to use POSIX semaphores to protect the counter variable.

## Lab 3: Condition Variables

Write a program that creates four threads and a counter.

Have one thread wait for input, with `scanf("%d", &val)`. After getting the value it should (safely) add that value to the counter.

Meanwhile, the other three threads should be be in a loop. In each loop, they should:

- Wait for the counter to be greater than zero.
- Decrement the counter; print a message with their thread ID (get it from `pthread_self()`) and the counter value.
- Sleep for one second.

You should hold a lock when looking at or changing the counter, but not at any other time - especially not when sleeping or waiting for user input!

If you want to be really good, try not even holding the lock when you are printing. Make sure that you don't refer to the counter outside of the lock though.

## Lab 4: Producer/Consumer

Write a multi-threaded program that has one or more producers and one or more consumers, each producer and consumer being represented by a thread.

The producers create a data event, which can be as simple as storing an index in a structure, while the consumers use the event.

There should be a maximum number of events that can be buffered by producers before consumers eliminate them.

The solution is implemented in terms of condition variables; you can probably can find other methods, such as using semaphores.

# Chapter 20

# Networking and Sockets

We'll get an introduction to using **sockets** for inter-process communication, both on one machine or across networks. We'll discuss the basic networking layers under **Linux**, and how sockets are used. We'll distinguish between the different types of sockets, and how they are used, and touch upon the question of using the proper byte order.

## 20.1 Networking Layers

Networking applications communicate with servers and clients which are also networking applications. These applications (or daemons) may either be on remote hosts or on the local machine.

For the most part these applications are constructed to be independent of the actual hardware, type of network involved, routing, and specific protocols involved. This is not a general rule, however, as sometimes the application may work at a lower level or require certain features.

# Network Layers

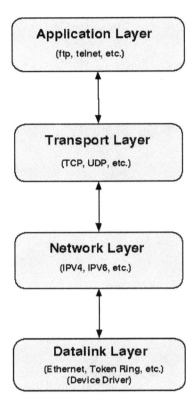

Figure 20.1: **Network layers**

Thus networking can always be seen as consisting of a number of stacked layers. This stack may be categorized in a number of ways, but a simple description appropriate for **Linux** (in which traffic moves both ways) would be:

- **Application Layer:** This can be familiar programs such as **ftp, http** and **smtp**, that communicate across the Internet, or programs such as **X** clients and servers that communicate either across the Internet or on the local machine, as well as any custom network application.

- **Transport Layer:** This is the method of data encapsulation, error checking protocols, etc. The two most common examples are: **streaming** (usually **TCP** (Transmission Control Protocol)) connection-oriented; and **datagram** (usually **UDP** (User Datagram Protocol)) connectionless. Other examples include **SLIP** and **PPP**.

- **Network Layer:** This describes how data is to be sent across the network, containing routing information etc. The most common protocols are **IPV4** (Internet Protocol Version 4) or the newer **IPV6**, and **Unix** for local machine communication. Other examples include **ARP** and **ICMP**

- **Datalink Layer:** This is the hardware part. It includes both the type of device (**Ethernet**, **Token Ring**, etc.) and the actual device driver for the network card.

Networking applications send and receive information by creating and connecting to **sockets**, whose endpoints may be anywhere. Data is sent to and received from sockets as a **stream**. This is true whether or not the underlying transport layer deals with connectionless un-sequenced data (such as **UDP**), or connection-oriented sequenced data (such as **TCP**). Note that various combinations of these layers are possible, such as **TCP/IP** or **UDP/IP**.

The basic data unit that moves through the networking layers and through the network is the **packet**, which contains the data but also has headers and footers containing control information. Within the kernel, the packet is described by a **socket buffer**, a data structure of type **sk_buff**.

These headers and footers contain information such as the source and destination of the packet, various options about priority, sequencing, and routing, identification of the device driver associated with the socket, etc.

When an application writes into a socket, the transport layer creates a series of one or more packets and adds control information. It then hands them off to the network layer which adds more control information, and decides where the packets are going; Packets going out on the network are handed off to the datalink layer and the device driver.

When packets of data are received by the datalink layer, it first sees if they are intended for the local machine, and if so it processes them and hands them off to the network layer, which then passes them through to the transport layer, which sequences the packets, and finally strips out the data and sends it back to the application.

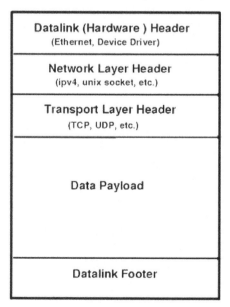

Figure 20.2: **Data Packet Encapsulation**

As packets move up and down through the networking layers, the kernel avoids repeated copying by passing pointers to the encapsulated data buffer, or payload, in the packet, while modifying headers and footers as necessary.

The outermost header and footer correspond to the **datalink** layer, which describes the hardware, device driver, and the hardware type of network, such as **Ethernet** or **Token Ring**. For instance, the **MAC** address will appear here.

The next layer describes the network protocol, such as **IPV4**, and the innermost header describes the transmission protocol, such as **TCP** or **UDP**.

For reasons of optimization, the network and transport layer are not as completely separated as they might be in principle. For instance the network layer implementations may each contain implementations of the transport layer, rather than passing always through a common code base. For instance, both **Internet** and local **Unix** sockets have their own datagram (connectionless) code.

## 20.2   What are Sockets?

Communication through a socket is generally bi-directional and can be multiplexed; i.e., data moves to and from a socket, and more than one process can access the socket in each direction (at least in principle.)

The processes communicating may be related (in the parent/child, or sibling thread senses), or be completely unrelated. They may reside on the same machine, or on nodes anywhere on a local or world-wide network. Many Unix functions (such as **ftp, finger, telnet,** or **lpr**) use sockets.

When a socket is created, it is associated with a so-called **communication domain**, or **protocol family**. For example, **Unix domain sockets**, use named pipes (**fifo's**), and are **bound**, or tied, to filesystem inodes. They are used for communication only on a local machine. **Internet** sockets are in the **IPv4** or **IPv6** communication domains, have no associated file system entries, and binding (or naming) them involves tying the socket to a specific Internet address (or range of addresses).

Each communication domain has its own way of specifying an **address**, be it a local inode on the filesystem, or a network address.

The **type** of communication describes how data should be encapsulated and sent from one socket to another; it is independent of the protocol family itself, although certain combinations of domain and type are more frequent, and others are not possible.

Two basic types are **stream sockets** (described as `SOCK_STREAM`), and **datagram sockets** (described as `SOCK_DGRAM`). These can also be considered as connection vs. connectionless. We'll describe them in detail shortly.

Finally, with each socket is associated a **protocol**. For instance, sockets of the **IP** domain are usually used with the streaming **T**ransmission **C**ontrol **P**rotocol (**TCP**), from whence comes the often used phrase **TCP/IP**. Note that the **IP** part deals with routing through the Internet, while the **TCP** part deals with data integrity; these are quite independent degrees of freedom.

One can also use datagram transmission, usually with **UDP** (**U**ser **D**atagram **P**rotocol), across the Internet, which leads to the combination **UDP/IP**.

Creation of a socket doesn't do much and doesn't establish any communication. In order for a socket to be used, something has to be plugged into it and a connection has to be made, which requires handshaking and agreement over protocols.

Basic documentation can be obtained by doing `man 7 socket` and `man 7 unix`.

## 20.3  Stream Sockets

A **stream socket** is **connection-oriented**; two sockets will be plugged into each other and before any data can flow back and forth, the connection must be established.

The most common type of stream socket has the `type` known as `SOCK_STREAM`.

In addition **Linux** supports the type known as `SOCK_SEQPACKET` which is similar except the packets of data are of fixed length and when reading from such a socket, only the amount of data requested is returned, and the rest discarded.

Stream sockets are **reliable**: the data integrity of packets is checked and if there is any corruption they are dropped. Packets which are not successfully sent and acknowledged are resent until success is achieved.

Data sent through steam sockets is **ordered**; while packets may take different times to reach their destination and arrive out of order, the kernel will reorder them upon arrival.

Communication is **full-duplex**; each end of a connection is free to read and write as long as permissions are appropriate.

The connected sockets may be on the same machine or on any two points of a network; this will change the communication **domain**, but not the type.

## 20.4  Datagram Sockets

Datagram sockets are **connectionless**; the two socket endpoints are not **connected** before transmission can start.

The most common type of datagram socket has the `type` known as `SOCK_DGRAM`.

In addition **Linux** supports the type known as `SOCK_RDM` (for **R**eliable **D**elivered **M**essages) which is similar except the packets are guaranteed to arrive.

Datagram sockets are **unreliable**: the data integrity of packets is not checked, and if any packets are dropped because of traffic or corruption they are not resent. It is up to the receiving application to maintain its own flow control.

Data sent through datagram sockets is **unordered**; if packets take different times to reach their destination and arrive out of order, the kernel will not reorder them upon arrival. Once again it is up to the receiving application to perform any ordering operations.

Communication is **full-duplex**; each end of a connection is free to read and write as long as permissions are appropriate.

The connected sockets may be on the same machine or on any two points of a network; this will change the communication **domain**, but not the type.

## 20.5   Raw Sockets

**Raw** sockets permit user-space implementation of the **IPV4** protocols. Layers in the **TCP/IP** stack are bypassed, and the socket sends and receives raw datagrams (excluding the link-level headers, such as for Ethernet.)

Only super-users can have access to raw socket facilities.

While many **Unix**-like operating systems have a raw socket implementation, the lack of standardization is such that portability is unlikely.

Raw sockets are used by networking utilities, such as **traceroute** and **ping**, and Internet security and filtering tools. They are also useful in the development of new protocol implementations.

## 20.6   Byte Ordering

When multi-byte values are sent over the network, all nodes must agree about how the bytes (or **octets** as they are usually called in network parlance) are to be ordered, if communication is to be effective.

The **network order** is that in which the high-order byte is at the starting address. This is also known as **Big-endian**, and is used natively on many architectures, such as all **Sun** platforms.

In the **Little-endian** order, the low-order byte is at the starting address. This is the also the native architecture on many platforms, including all **x86** machines.

Just to give an example, consider the 16-bit `short int` representation of the number `700 (0x02BC)`. Supposing it is stored in memory locations 1000-1001, we find:

Table 20.1: **Byte ordering**

| Order         | *1000 | *1001 |
|---------------|-------|-------|
| Little Endian | BC    | 02    |
| Big Endian    | 02    | BC    |

Note that there are even architectures which can run with either byte-ordering, although it cannot be changed on the fly.

Mistakes with byte order are quite common, and some can go undetected until an application is ported to another platform, or tested on a network which has machines of both byte-orderings.

For instance, while it is necessary to properly convert a 32 bit Internet address in order to make a connection, and such errors would tend to be caught, failing to convert a 16 bit port assignment may go undetected as long as the error is made **twice**; i.e., in both the client and the server.

Even when storing multi-byte values in local address structures, it is necessary to do the byte-swapping conversions; while it would be possible to have this done transparently to the application, in the kernel networking layers, this would go against the **Posix** specification which requires certain fields be maintained in network byte order.

The functions which accomplish the byte swapping are:

```
#include <netinet/in.h>

uint32_t htonl(uint32_t hostlong);
uint16_t htons(uint16_t hostshort);
uint32_t ntohl(uint32_t netlong);
uint16_t ntohs(uint16_t netshort);
```

Note that the bit-lengths are explicitly specified in the types. On **Linux** these are all coded as fast in-line assembly instructions.

On Big-endian architectures these operations become no-ops.

## 20.7  Labs

### Lab 1: Using netstat to Examine Connections.

The command line utility **netstat** is an all-purpose tool for examining the state of the various sockets and interfaces active on the system and can be used for other purposes as well, such as examining routing. Typing `netstat -h` will give a brief summary of possiblities.

Typing `netstat -ae` will give a quick summary of all the information. Typing `netstat -i` will give a summary by interface:

```
$ netstat -i
Kernel Interface table
Iface       MTU Met   RX-OK RX-ERR RX-DRP RX-OVR    TX-OK TX-ERR TX-DRP TX-OVR Flg
eth0       1500   0   98577      0      0      0    83195      0      0      0 BMRU
eth1       1500   0   11560      0      0      0    13574      0      0      0 BMRU
lo        16436   0     106      0      0      0      106      0      0      0 LRU
```

Note that typing `netstat -ie` will give the same output as `ifconfig`.

Typing

```
$ netstat  -ae --raw --tcp --udp
```

will show information about the state of **raw**,  **TCP**, and **UDP** sockets.

To obtain information about **Unix domain sockets**:

```
$ netstat  -ae --unix
```

and to gain global statistics:

```
$ netstat  -as
```

# Chapter 21

# Sockets - Addresses and Hosts

We'll discuss the use of different types of addresses in networking sock-
ets. We'll show how to convert addresses from one required form to another, and how to get information about hosts.

## 21.1   Socket Address Structures

Every kind of socket has an address structure associated with it. While a generic address structure is
defined (`struct sockaddr`) it is never used directly; it is used only as a generic pointer type. Thus
you'll often see programs doing machinations like:

```
struct sockaddr_un addr;
...
connect(sd, (struct sockaddr *)&addr, sizeof(addr) );
```

It would have been easier to use a `void *` pointer, but the socket functions which use addresses predate the **ANSI C** standardization.

There are many kinds of address structures; indeed there is one for each protocol family. For example, the above code fragment mentions that appropriate for the **Unix domain socket**, or local socket, which is defined as:

```
#include <sys/socket.h>
#include <sys/un.h>

#define UNIX_PATH_MAX    108

struct sockaddr_un {
    sa_family_t  sun_family;               /* AF_UNIX */
    char         sun_path[UNIX_PATH_MAX]; /* pathname */
};
```

Note that the first element is the type `sa_family_t`, and this feature is true for all address types. In this case the element `sun_family` must be set to AF_UNIX, or an error will result. The second element, `sun_path` gives the NULL-terminated pathname of the socket on the filesystem.

The other very common type is that for the Internet Protocol (**IP**), version 4, which looks like:

```
#include <sys/socket.h>
#include <netinet/in.h>

struct sockaddr_in {
    sa_family_t    sin_family; /* address family: AF_INET */
    u_int16_t      sin_port;   /* port in network byte order */
    struct in_addr sin_addr;   /* Internet address */
};

/* Internet address. */
struct in_addr {
    int_addr_t    s_addr;      /* address in network byte order */
};
```

Note that `int_addr_t` is just an unsigned 32-bit integer.

There is some some additional padding which brings the size up to that of the generic `sockaddr` type, which we need not concern ourselves with, except to note it should be zeroed when a structure is initialized.

Note that some implementations also include a `sin_len` field, which gives the length of the structure, but **Linux** does not support this and it is not required to by **Posix** specifications.

Once again the first element gives the address family; in this case it must always have the value AF_INET. The second element gives the **port** (which we'll discuss shortly) and must be in network byte order.

The third element is a structure of type `in_addr`, which contains only a 32-bit integer specifying the **IPV4** address in network byte order. Note that it is important that when working with this quantity you remember whether you are dealing with it as a structure or an integer. Thus either of the following references are legal:

```
struct sockaddr_in addr;
...
struct in_addr x = addr.sin_addr;    /* reference as a structure */
in_addr_t y = addr.sin_addr.s_addr; /* reference as an int */
```

We'll deal later with how to connect addresses in the conventional "dotted quad" notation (i.e., 192.168.1.100) or in the domain-name notation (i.e., www.coopj.com) with the actual 32-bit integer; this requires a number of conversion functions to go in all possible directions.

As stated, each protocol family has its own address structure, so if you crawl through system headers, you'll find definitions for structures of types like sockaddr_in6, sockaddr_ipx, sockaddr_rose, sockaddr_ax25, etc. But as noted, in every case the first element gives the address family, and any multi-byte values must be in network order.

## 21.2   Converting IP Addresses

The IP address structure contains the **s_addr** field, which is the 32 bit network ordered IP address. Addresses are usually given in the so-called "dotted-quad" notation, as a string, with each byte separated by a period, as in 192.168.1.1. The following routines exist for conversion of these names:

```
#include <sys/socket.h>
#include <netinet/in.h>
#include <arpa/inet.h>
#include <netdb.h>

struct in_addr {
    unsigned long s_addr;
}

int inet_aton(const char *cp, struct in_addr *inp);
char *inet_ntoa(struct in_addr in);
in_addr_t inet_addr(const char *cp);
```

Given a pointer to string containing the dotted-quad notation in its first argument, the function inet_aton() returns it to the structure of type **in_addr** pointed to by the second argument. Valid addresses yield non-zero return values while invalid addresses give zero.

The inet_addr() function does essentially the same thing, giving as its return value the binary address in network byte order. Invalid input leads to a return value of INADDR_NONE. However, this function is deprecated and should not be used in new code. It doesn't behave improperly when it is fed the valid address 255.255.255.255, as it returns -1 in that case.

The inet_ntoa() function performs the inverse operation, converting a network address in network byte order to a strings in dotted-quad format. Note that the string is returned in a statically allocated buffer which will be rewritten in any subsequent calls to the function, so if its value needs to be preserved, it should be copied.

Note that you cannot feed these functions addresses in the alphanumeric form, such as coopj.com. We'll show how to deal with those next.

## 21.3   Host Information

Up to now we have concentrated on numeric Internet addresses, or their representation in dotted-quad notation; i.e., 0XC0A80100 or 192.168.1.0. However, in many if not most circumstances we prefer to use **names** (such as coopj.com) instead of numbers for at least three reasons:

- They are easier to remember.

- Numbers may change while the name representation should be persistent.

- Moving to **IPV6** will preserve the names while making the numbers (in the new longer style) much harder to type in correctly.

The mapping between **IP** numbers and domain names is accomplished by the **D**omain **N**ame **S**ystem (**DNS**). We'll leave aside the question of how a **name server** is set up and whether or not and how the **bind** program is used (this is different than the **bind()** function call we'll discuss when we deal with servers).

Both servers and clients interact with **DNS** through a **resolver** library, the central functions of which are:

```
#include <sys/socket.h>
#include <netdb.h>

struct hostent *gethostbyname(const char *name);
struct hostent *gethostbyaddr(const void *addr, int len, int type);
```

gethostbyname() takes as input a host name (as either a name or an IP number in standard dot notation), and returns its **IP** address in the **hostent** structure pointed to by its return value.

gethostbyaddr() does the inverse process. Its first *addr argument is a pointer to an in_addr structure containing the binary address. This structure has a length given by the second argument, and third argument specifies the address family which must be AF_INET or AF_INET6.

Successful completion returns a pointer to a **hostent** structure, defined as:

```
struct hostent {
    char    *h_name;        /* official name of host */
    char    **h_aliases;    /* alias list */
    int     h_addrtype;     /* host address type */
    int     h_length;       /* length of address */
    char    **h_addr_list;  /* list of addresses */
}
#define h_addr  h_addr_list[0]  /* for backward compatibility */
```

The h_name element contains a pointer to the so-called **canonical** name of the host; this can be different than the actual host name if a specific service has been moved to another host, in a fashion transparent to the user; i.e., it could be ftp.coopj.com instead of coopj.com.

The h_aliases argument contains a NULL-terminated array of alternative names, or **aliases**, for the host.

The `h_addrtype` element can be either `AF_INET` for IPv4 or `AF_INET6` for IPv6.

The `h_length` element gives the length of the address, in bytes.

The last element, `h_addr_list` is a NULL-terminated array of network addresses (in network byte order) for the host. The name `h_addr` can be used as shorthand for the first member of this array, and dates back to an early implementation where there was no array.

Note that the address pointer is to an `in_addr` structure, not directly to the 32-bit binary address, so you'll have to do something like

```
struct *hostentry;
struct in_addr addr;
...
memcpy(&addr, hostentry->h_addr, hostentry->h_length);
printf("The address is %x\n", ntohl(addr.s_addr));
```

Note that all recent releases of **bind** permit specifying the `name` argument to be in dotted-quad form; i.e., the results of `gethostbyname("coopj.com")` and `gethostbyname("65.254.254.34")` are identical.

A word of caution is that both `gethostbyname()` and `gethostbyaddr()` may return pointers to static data, which may be overwritten by later calls, and are thus not re-entrant. Just copying the `hostent` structure is not sufficient, as it contains pointers. Thus a more careful and deeper copy is required.

If these functions fail, information about the cause can be obtained through the usual `perror()` function. However, it is also possible to use:

```
extern int h_errno;
void herror(const char *s);
const char *hstrerror(int err);
```

where `herror()` works in the same fashion as `perror()`, and `hstrerror()` retrieves a pointer to the associated error string associated with `err` (generally `h_errno`.) These functions are considered deprecated, but are widely used anyway.

The `h_errno` variable can be:

Table 21.1: **h_errno values**

| Error | Meaning |
|---|---|
| HOST_NOT_FOUND | Specified host unknown. |
| NO_ADDRESS, NO_DATA | The name is valid, but has no IP address. |
| NO_RECOVERY | Unrecoverable name server error. |
| TRY_AGAIN | Temporary error on name server; try again later. |

Note that if a particular host is known locally (i.e., specified in the `/etc/hosts` file), `gethostbyname()` will return successfully without actually contacting a name server to verify the information; it may thus be unreliable.

To inquire or change the host name of the local machine, one can use the functions:

```
int gethostname(char *name, size_t len);
int sethostname(const char *name, size_t len);
```

which return 0 on success. The second argument to the get function is the maximum length of the retrieved name; longer names are truncated. In the set function it is the actually length of the new name.

On the super-user can call `sethostname()`, for obvious reasons, but any user can retrieve the name through `gethostname()`.

## 21.4   Labs

### Lab 1: Examining Internet Addresses

Write a program that takes as an argument an Internet address in dot-quad notation, e.g., `127.0.0.1` or `192.168.1.100`.

The program should convert this to a binary address with `inet_aton()` and print out the result.

The program should convert this to a binary address with `inet_addr()` and print out the result.

The program should invert the result of `inet_aton()` with `inet_ntoa()` and make sure the original input comes back.

### Lab 2: Examining Host Entries

Write a program that takes as input an Internet address and returns information about its address, obtained with `gethostbyname()`.

Some good examples to try would be:

```
www.us.kernel.org
localhost
www.yahoo.com
google.com
coopj.com
```

For the address the program should print out:

- The address name, type, and length.
- Any aliases.
- The full list of addresses used by the host.

i.e., you should dump out the `hostent` structure.

For a little bit extra, print out the addresses in dotted quad notation, **without** using the helper functions.

Do all hosts fill in the `aliases` array?

Compare your results with what you get from typing:

```
host <address>
```

# Chapter 22

# Sockets - Ports and Protocols

We'll consider the use of **ports** and **protocols** with sockets, concentrating on how they are used and how to obtain information about them.

## 22.1 Service Port Information

Multiple processes may be using a given transmission protocol (generally **UDP** or **TCP**) at a given time. In order to differentiate between the various **services** operating concurrently, **port numbers** are assigned uniquely.

A port number is merely a 16-bit integer; we have already seen it pop up in the `sin_port` element of the socket address structure, where it is always stored in **network order**.

It may sound silly to emphasize this, but there is no physical aspect to a port, nothing to plug a cable into, just as there is no physical manifestation of a socket. It is a convenient concept to which one can draw mechanical analogues, however, just as is a socket.

It is important that all network programs agree about what port numbers are associated with particular services. Indeed a central registry is maintained by the Internet Assigned Numbers Authority (**IANA**). **http://www.iana.org/assignments/port-numbers** .

Ports 0-1023 are formally known as **Well Known Ports**. For instance **ftp** is assigned to port 21, and **http** to port 80.

These well known ports are **reserved**, in the sense that only a super-user process can assign these to a socket. This helps prevent a rogue server from trying to masquerade a service. However, non-super-user clients are perfectly capable of connecting to such sockets.

Ports 1024-49151 are known as **Registered Ports**. **IANA** does not control these ports but does register them and list their use. For instance **quake** is assigned to port 26000, and **traceroute** is assigned to port 33434.

Ports 49152-65535 are known as **Ephemeral Ports**, **Dynamic Ports**, or **Private Ports**. **IANA** has nothing to say about these values.

Ephemeral Ports are used by clients. They are meant to be short lived (through the life of the process at most.) A client never cares what the actual port value is, only that it be unique. This is guaranteed by the relevant transmission protocol, which takes care of assigning and releasing these dynamic objects.

The current list of port assignments is maintained in the file **/etc/services**. (On other operating systems the file may be elsewhere, but it is always at this location under **Linux**.) Looking at just a few lines near the top we see

```
.....
# service-name  port/protocol  [aliases ...]    [# comment]

tcpmux     1/tcp                       # TCP port service multiplexer
tcpmux     1/udp                       # TCP port service multiplexer
rje        5/tcp                       # Remote Job Entry
rje        5/udp                       # Remote Job Entry
echo       7/tcp
echo       7/udp
discard    9/tcp           sink null
discard    9/udp           sink null
.....
```

and note the following:

- The same port number is assigned by both the **UDP** and **TCP** transmission protocols for a given service. This is now official policy and is universal except for some historical exceptions.

- Even though some services only use one particular protocol, the port is delegated identically for both.

- The service name can also have **aliases**; thus references to the services **discard, sink** and **null** are treated identically.

- Appearance of an entry in the file in no way implies that the service is actually running.

All networking programs should reference this list of services (through library functions) to ascertain port numbers and protocols for a given service. If the port number changes, the program will not require recompilation.

The system calls that access the /etc/services file are:

```
#include <netdb.h>

struct servent *getservbyname(const char *name, const char *proto);
struct servent *getservbyport(int port, const char *proto);

struct servent *getservent(void);
void setservent(int stayopen);
void endservent(void);

struct servent {
    char *s_name;      /* official service name */
    char **s_aliases;  /* alias list */
    int  s_port;       /* port number */
    char *s_proto;     /* protocol to use */
}
```

Thus the call

```
serv_entry = getservbyname("ftp", "udp");
```

returns the structure describing the **ftp** service with the **UDP** protocol, and

```
serv_entry = getservbyport(htons(80),"tcp");
```

returns the structure describing **http** with the **TCP** protocol.

The function setservent() opens and rewinds /etc/services for reading; if stayopen=1, the file will not be closed between subsequent calls to the get functions.

Once the file has been opened, the function getservent() can be used to read it line by line, and the function endservent() closes the file when done.

Remember that port numbers must be passed to these functions, and are stored in the servent structure, in network byte order.

## 22.2   Protocol Information

Another file, **/etc/protocols**, connects the various Internet protocols with their numbered assignments. Its contents are also maintained by **IANA**, and the master document can be found at **http://www.iana.org/assignments/protocol-numbers**.

The functions for dealing with scanning this file are quite simple, and are:

```
#include <netdb.h>
```

```
struct protoent *getprotobyname(const char *name);
struct protoent *getprotobynumber(int proto);

struct protoent *getprotoent(void);
void setprotoent(int stayopen);
void endprotoent(void);

struct protoent {
    char  *p_name;      /* official protocol name */
    char  **p_aliases   /* alias list */
    int   p_proto;      /* protocol number */
}
```

Their use is completely straightforward and we won't examine them in any further detail.

## 22.3   Labs

### Lab 1: Addresses, Services and Protocols

Write a program to take three parameters:

- An IP address in dot-quad notation or a host name
- A service name or a port number
- A protocol name (**tcp** or **udp**)

From this information configure a `sockaddr_in` address structure. Test with parameters `localhost`, `www`, and `tcp`. You should get:

```
sin_family =            2
sin_addr   =   2130706433 (0x7F000001) (127.0.0.1)
sin_port   =           80 (0x00000050)
```

### Lab 2: Getting Services

Write a program that takes as arguments a **service** and a **port number**; e.g., you can test your program with something like:

```
lab finger 80
```

(Note: The service and port number need not agree.)

Use `getservbyname()` to find out what port number is bound to the service. Do this for both **TCP** and **UDP**.

Use `getservbyport()` to find out what service is bound to the port number. Do this for both **TCP** and **UDP**.

In both cases, print out any aliases for the service name.

## Lab 3: Getting All Services

Write a program that lists all services, together with their port numbers, possible protocols, and aliases, on your local machine.

# Chapter 23

# Sockets - Clients

We'll describe the structure of a network **client** using sockets. We'll delilneate the system calls made, and show how to create, connect to, and close sockets. We'll give simple examples of client programs for both unix domain and Internet sockets.

## 23.1   Basic Client Sequence

The first thing a client has to do is create a socket:

```
sd = socket (domain, type, protocol);
```

specifying the domain, type of socket, and protocol.

It then connects to the socket:

```
connect (sd, &serv_addr, addrlen);
```

specifying the address it wishes to communicate with.

It can then send or receive information through the socket:

```
read (sd, buf, nbytes);
write (sd, buf, nbytes);
```

using standard **Unix** reads and writes or the send and receive functions we'll discuss later.

Finally when done it should release the socket using the functions:

```
close (sd);
shutdown (sd, how);
```

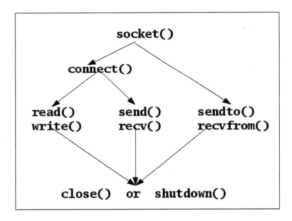

Figure 23.1: **Basic Socket Client Sequences**

Note: for connectionless protocols, such as for **UDP** datagrams, the **connect()** step is not required; input/output operations will use **sendto()**, **recvfrom()**.

## 23.2   socket()

All network activity begins with a call to the **socket()** function:

```
#include <sys/types.h>
#include <sys/socket.h>

int socket (int domain, int type, int protocol);
```

which on success returns a non-negative integer known as the **socket descriptor**, which is similar in many ways to a **file descriptor**.

However, unlike a file descriptor returned by the `open()` call, obtaining a socket descriptor successfully is not enough to be ready to do input/output operations. In the case of a typical network **client**, one needs to follow this up with a call to `connect()`. In the case of a typical network **server**, one needs the `bind()`, `listen()`, `accept()` sequence, and another descriptor will be generated first.

The `socket()` function takes three integer input arguments. The first of these is the `domain`, which specifies the protocol family (or communication domain) which describes how data should be sent out over the network. The permissible values are defined in **/usr/include/bits/socket.h**, (included from **/usr/include/sys/socket.h**) and are:

Table 23.1: **Socket domains**

| Domain | Value | Meaning |
|---|---|---|
| PF_UNSPEC | 0 | Unspecified |
| PF_LOCAL | 1 | POSIX name for PF_UNIX |
| PF_UNIX, PF_FILE | PF_LOCAL | Unix Domain Sockets |
| PF_INET | 2 | Internet Protocol (IPv4), Version 4 |
| PF_AX25 | 3 | Amateur Radio AX.25 Protocol |
| PF_IPX | 4 | Novell IPX |
| PF_APPLETALK | 5 | Appletalk |
| PF_NETROM | 6 | Amateur Radio NetROM |
| PF_BRIDGE | 7 | Multi-protocol Bridge |
| PF_ATMPVC | 8 | Access to Raw ATM PVCs |
| PF_X25 | 9 | ITU-T X.25 / ISO-8208 protocol |
| PF_INET6 | 10 | Internet Protocol (IPv6), Version 6 |
| PF_ROSE | 11 | Amateur Radio X.25 PLP |
| PF_DECnet | 12 | DECnet |
| PF_NETBEUI | 13 | Reserved for 802.2LLC project |
| PF_SECURITY | 14 | Security callback pseudo AF |
| PF_KEY | 15 | PF_KEY key management API (used for cryptography.) |
| PF_NETLINK | 16 | Kernel-User Interface Pseudo-device |
| PF_ROUTE | PF_NETLINK | Alias used to Emulate 4.4BSD |
| PF_PACKET | 17 | Low Level Packet Interface |
| PF_ASH | 18 | Ash |
| PF_ECONET | 19 | Acorn Econet |
| PF_ATMSVC | 20 | ATM SVCs |
| PF_SNA | 22 | Linux SNA Project |
| PF_IRDA | 23 | IRDA sockets |
| PF_PPPOX | 24 | PPPoX sockets |
| PF_WANPIPE | 25 | Wanpipe API sockets |
| PF_BLUETOOTH | 31 | Bluetooth sockets |
| PF_MAX | 32 | Maximum Value |

In some cases the above protocols are not fully implemented under **Linux** but space has been reserved for them in the table of communication domains.

The most important ones here (which we will concentrate on) are: `PF_LOCAL (PF_UNIX)`, for Unix domain sockets local to the machine, and `PF_INET, PF_INET6` for **IP** (**I**nternet **P**rotocol) versions 4 and 6.

Note that all these domains can be referred to with the prefix `AF_` in place of `PF_`, where `AF` stands for **A**ddress **F**amily and `PF` stands for **P**rotocol **F**amily. Historically the possibility was left open for a protocol family supporting multiple address families. However, this has never happened, so you can probably use either form, but strictly speaking you should be using the `PF_`-prefixed values for the `socket()` function.

The second argument to the `socket()` call is the **type** of socket and is enumerated in the same header file as the domain:

Table 23.2: **Socket types**

| Type | Value | Meaning |
|------|-------|---------|
| `SOCK_STREAM` | 1 | Sequenced, reliable, two way connection based byte stream, such as **TCP**. Out-of-band data transmission may be supported. |
| `SOCK_DGRAM` | 2 | Connectionless unreliable datagrams: messages of fixed maximum length, no guarantee of delivery or reordering. |
| `SOCK_RAW` | 3 | Raw network protocol interface, only for super-user. |
| `SOCK_RDM` | 4 | Reliably delivered messages, but ordering not guaranteed. |
| `SOCK_SEQPACKET` | 5 | Sequenced, reliable, two-way connection-based datagrams of fixed maximum length. Entire packets must be read with each reading system call. Not supported with `PF_INET`. |
| `SOCK_PACKET` | 10 | **Linux**-specific; get packets at the device level, used for **rarp** and some other things. Considered obsolete; from **Linux** 2.0 kernels. |

Not all combinations of **domain** and **type** are valid.

The most frequently used ones are `SOCK_STREAM` (used in **TCP**) and `SOCK_DGRAM` (used in **UDP**) either of which may be used in combination with `PF_INET(6)`.

The third argument to `socket()`, `protocol` specifies which protocol to use with the socket; normally there is only one kind of protocol provided for each protocol family, and a value of `0` passed to `socket()` selects that default. However, raw sockets have some other possibilities.

A common misunderstanding is to simply equate `SOCK_STREAM` with **TCP** and `SOCK_DGRAM` with **UDP**. While in practice this assumption is generally a good one, the `protocol` argument to `socket()` actually specifies the choice; using `0` gets the most common default behaviour.

The possible error returns to `socket()` are:

Table 23.3: **socket() error return values**

| Error | Meaning |
|-------|---------|

| EPROTONOSUPPORT | The type or the protocol is not supported. |
|---|---|
| EAFNOSUPPORT | The specified address family is not supported. |
| ENFILE | Not enough kernel memory to create a socket structure. |
| EMFILE | Process file table overflow. |
| EACCES | Permission denied. |
| ENOBUFS, ENOMEM | Insufficient memory to create socket. |
| EINVAL | Unknown protocol or protocol family unavailable. |

Remember, to get access to the specific error, you'll have to do something like:

```
#include <errno.h>
....
sd = socket (PF_INET, SOCK_STREAM, 0);
if( sd < 0 ){
    perror ("Failed to create the socket ");
    exit (errno);
}
```

## 23.3  connect()

Once a socket descriptor has been obtained with the `socket()` call, it is necessary for a client to use the `connect()` call to try and "plug in" something to the socket:

```
#include <sys/types.h>
#include <sys/socket.h>

int connect(int sd, const struct sockaddr *serv_addr, socklen_t addrlen);
```

All arguments are inputs and are not modified by `connect()`. The first argument is just the socket descriptor returned by `socket()`, while the second and third argument specify the **address** the socket will be connected to and its length.

Sometimes the type of the third argument appears as `int` instead of `socklen_t`. This is historical and while these types are the same under **Linux**, the proper type should be used.

The address and how it is used depend on what kind of protocol is being used for the socket. One never uses the generic `struct sockaddr`; a particular type of address is always cast this way, so you typically see code like:

```
struct sockaddr_un addr;
...
sd = socket(PF_LOCAL, SOCK_STREAM, 0);
...
if (connect (sd, (struct sockaddr *) &addr, sizeof (addr))) {
        perror ("Client connect");
        exit (EXIT_FAILURE);
    }
```

Each protocol deals with the address in its own way.

In the above case the use of SOCK_STREAM indicates one is attempting to make a connection-based linkup to a specific address (which is a host IP address and port or a path name) as specified in the second input parameter. This would be true also for a specification of SOCK_SEQPACKET. Connection-based protocols may use connect() only once for a given socket.

If instead the above example had used SOCK_DGRAM it would have established a connectionless association with the specified address; it is where datagrams are to be sent, and from where they are to be received.

A connectionless protocol can call connect() again to establish a new address association. Releasing all association can be done by connecting again, using AF_UNSPEC in the sa_family element of the address.

On success, connect() returns 0, and on failure returns -1 and sets errno appropriately. The possible error returns to connect() are:

Table 23.4: **connect() error return values**

| Error | Meaning |
|-------|---------|
| EBADF | Invalid value for socket descriptor given. |
| EFAULT | Address structure has an invalid address. |
| ENOTSOCK | Socket descriptor not associated with a socket. |
| EISCONN | Socket already connected |
| ECONNREFUSED | No one listening at remote address. |
| ETIMEDOUT | Connection timed out, perhaps because server is too busy. |
| ENETUNREACH | Network is unreachable. |
| EADDRINUSE | Local address already in use. |
| EINPROGRESS | A non-blocking socket; connection can not be completed at once. |
| EALREADY | A non-blocking socket; a previous connection attempt has not yet finished. |
| EAGAIN | No more free local ports. |
| EAFNOSUPPORT | Incorrect value in the sa_family field of the address |
| EACCES, EPERM | Either an attempt was made to **broadcast** with out the appropriate flags set, or a local firewall prevented the connection. |

After a connection has been made, the function

```
int getsockname (int sd, struct sockaddr *addr, socklen_t addrlen);
```

will supply information about the address and port number assigned to the connection.

## 23.4   close() and shutdown()

The simplest way to terminate use of a socket is to use the standard close() function:

```
#include <unistd.h>
int close (int sd);
```

In this case the argument is a socket descriptor, rather than the usual file descriptor, but the usage of `close()` is the same as it is when it is used on a file.

Any remote attempt to read or write on the socket after `close()` is called will result in an error. However, there may be some problems with just using `close()`.

The first limitation is that the way `close()` works on any descriptor is to decrement the reference count associated with it (the number of processes using it) and not perform the actual close until the count reaches zero. An example would be where a socket descriptor is created before a `fork()`, which means both parent and child would need to close it before it is actually released.

This release may be implicit when the process terminates, normally or abnormally, since the exit handling routines always close all open descriptors. Such a delay in releasing is probably what is desired, but you have no control over this with the simple `close()` function.

The second limitation arises from the full-duplex nature of the connection. Both directions are terminated at once with `close()`, but perhaps one wants to finish sending to the socket but would like to receive pending data for some time.

More control can be gained with the `shutdown()` function:

```
#include <sys/socket.h>
int shutdown (int sd, int how);
```

The parameter `how` can have the following values:

Table 23.5: **Socket shutdown methods**

| Value | Meaning |
|---|---|
| SHUT_RD | No more data will be received. Any data currently in the socket receive buffer is discarded. |
| SHUT_WR | No more data will be transmitted. Any data currently in the socket send buffer will be sent. |
| SHUT_RDWR | No more data will be received or transmitted. |

Note that `shutdown()` does not close the socket. It returns 0 on success, and the following possible errors:

Table 23.6: **shutdown() error return values**

| Error | Meaning |
|---|---|
| EBADF | `sd` is not a valid descriptor. |
| ENOTSOCK | `sd` describes a file, not a socket. |
| ENOTCONN | Socket not connected |

Note that it is also possible to set the `SO_LINGER` option on the socket, using the `setsockopt()` function we will discuss later. This gives more control to the `close()` method, enabling flushing the socket receive and send buffers before the actual release. In this case it is important to check the return value of `close()`, a step which is often neglected.

## 23.5   Unix Client

Here's a simple example of a `PF_UNIX` socket client.

It reads one line from standard input, sends it to the local socket, `/tmp/mysock`, and then terminates.

```
#include <stdlib.h>
#include <stdio.h>
#include <unistd.h>
#include <sys/socket.h>
#include <sys/un.h>

#define MSG_LEN 1024

int main (void)
{
    struct sockaddr_un uaddr;
    int msg_len, sd;
    char message[MSG_LEN];

    uaddr.sun_family = AF_UNIX;
    strcpy (uaddr.sun_path, "/tmp/mysock");

    sd = socket (PF_UNIX, SOCK_STREAM, 0);
    connect (sd, (struct sockaddr *)&uaddr, sizeof (uaddr));

    msg_len = strlen (fgets (message, MSG_LEN, stdin));
    write (sd, message, msg_len);

    close (sd);
    exit (EXIT_SUCCESS);
}
```

Note that unless you install a **server** to create the socket first, you can't really test this program.

## 23.6   Internet Client

Here's a simple example of a `PF_INET` socket client, in this case a client for **echo**, which has a service port = 7. The echo server protocol merely requires that whatever is sent just gets echoed back.

The program takes as its argument the server **IP** address (in name or dotted-quad notation), and then connects to it. Next it reads one input line from the terminal and sends it to the server. It then reads from the server the echoed output and prints it out.

```
/*
 * simple echo CLIENT
 * First make sure the echo SERVER is on
 * as root: check with:   chkconfig --list | grep echo
 *            turn on with: chkconfig echo on
 * Usage:  progname address, then type   a message to send
 */

#include <stdio.h>
#include <stdlib.h>
#include <errno.h>
#include <unistd.h>
#include <string.h>
#include <sys/types.h>
#include <sys/socket.h>
#include <netinet/in.h>
#include <netdb.h>
#define MSG_LEN 1024
#define PORT_NUMBER 7

int main (int argc, char **argv)
{
    int sd, msg_len;
    char message[MSG_LEN];
    struct sockaddr_in addr;
    struct hostent *hostent;

    sd = socket (PF_INET, SOCK_STREAM, 0);

    hostent = gethostbyname (argv[1]);
    addr.sin_family = AF_INET;
    addr.sin_port = htons (PORT_NUMBER);
    memcpy (&addr.sin_addr, hostent->h_addr, hostent->h_length);

    connect (sd, (struct sockaddr *)&addr, sizeof (addr));

    msg_len = strlen (fgets (message, MSG_LEN, stdin));
    write (sd, message, msg_len);

    memset (message, 0, MSG_LEN);
    msg_len = read (sd, message, MSG_LEN);
    write (STDOUT_FILENO, message, msg_len);

    close (sd);
    exit (0);
}
```

Note that in order to get this to work you'll need to make sure the echo service is turned on. For instance on many **Linux** distributions the super-user has to do:

```
chkconfig echo-stream on
chkconfig echo-dgram  on
service xinetd restart
```

If **xinetd** is not installed (check with **rpm -q xinetd**) it will need to be installed, perhaps with **yum install xinetd**.

## 23.7  Labs

### Lab 1: Simple Internet echo Client

Take the sample Internet **echo** client program, and make it more robust, checking for errors at each stage, such as creating the socket, connecting to it, and reading and writing from it.

Try it first on your local machine.  (Make sure the **echo** server is on with `chkconfig --list | grep echo`)

To work with other machines you may also have to open up your firewall to the echo port.

Once it is turned it on you should be able to run it with:

```
lab1_echo_client localhost
```

Try running it on any other Internet address you think the **echo** server might be running on. What happens if it is not?

### Lab 2: Simple Internet finger Client

Write a client that connects to the **finger** socket on some host, asks it for information and displays what it returns.

You can look in `/etc/services` to find out the **finger** socket's port.

You might get information on all users or only selected users.

A naked carriage return sent to the **finger** server will return information on all logged in users (if the host will allow it). A user name followed by a carriage return will return information on that user.

The sample solution is written to work with this usage:

```
lab2_finger_client host user1 user2 ....
```

Try it on the local host, and if you know any Internet sites where **finger** is still running, try there. If you want to be fancy you can get it to work with the standard **finger** syntax:

```
finger user1@host1 user2@host2
finger @host1 @host2
```

**Note:** By default the **finger** server may not be installed, and if it is it may not be enabled. To take care of both steps, one could do (as root):

```
yum install finger-server
chkconfig finger on
service xinetd restart
```

# Chapter 24

# Sockets - Servers

We'll describe the structure of a network **server** using sockets. We'll delilneate the system calls made, and show how to bind addresses to sockets, and listen and accept connections. We'll give simple examples of server programs for both unix domain and Internet sockets.

## 24.1  Basic Server Sequence

The first thing a server has to do is create a socket:

```
sd = socket (domain, type, protocol);
```

specifying the domain, type of socket, and protocol.

187

It then binds an address and a protocol to the socket:

```
bind (sd, &serv_addr, addrlen);
```

It then listens for clients trying to make connections:

```
listen (sd, backlog);
```

When it notices a client trying to make contact it has to accept the connection:

```
confd = accept (sd, &client_addr, addrlen);
```

It can then send or receive information through the socket:

```
read (confd, buf, nbytes);
write (confd, buf, nbytes);
```

using standard **Unix** reads and writes or the send and receive functions we'll discuss later.

When done with the client connection it should release it with:

```
close (confd);
```

Finally when done with all connections, it should release the socket with one of:

```
close (sd);
shutdown (sd, how);
```

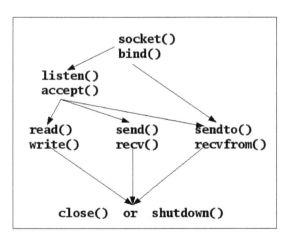

Figure 24.1: **Basic Socket Server Sequences**

Note: for connectionless protocols, such as **UDP**, the `listen()` and `accept()` steps are not required; input/output operations will use `sendto()`, `recvfrom()`.

## 24.2   bind()

The `socket()` function creates a socket, but does not by itself associate it with either an address, or if necessary, a service port. For this servers need to use the `bind()` function; for clients, address association usually begins with `connect()` (which does something **bind()**-like under the hood).

The prototype for `bind()` is:

```
#include <sys/types.h>
#include <sys/socket.h>

int bind (int sd, struct sockaddr *my_addr, socklen_t addrlen);
```

where the arguments are the same as for the `connect()` function, except one should note that the `const` modifier keyword has been removed from the address structure, which usually means its value can change. However, in this case **Linux** seems to disagree with the usual function `prototype` used on other operating systems, and indeed you can check that the address is in fact unchangeable.

One source of confusion is that the `bind()` function is often described as "assigning a name" to a socket. In fact, this function has nothing to do with "names" (such as `coopj.com`); it assigns addresses and protocols.

If one wants to **bind** a specific **IP** address and service port to an Internet server socket one would have something like:

```
int sd;
short int port = 50000;
struct sockaddr_in addr;
struct in_addr inaddr;
...
sd = socket (PF_INET, SOCK_STREAM, 0);
memset (addr, 0, sizeof(addr));
addr.sin_family = AF_INET;
addr.sin_port = htons (port);
addr.sin_addr.s_addr = inet_addr ("192.168.1.1");

bind (sd, (struct sockaddr *)&addr, sizeof(struct sockaddr));
```

where in the interest of brevity we've used the old-fashioned `inet_addr()` function rather than `inet_aton()`. Also note that we've been careful to zero out the address structure before using it and to make sure the service port is placed in proper network byte order.

However, it is possible to have the kernel choose both the service port and **IP** address automatically. If we select a service port of 0, the kernel will choose an **ephemeral** (dynamic) one from the available selection. If we desire to know what value was picked, we cannot examine the address structure after the call to `bind()`, because as we noted it will not change. To do this we would need something like:

```
struct sockaddr_in check;
int check_len;
...
bind (sd,...);
getsockname (sd, (struct sockaddr*)&check, &check_len);
printf ("selected port %d\n", ntohs(check.sin_port));
```

However, servers rarely want to do this since clients must also know the service port to which to connect. On the other hand, clients can also make calls to `bind()`; in fact the `connect()` function essentially does so implicitly and while doing so selects a dynamic port, the specific value of which rarely requires examination.

The **IP** address can also be allotted in automatic fashion, but here the rules are a little more complicated. If we do:

```
my_addr.sin_addr.s_addr = htonl (INADDR_ANY);
```

the kernel will fill in the **IP** address of the machine the server is running on.

Note, however, a machine may have more than one **IP** address. For instance a server may use a number of addresses to deal with different sub-networks. These addresses are **aliased**. Or the machine may have more than one network card, each with its own **IP** address.

In the case of **Unix Domain Sockets**, using **bind()** associates the socket with a filesystem entry, so you'll see code like:

```
struct sockaddr_un addr;
. . . .
sd = socket (PF_UNIX, SOCK_STREAM, 0);
addr.sun_family = AF_UNIX;
strcpy (addr.sun_path, "/tmp/mysock");
bind (sd, (struct sockaddr *)&addr, sizeof(addr));
```

On success `bind()` returns 0. The possible error returns are:

Table 24.1: **bind() error return values**

| Error | Meaning |
|---|---|
| EBADF | Invalid socket descriptor. |
| EINVAL | Socket already bound to an address. For `AF_UNIX` can mean `addrlen` is wrong, or not in the `AF_UNIX` family. |
| EACCES | Address is protected; user not super-user. For `AF_UNIX`, can mean no permission on part of the path. |
| ENOTSOCK | First argument is a file descriptor. |
| EROFS | Socket inode would be on a read-only file system. (`AF_UNIX` only.) |
| EFAULT | `my_addr` has an invalid pointer. (`AF_UNIX` only.) |
| ENAMETOOLONG | `my_addr` is too long. (`AF_UNIX` only.) |
| ENOENT | File does not exist. (`AF_UNIX` only.) |
| ENOMEM | Insufficient kernel memory available. (`AF_UNIX` only.) |
| ENOTDIR | Part of the path is not a directory. (`AF_UNIX` only.) |
| ELOOP | Too may symbolic links encountered. (`AF_UNIX` only.) |

One frequent problem that can cause `bind()` to fail is the kernel reporting that the address is already in use. This can happen because a server starts multiple processes to handle different client requests, or because the server has been restarted "too soon" after termination.

The way to get around this (which should be done for **all TCP** servers) is to set a socket option as:

```
int yes = 1;
setsockopt (sd, SOL_SOCKET, SO_REUSEADDR, &yes, sizeof(yes));
```

after the socket is created, and before the call to `bind()`. We'll discuss setting socket options in detail later.

## 24.3   listen()

The `listen()` function is called only by a server. It is called after `bind()` and it moves the socket into a **passive** state; i.e., the kernel should accept connections directed to this socket.

The prototype of the function looks like:

```
#include <sys/socket.h>

int listen (int sd, int backlog);
```

Only sockets of type `SOCK_STREAM` or `SOCK_SEQPACKET` can utilize the `listen()` call.

The first argument, `sd`, is a socket descriptor as obtained from `socket()`. The second parameter, `backlog`, is the number of connections allowed on the incoming queue.

Exactly what this means has varied from one operating system to another. In particular two queues are maintained:

- The **complete** connection queue contains entries for each client with whom the full handshake has been established.

- The **incomplete** connection queue contains entries for each client for which the process is not yet complete.

Under **Linux** the `backlog` parameter describes only the length of the **complete** connection queue. The maximum length of the **incomplete** connection queue can be read (or set by a super-user) by examining **/proc/sys/net/ipv4/tcp_max_syn_backlog**.

If `CONFIG_SYN_COOKIES` is set as a kernel configuration option, a socket will be protected from overload when too many connection attempts are made; clients can no longer detect an overloaded machine in this circumstance. Thus, denial of service through congestion is side-stepped. The maximum value is no longer effective and packets do not get dropped. See the **man** page for **tcp** for details.

On success `listen()` returns 0, and the possible error returns are:

Table 24.2: **listen() error return values**

| Error | Meaning |
|-------|---------|

| EADDRINUSE | Another socket is already listening on the same port. |
|---|---|
| EBADF | Invalid socket descriptor. |
| ENOTSOCK | First argument is a file descriptor. |
| EOPNOTSUPP | This type of socket doesn't support the listening operation. |

## 24.4   accept()

After calling `socket()`, `bind()`, and `listen()`, a server needs to call `accept()` to actually use the socket:

```
#include <sys/types.h>
#include <sys/socket.h>

int accept (int sd, struct sockaddr *addr, socklen_t *addrlen);
```

Only connection-based sockets can use `accept()`, those with types like `SOCK_STREAM`, `SOCK_RDM`, and `SOCK_SEQPACKET`.

On success, `accept()` returns a new socket descriptor (a non-negative integer), which is what will be used for subsequent input and output operations with the client that has connected.

On input, `addrlen`, the third parameter, points to a variable giving the size of the address structure pointed to by the second parameter. On return, it contains the actual length (in bytes) of the filled-in address structure. which may not be more than the initial value.

Unless the socket has been marked as **non-blocking** through `fcntl()` or `setsockopt()`, if no pending connections are queued, `accept()` will block until a client requests a connection.

If using `select()` or `poll()` with multiple socket descriptors, one would call these functions and then wait for an incoming connection. At that point `accept()` would get called and establish the full connection.

It is often the case that a server needs to handle requests from multiple clients as simultaneously as possible. There are a number of ways of designing such a **concurrent server**, such as creating a new child or a sibling thread for each request. We'll discuss this later.

The possible error returns to `accept()` are:

Table 24.3: **accept() error return values**

| Error | Meaning |
|---|---|
| EAGAIN          or EWOULDBLOCK | No connections present, a non-blocking socket. |
| EBADF | Invalid socket descriptor. |
| ENOTSOCK | First argument is a file descriptor. |
| EOPNOTSUPP | Socket is not of type `SOCK_STREAM`. |

| EFAULT | `addr` is a pointer to a non-writeable address. |
|---|---|
| EPERM | Connection forbidden by firewall. |
| EINTR | Interrupted by a signal before a valid connection was made. |
| ENOBUFS or ENOMEM | Insufficient memory (probably hitting socket buffer limits.) |

After a connection has been accepted, the function

```
int getpeername (int sd, const struct sockaddr *rem_addr, socklen_t addrlen);
```

will supply information about the address and port number of the remote peer connected to the socket.

## 24.5  Unix Server

Here's a simple example of a `PF_UNIX` socket server.

It loops endlessly waiting for new clients to connect. When they do, it will read one line of input from the local socket `./tmp/mysock`, and then echos it to standard output.

```
#include <stdlib.h>
#include <stdio.h>
#include <unistd.h>
#include <sys/socket.h>
#include <sys/un.h>

#define MSG_LEN 1024

int main (void)
{
    struct sockaddr_un uaddr;
    int rc, sd, cd;
    socklen_t alen = sizeof (struct sockaddr_un);
    char message[MSG_LEN];

    uaddr.sun_family = AF_UNIX;
    strcpy (uaddr.sun_path, "/tmp/mysock");

    sd = socket (PF_UNIX, SOCK_STREAM, 0);
    unlink ("/tmp/mysock");
    bind (sd, (struct sockaddr *)&uaddr, sizeof (uaddr));
    listen (sd, 5);

    for (;;) {

        cd = accept (sd, NULL, &alen);

        rc = read (cd, message, sizeof (message));
```

```
        write (STDOUT_FILENO, message, rc);

        close (cd);
    }

    close (sd);
    exit (EXIT_SUCCESS);
}
```

## 24.6   Internet Server

Here's a simple example of a `PF_INET` socket server, in this case an **echo** server.

Remember, the **echo** server protocol merely requires that whatever is sent just gets echoed back It loops endlessly waiting for new clients to connect.

You can test this with the simple **echo** client we showed, just changing the port number from the "official" value of 7, to the value PORT_NUMBER=7177 used below.

```c
#include <stdlib.h>
#include <stdio.h>
#include <unistd.h>
#include <string.h>
#include <sys/socket.h>
#include <netinet/in.h>
#include <netdb.h>
#include <arpa/inet.h>

#define MSG_LEN 1024
#define PORT_NUMBER 7177

int main (void)
{
    struct sockaddr_in addr, con_addr;
    int rc, sd, cd, yes = 1;
    socklen_t alen = sizeof (struct in_addr);
    char message[MSG_LEN];

    addr.sin_family = AF_INET;
    addr.sin_addr.s_addr = htonl (INADDR_ANY);
    addr.sin_port = htons (PORT_NUMBER);

    sd = socket (PF_INET, SOCK_STREAM, 0);

    setsockopt (sd, SOL_SOCKET, SO_REUSEADDR, &yes, sizeof (yes));
    bind (sd, (struct sockaddr *)&addr, sizeof (addr));
    listen (sd, 5);

    for (;;) {

        printf ("\nAccepting input on port %d\n", PORT_NUMBER);
        cd = accept (sd, (struct sockaddr *)&con_addr, &alen);
```

```
        rc = read (cd, message, sizeof (message));
        write (STDOUT_FILENO, message, rc);
        write (cd, message, rc);

        printf ("Received the end of input\n\n");
        close (cd);
    }

    close (sd);
    exit (EXIT_SUCCESS);
}
```

## 24.7  Labs

### Lab 1: Unix Client/Server with UDP.

Take the examples given for simple Unix domain socket **TCP** client and server programs (which can be found in the **SOLUTIONS/EXAMPLES** subdirectory tree) and convert them to work with **UDP**.

Once the server is running, any line of input typed to the client is merely echoed back by the server, and then the client terminates.

Test this by starting the server in one window, and then running the client in another. Try this first with the unaltered **TCP** programs, and then move on to your modified **UDP** ones.

Now test by starting two instances of the client, and then sending output first from the second one started, and then from the first one. In what order does the server get the input?

Do the same test with the **TCP** server examples. Are the results the same, or is the order inverted? Explain.

### Lab 2: Internet Client/Server with UDP.

Now the take the example Internet client and server programs and convert them from **TCP** to **UDP**. Test in the same way you did for the Unix domain socket programs.

Can your client program read back from the socket what it wrote to it? Try tracing your client with

```
strace client localhost
```

and try to see in detail what is happening.

# Chapter 25

# Sockets - Input/Output Operations

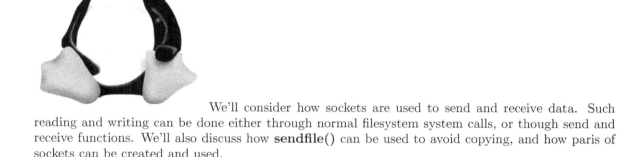

We'll consider how sockets are used to send and receive data. Such reading and writing can be done either through normal filesystem system calls, or though send and receive functions. We'll also discuss how **sendfile()** can be used to avoid copying, and how paris of sockets can be created and used.

## 25.1   write(), read()

Up to now, we have been somewhat cavalier about using `read()` and `write()` when dealing with socket descriptors. However, these functions behave somewhat differently than they do with normal file descriptors.

In particular, it is quite normal for a read or write operation to return fewer bytes than the nominal request. The probable reason is that the buffer limits may have been broached in either case (especially a write operation). Or in the case of a read operation not all of the data may have reached the socket yet.

This is quite similar to what happens when dealing with **pipes**, which should not be surprising. since a socket is basically a full-duplex pipe whose other end may be anywhere on the network.

Of course sometimes we ask to read a large number of bytes because we don't know in advance how many are coming in; in that case we may not want to use what follows.

An improvement to simply calling `read (sd, buf, nbytes)` would be something like:

```
char *tmp;
int rc, n = nbytes;
tmp = buf;

while ( ( rc = read (sd, tmp, n )) > 0 ){
      n    -= rc;
      tmp += rc;
      if (n <= 0 ) break;
}
```

or more tersely:

```
for (n=nbytes, tmp=buf; n>0 ; tmp +=rc, n -=rc )
    if ( ( rc = read (sd, tmp, n) ) <= 0 )
          break;
```

However, this isn't good enough. We haven't taken care of two possibilities:

- The read was interrupted by a signal; in this case we should keep going.

- The read encountered an end of data.

So, for an improvement, here is a (not very optimized ) wrapper function for **read()**:

```
ssize_t readit (int sd, char *buf, int nbytes){
    int n;
    char *tmp;

    tmp = buf;
    n = nbytes;

    while ( n > 0 ){
        int rc = read (sd, tmp, n);
        if ( rc > 0 ) { /* main case, successful read of some bytes */
            n    -= rc;
            tmp += rc;
            continue;
        }
        if ( rc == 0 ) /* end of file */
```

```
            break;
        /* reached here only if error, rc<0 */
        if (errno == EINTR) /* interrupted by a signal */
            continue;
        return (-1);
    }
    return (nbytes-n);
}
```

The equivalent `writeit()` function would be the same, except it doesn't have the statement

```
        if ( rc == 0 ) /* end of file */
            break;
```

Unless you have a non-blocking write operation, you shouldn't get zero anyway.

To keep things simple, we won't bother being this careful in our presentation unless we are sure we need to, but you should be aware that this kind of complication is pretty common.

## 25.2  send(), recv()

Writing and reading on a socket descriptor can also be done through the `send()` and `recv()` functions:

```
#include <sys/types.h>
#include <sys/socket.h>

int send (int sd, const void *buf, size_t len, int flags);
int recv (int sd,       void *buf, size_t len, int flags);
```

These functions require that the socket be **connected** either through `connect()` or `bind()` (possibly with `listen()`, `accept()`.) On success these functions return the number of bytes sent or received.

The first three arguments are just like those of `write()` and `read()`, but the last argument permits setting some flags for more control. Using `flags=0` gives a normal `write()` or `read()`.

The `flags` argument can control behaviour for each I/O request; control over every request can be done by setting socket options, using `fcntl()` or `ioctl()`. The permitted values for `flags` differs somewhat for the two functions.

For `send()` the value of `flags` can be a bitmask of the following values:

Table 25.1: **send() flags**

| Flag | Meaning |
|------|---------|
| MSG_OOB | Sends **out-of-band** data; both the type of socket (e.g., SOCK_STREAM) and the protocol (e.g., **TCP**), must support this. For **TCP**, it should be only one byte in length, and is considered as an urgent request. |
| MSG_DONTROUTE | The destination is on a local network, so don't route through a gateway. Generally used only by diagnostic or route programs. Equivalent to setting the socket option SO_DONTROUTE. |

| MSG_DONTWAIT | No blocking on the I/O operation; if the operation would block, EAGAIN is returned. This is equivalent to setting O_NONBLCOK through fcntl(), but just for this operation. |
| MSG_NOSIGNAL | Don't send a SIGPIPE signal on a stream socket when the other end breaks the connection; EPIPE is still returned as an error, however. |
| MSG_CONFIRM | Inform the link layer that a successful reply came from the other side. This works only on SOCK_DGRAM and SOCK_RAW sockets, and only for **TCP**. This is a **Linux** extension. |

For recv() the value of flags can be a bitmask of the following values:

Table 25.2: **send() flags**

| Flag | Meaning |
| --- | --- |
| MSG_OOB | Sends **out-of-band** data; both the type of socket (e.g., SOCK_STREAM) and the protocol (e.g., **TCP**), must support this. For **TCP**, it should be only one byte in length, and is considered as an urgent request. |
| MSG_DONTROUTE | The destination is on a local network, so don't route through a gateway. Generally used only by diagnostic or route programs. Equivalent to setting the socket option SO_DONTROUTE. |
| MSG_DONTWAIT | No blocking on the I/O operation; if the operation would block, EAGAIN is returned. This is equivalent to setting O_NONBLCOK through fcntl(), but just for this operation. |
| MSG_NOSIGNAL | Don't send a SIGPIPE signal on a stream socket when the other end breaks the connection; EPIPE is still returned as an error, however. |
| MSG_CONFIRM | Inform the link layer that a successful reply came from the other side. This works only on SOCK_DGRAM and SOCK_RAW sockets, and only for **TCP**. This is a **Linux** extension. |

The error returns from send() and recv() contain mostly standard errors for sockets and the protocols used. Full details can be obtained from the **man** pages.

## 25.3   sendto(), recvfrom()

Another method of writing and reading on a socket descriptor is provided by the sendto() and recvfrom() functions:

```
#include <sys/types.h>
#include <sys/socket.h>

int sendto   (int sd, const void *buf, size_t len, int flags,
```

```
                const struct sockaddr *to,     socklen_t tolen);
int recvfrom (int sd,         void *buf, size_t len, int flags,
            struct sockaddr *from, socklen_t *fromlen);
```

On success these functions return the number of bytes sent or received.

The first four arguments are identical to those of `send()` and `recv()`, and `flags` can take the same values.

The last two arguments specify the target address in the case of `sendto()`, or the address from which data is being received in the case of `recvfrom()`. In the sending case these values are unmodified; in the receiving case they are filled in with the address as in the case of `accept()`.

Note that in `recvfrom()`, the final argument is a pointer to the address length; before calling the function it should be set to the size of the address structure being passed; on return it contains the actual address length.

In a client, it is not necessary to `connect()` to a socket when using these functions; i.e., the call to `sendto()` replaces the `connect()`, `send()` combination.

In a server, it is not necessary to `listen()` and `accept()`; the function `recvfrom()` replaces those functions followed by `recv()`.

These functions are not normally used with **TCP**, although in principle, there is no reason they cannot be.

The error returns from `sendto()` and `recvfrom()` contain mostly standard errors for sockets and the protocols used. Full details can be gotten from the **man** pages.

## 25.4   sendmsg(), recvmsg()

The most general functions for writing and reading on a socket descriptor are **sendmsg()** and **recvmsg()**; indeed **send()** and **sendto()** are implemented as wrappers around **sendmsg()**, and similarly for the receiving functions.

The prototypes for these functions are:

```
#include <sys/types.h>
#include <sys/socket.h>

int sendmsg (int sd, const struct msghdr *msg, int flags);
int recvmsg (int sd,       struct msghdr *msg, int flags);
```

where the third argument, `flags` is the same as for the other sending and receiving functions, and all the dirty work occurs through the pointer to the `msghdr` structure:

```
struct msghdr {
    void        * msg_name;     /* optional address */
    socklen_t     msg_namelen;  /* size of address */
    struct iovec * msg_iov;     /* scatter/gather array */
    size_t        msg_iovlen;   /* # elements in msg_iov */
    void        * msg_control;  /* ancillary data, see below */
```

```
    socklen_t    msg_controllen; /* ancillary data buffer len */
    int          msg_flags;      /* flags on received message */
};
```

The first two elements point to the address of the target or the sending party and its length; they need only be used for unconnected sockets.

The `msg_iov` argument points to an scatter-gather array of a length given by the `msg_iovlen` argument, used in the same way as in the `readv()`, `writev()` system calls. Note the `iovec` structure contains two elements; a starting address and a length.

During a send, the data in the chain of `iovec` structures is treated as it were one long buffer. During a receive, each of the structures is filled until the data is completely peeled out. See the **man** pages for `readv()`, `writev()` for more details.

The next two elements permit the sending of **ancillary data**, or **control information**. A message is of the form

```
struct cmsghdr {
    socklen_t cmsg_len;    /* data byte count, including header */
    int       cmsg_level; /* originating protocol */
    int       cmsg_type;  /* protocol-specific type */
    unsigned _char  cmsg_data[]; */
};
```

and should be created and accessed with the macros defined in the **man** page for **cmsg()**.

An in-depth description of sending and receiving ancillary data would take too much time, so we recommend reading the `cmsg` documentation to fill in the details.

The final element in the `msghdr` structure is `msg_flags`. For `sendmsg()` it is not used, but for `recvmsg()` it can contain the following values on return:

Table 25.3: **sendmsg() flags**

| Flag | Meaning |
|------|---------|
| MSG_EOR | Indicates an **end of record** was reached; used generally with `SOCK_SEQPACKET` sockets. Not used for **TCP** or other byte-stream protocols. |
| MSG_TRUNC | The datagram had to be truncated because there was not enough room in `iovec` structures. |
| MSG_CTRUNC | Control data was discarded because `msg_controllen` was not big enough. |
| MSG_OOB | **out-of-band** data was received. Note the `flags` variable can not be altered as it is passed by value, so this situation is recorded here. |
| MSG_ERRQUEUE | An extended error was retrieved from the **socket error queue**. |
| MSG_DONTWAIT | If this value was set in `flags` it will be set here. |

## 25.5   sendfile()

Suppose you want to copy data from one file to another in an application. The simple way to do it would be something like:

```
rc = read  (fd1, buf, NBUF);
rc = write (fd2, buf, rc )
```

However, this is not very efficient for at least two reasons:

- It requires two system calls, each of which requires the kernel switching in and out of kernel-mode from user-mode.
- It requires temporary storage in a buffer, which is then merely emptied out, requiring an extra copy operation and wasting of memory.

The sendfile() function offers a way to handle this more efficiently:

```
#include <sys/sendfile.h>

ssize_t sendfile (int out_fd, int in_fd, off_t *offset, size_t count);
```

The data will be copied directly from file descriptor in_fd to file descriptor out_fd, starting from offset in the input file, and copying count bytes.

While the value of offset will be incremented by the number of bytes read, the file position will not change; in this sendfile() operates similarly to the pread() and pwrite() system calls.

Thus the above code fragment now becomes:

```
rc = sendfile (fd2, fd1, 0, NBUF);
```

While either file descriptor may refer to a socket, it is difficult and rarely required to copy from a socket to a file; the inverse operation, sending a file down a socket is more useful.

In this case **Linux** makes full use of **zero-copy** networking when using sendfile(). This means the file is sent directly out to the network without any copying in the kernel as well.

Kernel Version Note     Kernel Version Note

- In the 2.6 kernel, sendfile() won't work if the output descriptor does not describe a **TCP** socket.

When successful, `sendfile()` returns the number of bytes written to the output descriptor. On failure, the possible error codes are:

Table 25.5: **sendfile() error return values**

| Error | Meaning |
|---|---|
| EBADF | The input file not open for reading or output file not open for writing. |
| EINVAL | Invalid or locked descriptor. |
| ENOMEM | Insufficient memory to read from the input descriptor. |
| EIO | Unspecified error while reading the input descriptor. |

One should beware that other operating systems have versions of `sendfile()` or `sendfile()`-like functions which have different prototypes and usage than under **Linux**. Thus you have to be very careful if trying to write any kind of portable code.

## 25.6   socketpair()

The function `socketpair()` creates a pair of **connected** sockets:

```
#include <sys/types.h>
#include <sys/socket.h>

int socketpair (int domain, int type, int protocol, int sv[2]);
```

where **domain** must have the value `PF_LOCAL`, type can be `SOCK_DGRAM` or `SOCK_STREAM`, and `protocol` must be 0; i.e., one must have Unix domain sockets.

The pair of sockets is returned in the final argument.

This function works very much like the `pipe()` command that works with unnamed pipes. What is written into one socket is read out of the other.

Unlike the endpoints created by the `pipe()` command, however, those created by `socketpair()` are `full-duplex`; one can read **and** write to **both** descriptors.

## 25.7   Labs

### Lab 1:  Using send() and recv()

Take the examples given for simple Unix domain socket stream client and server programs and convert them to work with `send()` and `recv()`.

Test them as usual.

This may seem a little more than necessary but we are going to use the codes in the following labs.

## Lab 2: Using sendto() and recvfrom() for TCP.

Take your Internet solutions for the previous problem and convert them to work with **sendto()** and **recvfrom()**, and test them as usual.

For extra work, do the same thing with the Unix domain sockets. Does this work?

## Lab 3: Using sendto() and recvfrom() for datagrams.

Now provide solutions for both Unix domain and Internet sockets that work with **sendto()** and **recvfrom()**, and test them as usual.

## Lab 4: Using sendfile().

Write a program that opens a file and copies it to a socket, using **TCP** over the Internet. Use port 7177 as before, and by default you can connect to the localhost.

In order to do this you'll also need a server program to receive the data. You can adopt the previous Internet **TCP** server to do this. You just need to make the modifications that the data read go to an output file, and that it not write back to the client.

The input file (called **infile** by default) can be first filled with zeros, with a command like:

```
dd if=/dev/zero of=infile bs=1024 count=8192
```

which would create an 8 MB file.

You may do the I/O in a number of chunks (given by the third argument, which can be 1 by default), and repeat the whole operation a number of times given by the fourth argument (perhaps 10 by default) in order to produce better averaged timing information.

Now make small adaptations to the program to have it use **sendfile()** instead of the **read()** / **write()** combination in the first program.

In our sample solution, we have combined this into one program which takes as its first argument either **on** or **off**. You can compare the performance of the two methods by starting the server program and then doing:

```
time lab4_sendfile_client off [infile] [hostname] [nchunks] [nreps]
time lab4_sendfile client on  [infile] [hostname] [nchunks] [nreps]
```

and comparing the results.

You'll probably want to do this several times, making sure your system is lightly loaded. The **time** command will report on real (or wall clock), user, and system time. The system time may not be reliable, so to be rough, just concentrate on the wall clock.

If you want to get fancier you can put timing instrumentation in your code using **gettimeofday()** or a similar function.

**Note:** It is quite possible your timings will be limited by disk I/O and not the network transmission. In order to make sure this is not the case, work with a **ram disk**. You can do this by:

```
mkdir ramdisk
mount -t tmpfs none ./ramdisk
```

and then make sure your data file is on the ramdisk.

## Lab 5:  Using socketpair() on a socket

Using `socketpair()` write a simple program that creates a pair of connected sockets.

Write an identifying message into each socket, clear it, and then read from the socket.

Print out what is sent to and read from the sockets. Are you getting full duplex operation?

# Chapter 26

# Sockets - Options

We'll show how socket behaviour can be modified through the use of the **fcntl()** and **ioctl()** system calls on open socket descriptors. We'll also consider examining and modify socket options directly.

## 26.1 Getting and Setting Socket Options

There are a number of ways to get and set options for sockets. For a particular sending or reception of a packet, one can set flag values to control behaviour.

The most general form for getting and setting options is to use the `getsockopt()` and `setsockopt()` functions.

It is also possible to set options by using the `fcntl()` (file control) and `ioctl()` (input/output control) functions.

## 26.2   fcntl()

The `fcntl()` function (the name stands for **file control**) is used to control a number of characteristics of descriptors. In the following we limit our attention to those of interest when the descriptor is associated with a socket.

`fcntl()` can be used a number of ways to influence or modify the way a socket descriptor is used:

```
#include <unistd.h>
#include <fcntl.h>

int fcntl (int sd, int cmd);
int fcntl (int sd, int cmd, long arg);
```

What `fcntl()` does depends on the value of `cmd`:

Table 26.1: **fcntl() parameters**

| Flag | Operations |
|------|-----------|
| F_GETFL | Read all the flags of the file descriptor and give them as the return value. |
| F_SETFL | Set the file descriptor's flags to **arg**; |
| F_GETOWN | Find out the process ID of the socket **owner**; i.e., who is to receive the signals `SIGIO` and `SIGURG`, and give it as the return value. |
| F_SETOWN | Set the socket owner. |
| F_GETSIG | Find out what signal is sent when I/O becomes possible. |
| F_SETSIG | Set the signal to be sent when I/O becomes possible. A value of 0 sets this to `SIGIO`. The return value is the signal to be sent, or zero if `SIGIO`. |

The only flags that can be set for a socket are:

- `O_NONBLOCK`: Set the socket for non-blocking operation.

- `O_ASYNC`: Send the `SIGIO` signal whenever input or output becomes possible on the descriptor. Note the signal to be sent can be modified. This flag is not available on all operating systems.

A common mistake is to not preserve the unmodified flag values when using `fcntl()`. For example the following code avoids this problem:

```
flags = fcntl (sd, F_GETFL, 0);
fcntl (sd, F_SETFL, flags | O_NONBLOCK);
```

The signal `SIGURG` is sent when **out-of-band** data arrives on a socket. (This will cause `select()` to report an **exceptional condition**.) The use of `F_SETSIG`, `F_GETSIG` is **Linux**-specific, and generally not portable.

When a socket is created it is considered as not having an owner. But when a new one is created from a listening socket, the owner is inherited from the listening socket by the connected socket.

# 26.3　ioctl()

The `ioctl()` function (the name stands for **input/output control**) can be used for almost any hardware device and many kernel facilities, to examine and set behaviour.

The prototype of this function is:

```
#include <sys/ioctl.h>
int ioctl (int sd, int command, char *argp);
```

where the third argument is optional, depending on the value of the second argument, `command`.

Restricting ourselves to those possible commands that are directly of interest to sockets, we have:

Table 26.2: **Socket ioctl commands**

| Command | Meaning |
|---------|---------|
| SIOCGSTAMP | Return in the third argument a `struct timeval` a timestamp for the last packet passed to the user on this socket. |
| SIOCSPGRP | Set the process (or group) to receive the `SIGIO` and `SIGURG` signals; in this case the third argument points to a process ID. This is equivalent to using `fcntl()` with `F_SETOWN`. |
| FIOASYNC | Reset the value of the `O_ASYNC` flag; the third argument is the flag. This is equivalent to using `fcntl()` with `F_SETFL` and `O_ASYNC`. |
| SIOCGPGRP | Get the current process (or group) receiving the signals. This is equivalent to using `fcntl()` with `F_GETOWN`. |

Note that the last three duplicate the abilities of `fcntl()`, and as far as **Posix** is concerned, the use of `ioctl()` is deprecated in favor of it. However, you are quite likely to encounter code that is using the `ioctl()` interface.

There are many other commands which are of interest to networking in general, rather than just sockets. These have to do with routing and interfaces. See `man 7 socket` for detailed information.

# 26.4　getsockopt() and setsockopt()

In order to examine or modify the characteristics of a socket, one uses the functions:

```
#include <sys/types.h>
#include <sys/socket.h>

int getsockopt (int sd, int level, int optname, void *optval, socklen_t *optlen);
int setsockopt (int sd, int level, int optname, const void *optval, socklen_t optlen);
```

The socket must have previously been opened with `sd` being a valid socket descriptor.

The `level` argument indicates the general type of option being manipulated. The value `SOL_SOCKET` works at the socket level, the value `IPPROTO_IP` works at the **IPV4** level, etc.

The particular option being examined or set is denoted by the `optname` argument, while `optval` points to a buffer that either contains the value of option to be set, or returns the present value. The length of that buffer is returned in the last argument by the get function, and is supplied in the set function. (Note that in `setsockopt()` this last argument is **not** a pointer!)

For most socket-level options `optval` is either an integer value, and in the case of boolean on/off situations a value of 1 turns it on, and 0 turns it off. Remember we enabled a socket for immediate reuse with the code:

```
int yes=1;
setsockopt (sd, SOL_SOCKET, SO_REUSEADDR, &yes, sizeof(yes));
```

as a typical example.

The socket level options **Linux** understands are listed by `man 7 socket`, and are:

Table 26.3: **Socket options**

| Value | Type | Meaning |
|-------|------|---------|
| SO_KEEPALIVE | int | Periodically check to see if the connection is still alive. |
| SO_OOBINLIN | int | Out of band data should be left in line. |
| SO_RCVLOWAT SO_SNDLOWAT | int | Receive and Send buffer low water marks; the minimum bytes in the buffer before the data is passed to the protocol or the user. Under **Linux** this value is always 1. |
| SO_RCVTIMEO SO_SNDTIMEO | struct timeval | Receive and Send timeouts, before errors are reported. These can not be modified under **Linux**. |
| SO_BSDCOMPAT | int | Enable **BSD** bug compatibliity; obsolete and only for **UDP**. |
| SO_PASSCRED | int | Enable reception of the SCM_CREDENTIALS control message. |
| SO_PEERCRED | struct ucred | Return credentails of a foreign process connected to the socket. Only for PF_UNIX and can only be examined, not set. |
| SO_BINDTODEVICE | char * | Bind the socket to a particular device (such as eth0). Passing an empty string releases a binding. |
| SO_DEBUG | int | Enable debug tracing. Only for super-users. |
| SO_REUSEADDR | int | Allow reuse of local addresses |
| SO_TYPE | int | Get the socket type (e.g., SOCK_STREAM). |
| SO_DONTROUTE | int | Bypass routing table; used only for directly connected hosts. |
| SO_BROADCAST | int | Enable to receive or send broadcast datagrams. |
| SO_SNDBUF | int | Get or set the maximum socket send buffer. See /proc/sys/net/core/wmem_default and /proc/sys/net/core/wmem_max. |
| SO_RCVBUF | int | Get or set the maximum socket receive buffer. See /proc/sys/net/core/rmem_default and /proc/sys/net/core/rmem_max. |

| SO_LINGER | struct linger | When enabled, closing the socket delays return until all queued messages have been sent or the timeout has passed. The structure contains the timeout value. |
| SO_PRIORITY | int | Set a priority for all packets on the socket. |
| SO_ERROR | int | Get and clear the pending socket error. |

Information on the various **TCP** socket options (level=SOL_TCP) can be obtained by seeing `man 7 tcp`. Information on the various **IP** socket options (level=SOL_IP) can be obtained by seeing `man 7 ip`.

Some socket options can also be set by using the `fcntl()` or `ioctl()` functions, or setting flags in the various sending and receiving functions.

# 26.5   Labs

### Lab 1: Examining socket options

Write a program that uses `getsockopt()` to examine the default options for a **TCP/IP** socket.

Just open a socket (you don't have to do anything with it, like connecting), and then using the option names available in **/usr/src/linux/arch/x86/include/asm/socket.h**, obtain their values.

Note that most of the options have an integer value, but some are not, such as those which are given in a `timeval` data structure.

Print out the symbolic name along with the integer option number.

For the above you'll use `SOL_SOCKET` for the `level` parameter. You can also try other values such as SOL_IP. Look at the **man** pages for **socket(7), tcp(7), ip(7), unix(7)**, etc. to get some ideas.

# Chapter 27

# Netlink Sockets

We'll discuss the use of **netlink** sockets, explaining what they are, how to connect to them, and how to send messages through them.

## 27.1 What are netlink Sockets?

**Netlink** sockets provide a convenient method of transferring information between the kernel and user-space, or between various kernel subsystems.

Because they use the well established socket infrastructure they afford a relatively safe and well known interface, which often is preferable to either more old-fashioned methods such as **ioctl** commands, or the use of various pseudo-filesystems, such as **proc** or **sysfs**.

**Netlink** sockets are most often used for network system administration and monitoring. For instance they provide flexible advanced methods for controlling firewalls and routing.

The messages transferred are datagrams, and as with **UDP** this is not a reliable protocol. This means if a message can not be delivered (perhaps due to a lack of required memory) it is dropped. It is up to the sender and recipient to handle proper acknowledgments of receipt and requests for resending.

A message consists of a byte stream with one or more headers (described by `nlmsghdr` data structures), together with a data payload. We'll discuss details.

Messages are sent with the `sendto()` and `sendmsg()` standard socket library functions, and are received by the `recvfrom()` and `recvmsg()` functions.

For an excellent description and tutorial on working with **netlink** sockets, see **http://people.redhat.com/nhorman/papers/netlink.pdf** by Neil Horman at **Red Hat**.

Applications using netlink sockets can make use of **libnl**, a library providing an interface for raw netlink messaging and various netlink family specific interfaces. It can be downloaded with documentation from **http://people.suug.ch/ tgr/libnl/**.

## 27.2   Opening a netlink Socket

One creates a **netlink** socket in the usual way:

```
#include <linux/types.h>
#include <sys/socket.h>
#include <linux/netlink.h>

netlink_socket = socket (PF_NETLINK, type, netlink_family);
```

The `type` should be `SOCK_RAW`. The kernel will accept `SOCK_DGRAM` as well, but will not distinguish between them.

The last argument, `netlink_family`, is what is usually what is described as the `protocol` in the general `socket()` system call, so it can be confusing.

`netlink_family` can be one of the following:

Table 27.1: **Netlink families**

| netlink_family | Description |
|---|---|
| NETLINK_ROUTE | Receive routing packets and modify the routing table. (IPV4) |
| NETLINK_SKIP | Reserved for **ENskip.** |
| NETLINK_USERSOCK | Reserved for future user-space protocols. |
| NETLINK_FIREWALL | Receive packets for firewall code. (IPV4) |
| NETLINK_TCPDIAG | For monitoring **TCP** sockets. |
| NETLINK_NFLOG | For **netfilter** and **iptables** logging. |
| NETLINK_ARPD | Manage the **ARP** table (**A**dress **R**esolution **P**rotocol). |
| NETLINK_ROUTE6 | Receive routing packets and modify the routing table. (IPV6) |
| NETLINK_IP6_FW | Receive packets for firewall code. (IPV6) |
| NETLINK_DNRTMSG | **Decnet** routing messages. |
| NETLINK_TAPBASE – NETLINK_TAPBASE+15 | 16 instances of the **ethertap** device, a pseudo-network tunnel device for simulating an Ethernet driver. |

Note that the list of families in the **man** page for **netlink** is out of date.

The usual network system calls such as `connect()` and `bind()` require a pointer to an address structure generically cast to the type `struct sockaddr` . For **netlink** sockets the actual address structure is:

```
struct sockaddr_nl
{
    sa_family_t nl_family;    /* AF_NETLINK */
    unsigned short nl_pad;    /* zero */
    pid_t       nl_pid;       /* process pid */
    __u32       nl_groups;    /* multicast groups mask */
};
```

where `nl_family` is always `AF_NETLINK` and `nl_pad` is for internal kernel use and should not be modified.

The process owning the socket is described as `nl_pid`; the sending process should set this field. The kernel sets this to describe the process to receive the message, or to zero for either multicast messages or those destined for internal delivery.

The **nl_groups** field is used for multicasting. It is a bit-mask describing 32 multicast groups it may wish to listen to; by default the bits are all cleared. Each protocol family has its own set of 32 multicast groups.

## 27.3   netlink Messages

A **netlink** message is described by the following **nlmsghdr** data structure:

```
struct nlmsghdr
{
    __u32       nlmsg_len;    /* Length of message including header */
    __u16       nlmsg_type;   /* Message content */
    __u16       nlmsg_flags;  /* Additional flags */
    __u32       nlmsg_seq;    /* Sequence number */
    __u32       nlmsg_pid;    /* Sending process PID */
};

struct nlmsgerr
{
    int              error;
    struct nlmsghdr msg;
};
```

Note that the data **payload** directly follows the message, and **nlmsg_len** describes the full length including the header.

The type of message is indicated by **nlmsg_type**

Table 27.2: **Netlink message types**

| Message Type | Description |
|---|---|
| NLMSG_NOOP | Ignore the message. |
| NLMSG_ERROR | The message signals an error; the payload contains a nlmsgerr data structure describing it. |
| NLMSG_DONE | The message is the terminator of a multipart message. |
| NLMSG_OVERRUN | Signals data was lost. |

In addition each netlink family (or protocol) has other types relevant only to it.

The nlmsg_flags can also have protocol dependent values, as well as a bit mask of the following standard values:

```
#define NLM_F_REQUEST    1    /* It is request message.       */
#define NLM_F_MULTI      2    /* Multipart message,
                                 terminated by NLMSG_DONE */
#define NLM_F_ACK        4    /* Reply with ack, with zero or error
                                 code */
#define NLM_F_ECHO       8    /* Echo this request            */

/* Modifiers to GET request */
#define NLM_F_ROOT       0x100   /* specify tree root    */
#define NLM_F_MATCH      0x200   /* return all matching  */
#define NLM_F_ATOMIC     0x400   /* atomic GET           */
#define NLM_F_DUMP       (NLM_F_ROOT|NLM_F_MATCH)

/* Modifiers to NEW request */
#define NLM_F_REPLACE    0x100   /* Override existing          */
#define NLM_F_EXCL       0x200   /* Do not touch, if it exists */
#define NLM_F_CREATE     0x400   /* Create, if it does not exist */
#define NLM_F_APPEND     0x800   /* Add to end of list         */
```

nlmsg_seq field should be a serial message counter, used to aid in correlating acknowledgments. The nlmsg_pid is as discussed before.

The data passed to and from netlink sockets should only be accessed using the following macros:

Table 27.3: **Netlink macros**

| Macro | Description |
|---|---|
| int NLMSG_ALIGNTO | Alignment value (set to 4). |
| int NLMSG_ALIGN(size_t len) | Rounds the length of a message up for alignment. Used internally. |
| int NLMSG_LENGTH(size_t len) | Given the length of the ancillary data, returns the size of the payload plus the header, rounded up for alignment. Used to set nlmsg_len. |

| int NLMSG_SPACE(size_t len) | Returns aligned size of passed length. Like NLMSG_LENGTH but does not include the size of the message header |
|---|---|
| void *NLMSG_DATA(struct nlmsghdr *nlh) | Gives a pointer to the ancillary data contained in the structure. |
| struct nlmsghdr *NLMSG_NEXT(struct nlmsghdr *nlh) | For multiple response messages, points to the next message. |
| int NLMSG_OK(struct nlmsghdr *nlh, int len) | Used to ensure one of multiple messages is received properly. |
| int NLMSG_PAYLOAD(nlmsghdr *nhl, int len) | Returns the length of the ancillary data payload. |

## 27.4  Labs

### Lab 1: Using Netlink to monitor routing changes.

We give you a program which is capable of monitoring (through **netlink**) routing table operations: **lab1_nl_routing.c**. Compile and execute.

Add, delete, and modify routes on your system and see how the program responds. If you stop and restart your network (with `service network restart`) you should see some messages. Or you can try some commands such as

```
route add -net 192.56.76.0 netmask 255.255.255.0 dev eth0
route add -host 123.213.221.231 eth0
route add -net 10.13.21.0 netmask 255.255.255.0 gw 192.168.1.254 eth0
```

If you are ambitious, modify the code to obtain more information about the requests.

### Lab 2: Using Netlink to send kernel messages to an application.

We give you a kernel module ( **lab2_nl_sender.c**) that sends messages to a netlink socket to be monitored by a user application ( **lab2_nl_receive_test.c**).

Compile and test the two programs. Try sending multiple messages through straightforward modifications.

# Chapter 28

# Sockets - Multiplexing and Concurrent Servers

We'll discuss how sockets can be used for multiplexed and asynchronous I/O. We'll consider the use of **select()**, **poll()**, **pselect()**, **ppoll()** and **epoll** for working with groups of socket descriptors simultaneously. We'll show how signal driven I/O can be used effectively. Finally we'll consider how to write concurrent servers.

## 28.1   Multiplexed and Asynchronous Socket I/O

An application may have a need to handle input from and/or output to a number of different sources simultaneously. These may correspond to file descriptors, socket descriptors, or a combination of the two. For instance, concentrating on reading:

- A client or server may be waiting for input from a terminal or a file or pipe.

- A server may be listening for new connections which it can `accept()`.

- A client or server may be ready to accept input from connected sockets, or from connectionless sockets.

In most cases by default I/O is a **blocking** operation: an application will not return from a reading system call until data is present, either any amount at all or until the low-water mark has been passed. While the application is blocked it can't do anything else.

An application can do **non-blocking** operations, but often this requires it to do frequent **polling**; i.e., it sits in a loop checking every so often for input. This can often be a big waste of CPU cycles.

There are several methods an application can choose that may perform better than these two choices:

- Multiplexing can be done using `select()`, `pselect()`, or `poll()`. This is still a variation on **polling** but permits waiting on a number of different I/O channels, and can be optimized by the kernel rather than an application. The newer **Linux**-specific method termed **epoll** scales the best to large numbers of descriptors.

- An application can use **signal-driven** I/O; when action needs to be taken with respect to a descriptor, the I/O activity can be taken care of by a signal handler. This removes the `polling` activity, but requires a lot of signal activity.

- An application can use true **asynchronous** I/O; here I/O operations are initiated and the return happens before completion. A signal indicates the end of the I/O activity, rather than the start.

- A server can be written to handle concurrent operations by either forking children for each channel that needs to be handled, or by launching light weight threads for that purpose. This can be done in parallel with some of the other techniques as well.

There is no "one size fits all" approach for all applications, in that the I/O channels may be open for a short time or a long time, there may be many simultaneous requests or just a few, etc.

## 28.2   select()

The `select()` function works with a set of file descriptors and/or socket descriptors, thus providing multiplexing and asycnrhronous input and output.

With `select()`, one can wait for a specified time until data is ready to be read, or written, or an exception is noted:

```
#include <sys/types.h>
#include <sys/time.h>
#include <unistd.h>

int select (int n, fd_set *readfds, fd_set *writefds, fd_set *exceptfds,
            struct timeval *timeout);

struct timeval {long tv_sec, long tv_usec};
```

The argument n gives the number of file descriptors to check, which should be one higher than the highest file descriptor (since they start with 0.) The **Linux** kernel has a limit of __FD_SETSIZE=1024 file descriptors that can be used for select().

The arguments readfds, writefds, exceptfds are pointers to so-called **descriptor sets**, which are stored in the fd_set data type, which signal to the kernel which descriptors are to be watched for what kind of action.

When data is ready to be read on a descriptor, the appropriate bit is set in the read set. When a descriptor is ready for input, a bit is set in the write set. When there is a socket error, both bits can be set. Bits in the exception set are set when out-of band data arrives.

The following macros operate on these sets:

Table 28.1: **Select set macros**

| FD_ZERO(fd_set *set); | Clear all bits in set. |
|---|---|
| FD_CLR(int fd, fd_set *set); | Turn off bit for fd in set. |
| FD_SET(int fd, fd_set *set); | Turn on bit for fd in set. |
| FD_ISSET(int fd, fd_set *set); | Test bit for fd in set. |

The argument timeval gives the maximum time period select() should wait for one of the file descriptors to indicate a change in its status. If one or more are ready before the period has expired, the function returns at that time. The two elements of the structure give the expiration period in seconds and microseconds.

If timeval = NULL, the wait period is infinite, although it can be interrupted by a signal. If tv_sec = tv_usec = 0, the return is immediate; i.e., the function does a non-blocking check.

Any of the descriptor sets can be a **NULL** pointer; if all three are, then select() works as a higher precision timer than the simple sleep() function; this trick is often exploited.

Under **Linux** the argument timeout is modified to reflect the amount of time not slept. Most other operating systems do not do this, so to be safe don't use this variable after the function returns. Keep in mind the descriptor sets themselves are modified during the system call so they need to be reinitialized each time select() is called.

On success, select() returns the number of descriptors that are ready for some kind of action; if a file descriptor is ready for both read and write it would add 2 to the return value under **Linux**; on some other operating systems only 1, so once again don't use this value in any important way. A return value of 0 indicates the time limit expired before any file descriptor was ready. A return value of -1 indicates an error. Note that if a signal is caught before a file descriptor flips its state, this can happen.

Note that upon timeout the file descriptor set is cleared. If select() is to be called **again** after timeout, another FD_SET operation will be required. This approach can be suitable if the input is partially event-driven (via file input) and partially polled (via periodic timeouts).

The select() function is most often used with **pipes** and **sockets**, rather than regular files. For these kinds of filesystem inodes, read and write calls may block while waiting for other processes to complete certain actions. This function is therefor useful in constructing *event-driven* code.

## Example:

```
#include <stdio.h>
#include <unistd.h>
#include <stdlib.h>
#include <fcntl.h>
#include <sys/time.h>
#include <sys/types.h>
#include <sys/select.h>

int main (void)
{
    fd_set fd_rset;
    struct timeval timeout = { 8, 5000 };
    int rc, fd;

    fd = open ("./afifo", O_RDONLY | O_NONBLOCK);

    FD_ZERO (&fd_rset);
    FD_SET (fd, &fd_rset);

    if ((rc = select (fd + 1, &fd_rset, NULL, NULL, &timeout)) < 0) {
        printf ("error in select()\n");
        exit (EXIT_FAILURE);
    }
    printf (" select returned with rc=%d\n", rc);

    if (rc > 0 && FD_ISSET (fd, &fd_rset))
        printf ("Data ready for reading on fd=%d\n", fd);
    if (rc == 0)
        printf ("No data found\n");
    exit (EXIT_SUCCESS);
}
```

The select() function doesn't scale well as the number of descriptors increases (as we will soon detail.) The method we discuss next, poll(), is newer and fares somewhat better but has limitations as well.

# 28.3  poll()

The `poll()` function has essentially the same functionality as `select()`:

```
#include <sys/poll.h>

int poll (struct pollfd *ufds, unsigned int nfds, int timeout);
```

The `timeout` parameter gives the time to wait in milliseconds. A value of 0 means return immediately (don't block), while any negative value means wait indefinitely.

This function works on an array of length `nfds` of data structures of type

```
struct pollfd{
    int fd;        /* file descriptor */
    short events;  /* requested events */
    short revents; /* returned events */
}
```

In the data structure, the `fd` element gives the file descriptor to examine; a negative value means to ignore.

The `events` element is a bitmask of the events to be checked. It is composed of the following possibilities:

Table 28.2: **Polling events**

| Value | Meaning |
|---|---|
| POLLIN | Normal or priority band data can be read. |
| POLLRDNORM | Normal data can be read. |
| POLLRDBAND | Priority band data can be read. |
| POLLPRI | High priority data can be read. |
| POLLOUT | Normal data can be written. |
| POLLWRNORM | Normal data can be written. |
| POLLWRBAND | Priority band data can be written. |
| POLLMSG | Non standard value |

Under most circumstances, one would just use `POLLIN` to check if there is data to be read, and `POLLOUT` to see if data can be written.

The `revents` element in the data structure is filled in by `poll()` with the reason for the function return (e.g., `POLLIN`, `POLLOUT`). It can also have one of the following values which indicate various problems:

Table 28.3: **Polling return events**

| Value | Meaning |
|---|---|
| POLLERR | An error has occurred. |
| POLLHUP | The socket has hung up. |
| POLLINVAL | Invalid descriptor |

The return value of `poll()` is the number of structures which have non-zero values in their `revents` elements. A value of 0 implies the call timed out, and a value of -1 indicates an error (including `EINTR`, which means a signal has occurred.)

## Example:

```
#include <stdio.h>
#include <unistd.h>
#include <stdlib.h>
#include <fcntl.h>
#include <sys/poll.h>

int main (void)
{
    struct pollfd ufds[1];
    int timeout = 8050, rc, fd;

    /* Watch stdin for input, stdout for output. */

    fd = open ("./afifo", O_RDONLY | O_NONBLOCK);

    ufds[0].fd = fd;
    ufds[0].events = POLLIN;

    if ((rc = poll (ufds, 1, timeout)) < 0) {
        printf ("error in poll()\n");
        exit (EXIT_FAILURE);
    }

    printf (" poll returned with rc=%d\n", rc);

    if (rc > 0 && (ufds[0].revents & POLLIN))
        printf ("Data ready for reading on fd=%d\n", fd);
    if (rc == 0)
        printf ("No data found\n");

    exit (EXIT_SUCCESS);

}
```

There are some advantages to using the `poll()` call over `select()`. In particular there is no fixed limit to the number of descriptors that can be watched (although there will still be a limit on the number of file descriptors a process can have, we don't have to worry about the size of the descriptor set.)

In fact, under **Linux**, since the 2.2 kernel `select()` has been implemented internally as a wrapper around `poll`.

## 28.4   pselect() and ppoll()

An enhancement of the `select()` function is provided by the `pselect()` function:

```
#include <sys/select.h>
#include <sys/time.h>
$include <sys/types.h>
#include <unistd.h>

int pselect (int n, fd_set *readfds, fd_set *writefds, fd_set *exceptfds,
             const struct timespec *timeout, const sigset_t *sigmask);
```

There are three differences as compared to `select()`:

- Instead of a `struct timeval`, it uses

```
struct timespec {
    long    tv_sec;   /* seconds */
    long    tv_nsec;  /* nanoseconds */
};
```

  which has nanosecond resolution (which does not imply your system can properly resolve this.)

- The `timeout` parameter is not changed by the function.

- The `sigmask` parameter can be used to set a temporary signal mask (which signals should be blocked) while `pselect()` is called. (You can see **man sigprocmask** for a synopsis of how to handle signal masks.)

Similarly for `poll()` one can use as an alternative the enhanced function

```
#include <poll.h>

int ppoll(struct pollfd *fds, nfds_t nfds, const struct timespec *timeout,
          const sigset_t *sigmask);
```

where the two new arguments function exactly as in `pselect()`.

## 28.5   epoll

Both `select()` and `poll()` suffer in performance when the number of file (socket) descriptors being watched becomes large.

Because these calls return only the knowledge that one or more descriptors is ready for action, but not which, the application has to check each one in a loop. Thus the time taken scales directly with the number; i.e., they are **O(N)** in mathematical terms.

The 2.6 kernel introduces the new `epoll` set of system calls, for which the time taken to locate the descriptor ready for action is independent of the number; i.e., it is **O(1)** algorithmically.

The relevant functions and data structures for user applications are to be found in **/usr/include/sys/epoll.h**.

```
#include <sys/epoll.h>

int epoll_create (int size);
int epoll_ctl (int epfd, int op, int fd, struct epoll_event *event);
int epoll_wait (int epfd, struct epoll_event *events, int maxevents, int timeout);

typedef union epoll_data
{
  void *ptr;
  int fd;
  uint32_t u32;
  uint64_t u64;
} epoll_data_t;

struct epoll_event
{
  uint32_t events;
  epoll_data_t data;
}
```

First one calls `epoll_create()`, passing in the maximum number of file descriptors the process will need to manage. This functions returns a special file descriptor (**epfd**) which is used as input for the other functions, and which should have a normal `close()` applied to it when done.

The function `epoll_ctl()` should then be called for **each** file descriptor of interest, where op can be:

Table 28.4: **epoll operations**

| EPOLL_CTL_ADD | Add a file descriptor. |
|---|---|
| EPOLL_CTL_DEL | Remove a file descriptor. |
| EPOLL_CTL_MOD | Change the `epoll_event` structure for a file descriptor. |

Note the `epoll_event` has a data structure embedded in it that is a union so it can be used in different ways. Thus using it as `void *ptr` it can hold as much detailed information about the file descriptor and activity as you choose to use.

The `events` field of the data structure is a bit mask of what events would inspire attention. For instance the value `EPOLLIN | EPOLLOUT` would indicate the file is available for read and/or write operations. (See **man epoll_ctl** for the full set of event types.)

Not that set up is done, one can enter into a loop around `epoll_wait()` which will wait until one to `maxevents` are available for as long as `timeout` milliseconds. If `timeout` = NULL, there is no blocking and an immediate return, and if `timeout` = -1 the wait is infinitely long.

The return value of `epoll_wait()` is the number of ready descriptors, and the `events` argument will point to an array of structures describing each event. Thus there is no longer any need to walk down the entire list of file descriptors to process events. Thus the algorithm scales as **O(1)**.

### Example:

```
#include <stdio.h>
#include <unistd.h>
#include <stdlib.h>
#include <fcntl.h>
#include <string.h>
#include <sys/epoll.h>

int main (void)
{
    int timeout = 8050, rc, fd, epfd, maxevents = 1;
    struct epoll_event ep_sd, ep_event;

    /* Watch stdin for input, stdout for output. */

    fd = open ("./afifo", O_RDONLY | O_NONBLOCK);

    ep_sd.data.fd = fd;
    ep_sd.events = EPOLLIN;

    epfd = epoll_create (1);
    epoll_ctl (epfd, EPOLL_CTL_ADD, fd, &ep_sd);

    if ((rc = epoll_wait (epfd, &ep_event, maxevents, timeout)) < 0) {
        printf ("error in epoll()\n");
        exit (EXIT_FAILURE);
    }

    printf (" epoll returned with rc=%d\n", rc);

    if (rc > 0 && (ep_event.events & EPOLLIN))
        printf ("Data ready for reading on fd=%d\n", ep_event.data.fd);

    if (rc == 0)
        printf ("No data found\n");

    exit (EXIT_SUCCESS);

}
```

## 28.6   Signal Driven and Asynchronous I/O

**Signal-driven I/O** can be used to avoid blocking and polling as an alternative to `select()`, `poll()`, and `epoll`.

First the socket must be **enabled** for signal-driven I/O; this means setting the **socket owner**; i.e., determining which process should receive the SIGIO signal when the socket has activity.

Remember that we can set this with fcntl() or setsockopt(). Under **Linux** we can also set the signal itself.

A signal handler has to be installed, preferably with the sigaction() system call (rather than the weaker and less reliable signal() system call.)

The signal handler can then either read the data (with recvfrom() for example) and perhaps notify the main program that data is available, or it can notify the main program to read the data. Meanwhile the main program just sits in a loop.

Under true **asynchronous I/O**, the operation is somewhat the reverse. The I/O operation is initiated and the program continues to execute. When the I/O operation is done, a signal is generated to signify completion.

This can be done through the explicit use of signals, but the more advanced implementation uses the **AIO** interface, whose functions are defined in **/usr/include/aio.h**. There are special functions for reading, writing, and other necessities.

## 28.7   Concurrent Servers

The **concurrent server** model permits a server to handle multiple requests simultaneously, while preventing blocking in one of them from stalling the entire operation.

The basic idea is to have the main parent process listen for connections and then whenever one is accepted, to create a child process to handle that connection. When there is no more work to do for the client the child process terminates.

This creates code that looks like:

```
sd = socket(...)
....
listen(...);
....
for ( ; ; ){
    cd = accept(...);
    pid = fork();

    if (pid==0) { /* child process */
       close(sd);
       handle_the_client();
       close(cd);
       exit(0);
    }
    close(cd);
}
```

All the real work will be done by the handle_the_client() function.

Note that the child inherits a copy of all file (and socket) descriptors across the fork and thus should close the socket descriptor while working on the descriptor returned by accept().

This is a very common and well established model; it permits the server to handle many clients at once.

However, creating a process is not a cheap operation. It makes sense when there is a significant amount of work to do for each client, and/or when the length of time the client process might require the server is lengthy. Yet often the client request may be short lived or trivial.

In this case, the concurrent server can be implemented in terms of a multi-threaded model, in which the children are so-called **light weight processes**, or **LWP**'s.

In this kind of multi-threaded parallel implementation, the sibling processes all share the same file descriptor space, memory, signal handlers and other attributes. Thus multi-threading may be the way to go when the child needs to communicate back to the parent after processing the request, perhaps by making the data available.

A code fragment showing how a multi-threaded concurrent server using the Posix Threads library (**pthreads**) might look would include:

```
/* Don't forget to compile with -pthread */

#include <pthread.h>

sd = socket(...)
....
listen(...);
....
for ( ; ; ){
    cd = accept(...);
    pthread_create(&thr[cd], NULL, handle_the_client, &Data[cd]);
    pthread_detach(&thr[cd]);
}
....
```

When the thread is started up, it will execute the `handle_the_client()` function. Note it doesn't do a `close()` on the socket descriptor; threads share their descriptor space and this would close it in the server too! Obviously, some care is required that the threads don't get in each other's way.

## 28.8   Labs

### Lab 1: I/O Multiplexing and select()

Write a program that takes some files names as arguments. It should open each file, and then scan each one for incoming data.

When any file has data ready to read it should print out the filename as well as the data. Loop indefinitely, printing the data from each file as it comes.

Test the program by creating two named pipes with the `mkfifo` command:

```
mkfifo file1
mkfifo file2
```

(we'll discuss this when we discuss **pipes**) and opening up three shell windows (or using three virtual terminals if you don't have **X** running).

In two windows, type `cat > file1` and `cat > file2`; in the third window, run your program. You should be able to type "Hello" in the first window, and see "file1 says: Hello" come from your test program, then type "Goodbye" in the second window and see "file2 says: Goodbye", etc.

Some hints:

- Print out the name of each file as you open it. Remember that if you try to open a **fifo** for reading, and nobody has it open for writing, you will stop dead right there! This is an easy mistake to make and printing each filename you open will make it obvious when this happens.

- You don't have to worry about files being closed if you don't want to. For extra credit, have your program "forget" about closed files when you hear that they are closed, but this can be tricky so don't worry about it if you don't want to.

- Don't forget that the first argument to `select()` should be the highest file descriptor that is set in your file descriptor set **plus one**, not the number of files set! This is very important!

Implement the program using `select()`.

Implement the program using **epoll**.

## Lab 2:  Concurrent Servers

Take your code for a simple Internet **TCP** server, and adapt it to handle multiple simultaneous connections using `select()`.

Set a maximum number of simultaneous connections to permit.,

Make sure you examine the listening socket descriptor so you can accept new connections, as well as listen for incoming data on existing connections.

To test the server, adapt your simple Internet **TCP** client to open multiple sockets, and then send data to them in random order. You can do this with something like:

```
srand(seed);
....
sd_to_writeto = rand()%number_of_connections;
```

What happens if you try to open more connections than your server will permit?

Implement the server using:

- `select()`.

- `poll()`.

- The **epoll** set of functions.

- `fork()`.

- You'll need to create a child for each new incoming connection.

- You'll have to be careful to reap children when they terminate. Otherwise they will become **zombies** and you will be limited in the number of connections you can open.

- To do this you'll most likely want to use some combination of `waitpid()` and installing a signal handling routine for `SIGCHLD`.

- The **pthread** library.

  - Create multiple threads, using `pthread_create()` to create a light weight process, or thread, for each new incoming connection.

  - Make sure you **detach** the thread when you create it, either by using `pthread_detach()` or setting the attributes with `pthread_attr_init()`, `pthread_attr_setdetachstate()`. Alternatively, you can wait for the thread to complete with `pthread_join()`.

  - Be careful about any global variables that can be affected in multiple threads, using `pthread_mutex_lock()` when necessary.

  - Make sure you compile with `-pthread`.

To compare results you may wish to insert some timing functions in the client program. If you do, start the timers when all clients have been opened, and stop them before they close, as otherwise you'll just be timing how long it takes to open and close the connections, which is a different metric.

Fill out the following table with your timing results. You might try 1000 connections with 10000 random client accesses.

Table 28.5: **Concurrent server results**

| Method | Time |
|--------|------|
| select | |
| poll | |
| fork | |
| pthread | |
| epoll | |

**Warning:** You may run into trouble with exceeding your limits on open file descriptors, and maximum memory use. These can be modified with the **ulimit** command (although only **root** can increase the limits.) Memory usage can be cut by limiting stack size.

# Chapter 29

# Inter Process Communication

We'll learn about three methods of **IPC**: shared memory, semaphores, and message queues, and their **System V** and **POSIX** implementations.

## 29.1   Methods of IPC

Broadly speaking, the term **Inter Process Communication** (**IPC**) includes any method that exchanges information or promotes cooperation among more than one process.

This includes pipes, networks. Unix domain sockets, etc., as well as the following three mechanisms that are often taken as a group and always connect processes only on a local machine, which may or may not have a parent-child relationship:

- **Shared Memory** allows one process to allocate memory to which other processes can attach and detach. The processes communicate directly through this sharing. This is the fastest **IPC** method. Careful synchronization is essential to preserve integrity and avoid race conditions.

233

- **Semaphores** are used by processes to signal each other when a resource is either available or unavailable due to concurrent use. One invokes **down** operations to gain access and **up** operations to let others gain access. Semaphores differ from other locking devices in that they are **counters** rather than binary; i.e., more than one (but less than some limiting number of processes) may share simultaneous access.

- **Message Queues** are used to exchange data among processes without using pipes. Depending on the implementation, messages may be retrieved according to priority, type, and/or first-in, first-out (**FIFO**) order.

There are two available standardized **IPC** implementations available on **Linux** systems: **System V IPC** and **POSIX IPC**. We will discuss both in detail as well as contrast them.

In both of these implementations these three mechanisms are closely linked. For instance, one basic system call, ipc(), can be used to invoke all three System V methods. Furthermore, all the POSIX IPC methods are implemented using pseudo-filesystems (on **Linux**) and can be examined and modified with normal file utilities.

When used improperly, **IPC** methods can cause **leaks** in system resources such as memory. By **design** it is possible for an **IPC** object to remain in existence even after all processes which have used it have terminated. The System V implementation is particularly clumsy in this regard, and inconsistencies between the methods used to remove the various kinds of objects leads to further programming errors, such as removing objects currently in use, thereby corrupting or terminating the processes using them.

The **IPC** methods are relatively old and predate large scale use of multi-threaded programming as well as many methods of network programming currently in use. If you need to have a lot of **IPC** usage, going over to a multi-threaded (or network) design may be a much cleaner and more efficient choice.

Both System V IPC and POSIX IPC can be configured in or out during **Linux** kernel configuration; they are not mandatory.

## 29.2　System V IPC

Implementation of System V **IPC** is **not** part of the **POSIX** standard, and not part of **ANSI C**. However, it is required for an operating system to be certified as **Unix**.

While these mechanisms may not be the best first choice for modern applications, if you have to maintain or port any legacy programs, you'll quite likely need to know System V **IPC**.

All the System V **IPC** methods share certain structures and flags and have others which are closely related. Such features include use of a unique **key** to identify the shared resource (provided by input) and the use of a unique **identifier** which is then generated by the kernel to be used as a handle.

## Identifiers

Each **IPC** object (a shared memory segment, semaphore set, or message queue), has associated with it a unique identifier. a system-generated non-negative integer based on a user-supplied **key**.

Two **IPC** objects of different kind can have the same ID (e.g., a message queue and a semaphore set), but two objects of the same type can never share an ID.

The first process accessing the structure (perhaps the server) creates the ID from the key; subsequent processes (perhaps the clients) attaching to the **IPC** structure fetch it using the key.

## Keys

Obtaining a unique **ID** requires use of a unique key. All processes accessing the **IPC** structure must agree upon the key.

The key may be arrived at in a number of ways:

- It may be hard coded into the application(s). This can lead to collisions and security holes.

- The first process can initiate a new **IPC** structure with a key of IPC_PRIVATE and store the returned ID in a file which other processes can then read. One disadvantage is that file operations are required.

- If the processes have a parent-child relationship, the parent can use IPC_PRIVATE and the child will have the identifier after the fork(). The child can then also pass the ID as an argument if and when it exec()'s a new program.

- The function ftok() can be used to generate a key. It requires as arguments a pathname and *project ID*. This is not particularly an advantage over the other methods. Likewise any other commonly agreed upon algorithm can be used. This is an ancient method whose use is hard to justify today.

The functions that create (or attach to) a new **IPC** object (shmget(), semget(), and msgget()) have a flag argument. A new **IPC** object can be created only if the key is IPC_PRIVATE, or the key is not already used by an existing **IPC** object, and the IPC_CREAT bit of flag is set.

If the **IPC** object already exists access will be given to it when the right key is given, and a new ID not generated, even if the IPC_CREAT flag is set. However, if the IPC_EXCL flag is also set, an error will result if the object already exists.

## Permission Structure

Every **IPC** object has an ipc_perm() structure, defined as:

```
struct ipc_perm
{
  key_t  key;   /* IPC key */
  uid_t  uid;   /* owner   user  id */
  gid_t  gid;   /* owner   group id */
```

```
  uid_t  cuid;  /* creator user  id */
  gid_t  cgid;  /* creator group id */
  mode_t mode;  /* access modes */
  unsigned short seq;    /* slot usage sequence number */
};
```

The owner and creator of the structure may be different; hence both the group and user identification fields appear.

Access modes control whether or not reading and/or writing (altering) are allowed.

`seq` is a counter that gets incremented, every time an **IPC** object is released, by the maximum number of **IPC** objects permitted; it can safely be ignored.

When an **IPC** structure is created, all fields other than `seq` are initialized.

Subsequently, the `uid`, `gid`, `cuid`, `cgid`, and `mode` fields can be modified by the appropriate function call for each **IPC** mechanism: `shmctl()`, `semctl()`, or `msgctl()`. Of course, the caller must be either the creator of the **IPC** object or superuser.

## ipcs

This command reports on the status of all System V **IPC** objects. Typing `ipcs -h` gives the following usage message:

```
ipcs provides information on ipc facilities for which you have
      read access.
Resource Specification:
          -m : shared_mem
          -q : messages
          -s : semaphores
          -a : all (default)
Output Format:
          -t : time
          -p : pid
          -c : creator
          -l : limits
          -u : summary
-i id [-s -q -m] : details on resource identified by id
usage : ipcs -asmq -tclup
        ipcs [-s -m -q] -i id
        ipcs -h for help.
```

Note that the **key** is listed:

```
$ ipcs -m

------ Shared Memory Segments --------
key         shmid    owner    perms    bytes    nattch    status
0x7b056858 1         coop     600      1024     3         dest
```

Note that system limits are generated by: `ipcs -l`.

You can get similar information directly from the kernel by examining the files under **/proc/sysvipc**.

## ipcrm

`ipcrm` can remove **IPC** objects. Its usage is:

```
ipcrm [ shm | msg | sem ] id
```

The identifier can be retrieved by using `ipcs`.

The user must have proper ownership.

If one tries to remove a shared memory object in use, it will be marked as destroyed but may remain while other attachments remain. If one tries to remove a semaphore or message queue object, the removal is immediate.

## 29.3 Posix IPC

The **POSIX IPC** implementation is newer than that of **System V IPC**. In fact it was incomplete in **Linux** until the 2.6 kernel added POSIX message queues.

It shouldn't be surprising that it is careful to avoid some of the incoherence in its older competitor's design. For example, each mechanism's function for removing an object (`shm_unlink()`, `mq_unlink`, `sem_unlink()`) only **marks** the object for deletion, which can occur only when the object's usage count vanishes.

Each object is created with an open function (`shm_open()`, `sem_open()`, `mq_open()`) which takes a name as an identifier, not a key. This name should begin with a slash (and contain no others) and the choice is left open to the implementation about whether the **named IPC** object has a filesystem representation.

**Linux** has chosen this route, and all shared memory and semaphore objects can be found under `/dev/shm`. Message queues need to be mounted somewhere using the **mqueue** filesystem, such as in

```
mount -t mqueue none /dev/mqueue
```

Note that the semaphore interface also permits unnamed semaphores, but they are intended to be used only between threads of a multi-threaded application.

## 29.4   Labs

### Lab 1: Examining System V IPC Activity

To get an overall summary of **System V IPC** activity on your system, do:

```
$ ipcs
------ Shared Memory Segments --------
key         shmid       owner       perms       bytes       nattch      status
0x00000000 0            root        777         135168      1
0x00000000 393217       coop        600         393216      2           dest
0x00000000 425986       coop        600         393216      2           dest
0x00000000 262147       coop        600         393216      2           dest
0x00000000 294916       coop        600         393216      2           dest
0x00000000 327685       coop        600         393216      2           dest
0x00000000 360454       coop        600         393216      2           dest
0x00000000 458759       coop        600         393216      2           dest
0x00000000 491528       coop        600         393216      2           dest
0x00000000 524297       coop        600         393216      2           dest
0x00000000 557066       coop        600         393216      2           dest
0x00000000 819211       coop        600         393216      2           dest
0x00000000 622604       coop        600         393216      2           dest
0x00000000 655373       coop        600         393216      2           dest
0x00000000 3833870      coop        600         393216      2           dest
0x00000000 753679       coop        600         393216      2           dest
0x00000000 786448       coop        600         393216      2           dest
0x00000000 950289       coop        600         12288       2           dest
0x00000000 983058       coop        600         393216      2           dest
0x00000000 1015827      coop        600         12288       2           dest
0x00000000 3866644      coop        600         393216      2           dest
0x00000000 3407893      root        644         790528      2           dest
0x00000000 3440662      root        644         790528      2           dest
0x00000000 3473431      root        644         790528      2           dest

------ Semaphore Arrays --------
key         semid       owner       perms       nsems

------ Message Queues --------
key         msqid       owner       perms       used-bytes   messages
```

Note that the currently running shared memory segments all have a key of 0 which means IPC_PRIVATE, and all but one are marked for destruction when there are no further attachments. Later when you are doing exercises you should repeat this command to see the results.

One can gain further information about the processes that have created the segments and last attached to them with:

```
$ ipcs -p

------ Shared Memory Creator/Last-op --------
shmid       owner       cpid        lpid
0           root        3867        31573
393217      coop        4076        19499
```

```
425986      coop        4074       3867
262147      coop        4076       19499
294916      coop        4703       3867
327685      coop        4705       3867
360454      coop        4074       3867
458759      coop        4383       5516
491528      coop        4070       3867
524297      coop        4070       3867
557066      coop        4738       3867
819211      coop        5012       3867
622604      coop        4835       3867
655373      coop        4837       3867
3833870     coop        21958      3867
753679      coop        4987       4466
786448      coop        5012       3867
950289      coop        4070       3867
983058      coop        4703       3867
1015827     coop        4703       3867
3866644     coop        21958      3867
3407893     root        3867       17031
3440662     root        3867       17031
3473431     root        3867       17031


------ Message Queues PIDs --------
msqid       owner       lspid      lrpid
```

so by doing:

```
$ ps ax | grep -e 3867 -e 5012

 3867 tty7     Ss+    1:30 /usr/bin/Xorg :0 -br -audit 0 -auth /var/gdm/:0.Xauth -nolisten tcp vt7
 5012 ?        Sl     0:20 /usr/lib64/thunderbird-2.0.0.22/thunderbird-bin
22162 pts/0    S+     0:00 grep -e 3867 -e 5012
```

we see **thunderbird** is using a shared memory segment created by the **X** server.

Do this on your system and identify the various resources being used and by who.  Are there any potential leaks on the system?

# Chapter 30

# Shared Memory

We'll learn how to use shared memory under **Linux**; how to create and attach (detach) to shared memory regions, and control operations.

## 30.1  What is Shared Memory?

**Shared Memory** is the most commonly used and the fastest of the three **IPC** methods.

One process allocates a memory region and then others attach to and detach from it. Synchronization is important and may require various kinds of locking mechanisms, such as semaphores.

Often the region creator functions as a **server** and subsequent attachees are **clients** with read-only access. In this case synchronization becomes simple.

One has to be particularly careful to have programs **remove** shared memory segments when they are no longer needed by any process. This may not done automatically and memory leaks can result.

Note that **detaching** is **not** the same as **removing**.

An alternative method of using shared memory which is very useful when the processes possess a parent/child relationship, is **anonymous memory mapping**, which we have already discussed. This can provide a cleaner alternative in which the shared segment will be removed as soon as all processes using it have unmapped it or exited.

In fact, the **Linux** kernel implementations of both System V and POSIX shared memory are based on memory mapping.

## 30.2   System V Shared Memory

The functions for dealing with **System V** shared memory objects are:

```
#include <sys/types.h>
#include <sys/ipc.h>
#include <sys/shm.h>

int  shmget (key_t key, int size, int shmflg);
void *shmat (int shmid, void *shmaddr, int shmflg )
int   shmdt (void *shmaddr)
int  shmctl (int shmid, int cmd, struct shmid_ds *buf);
```

The `shmflg` argument to `shmget()` contains the usual permission bits (such as 0644) which may be combined with `IPC_CREAT` when creating a new object. If `IPC_EXCL` is also specified, failure results if the object already exists. If `IPC_CREAT` is not specified the entire argument is ignored.

If `IPC_PRIVATE` is given for the `key`, a new segment can also be created. If neither `IPC_CREAT` or `IPC_PRIVATE` is specified, one one attaches to a previously existing segment.

The `size` argument is rounded up to be a multiple of the size of a page of memory (which can be obtained with `getpagesize()`) which yields 4 KB on **x86**.

The successful return value of `shmget()` is a valid shared memory identifier (generated from the `key` argument) to be used as an argument for the other functions.

In order to use the shared memory segment, one has to attach to and detach from it with `shmat()` and `shmdt()`.

Besides the shared memory identifier, `shmat()` takes as an argument `shmaddr`, a preferred address for the segment. Usually one specifies `NULL` for this value, which allows the system to choose the address of the shared memory segment. The other argument, `shmflg` is not the same as the one passed to `shmget()`, and can be `SHM_RND` or `SHM_RDONLY`. (You can have read-only, but no write-only segments.) The `SHM_RND` value is important only when `shmaddr` is specified.

Further control of the shared memory segment is done with the `shmctl()` function, which applies instructions according to the `cmd` argument on a structure of type `shmid_ds`:

```
struct shmid_ds {
    struct   ipc_perm shm_perm;  /* operation perms */
    int      shm_segsz;          /* size of segment (bytes) */
    time_t   shm_atime;          /* last attach time */
```

```
time_t   shm_dtime;      /* last detach time */
time_t   shm_ctime;      /* last change time */
unsigned short shm_cpid; /* pid of creator */
unsigned short shm_lpid; /* pid of last operator */
short    shm_nattch;     /* no. of current attaches */
        /* the following are private */
unsigned short   shm_npages; /* size of segment (pages) */
unsigned long   *shm_pages;
struct shm_desc *attaches;   /* descriptors for attaches */
};
```

`cmd` can have the following values:

Table 30.1: **System V shared memory shmctl() parameters**

| Value | Meaning |
|---|---|
| IPC_STAT | Retrieve `shmid_ds` structure and put in `buf`. |
| IPC_SET | Set values of the `shm_perm` member of the `shmid_ds` structure to that in `buf`. |
| IPC_RMID | Mark the shared memory segment for removal. |
| SHM_LOCK | Prevent swapping of the segment. (Super user only). |
| SHM_UNLOCK | Allow swapping of the segment. (Super user only). |

Note that using `IPC_RMID` will not actually remove the segment; this will only happen all processes have detached from it. This is different than the other **System V IPC** mechanisms for which removal is immediate.

The following limits are associated with shared memory segments:

Table 30.2: **System V shared memory limits**

| Parameter | Value | Meaning |
|---|---|---|
| SHMMAX | 32 MB | Maximum size for a segment. |
| SHMMIN | 1 B | Minimum size for a segment. |
| SHMMNI | 4096 | System wide maximum number of segments. |
| SHMSEG | SHMNI | Maximum number of segments for process. |
| SHMALL | (SHMMAX/PAGE_SIZE*(SHMMNI/16)) = 2 M (8 GB) | System wide maximum for shared memory pages. |

Here's an example of a minimal program that sets up a shared memory segment, attaches to it, detaches from it, and marks the shared memory segment for removal:

```
#include <unistd.h>
#include <stdlib.h>
#include <sys/ipc.h>
#include <sys/shm.h>
#include <string.h>

int main (int argc, char *argv[])
{
    int shmid;
    void *shared_mem;

    shmid = shmget ((key_t) 89, getpagesize (), 0666 | IPC_CREAT);
    shared_mem = shmat (shmid, (void *)0, 0);
    strcpy (shared_mem, "a string");

    /* do something */ sleep (5);

    shmdt (shared_mem);
    shmctl (shmid, IPC_RMID, 0);
    exit (0);
}
```

## 30.3  POSIX Shared Memory

**POSIX** shared memory objects are created, opened and removed with:

```
#include <sys/types.h>
#include <sys/mman.h>

int shm_open (const char *name, int oflag, mode_t mode);
int shm_unlink (const char *name);
```

Although **Linux** doesn't require it, `name` should start with a / and have no others embedded. When the shared memory segment exists it will be visible under `/dev/shm`.

The `oflag` argument to `shm_open()` must include either `O_RDONLY` or `O_RDWR` and can be combined with:

- `O_CREAT`: Create the shared memory object if it does not exist. In this case the `mode` argument contains the usual permission bits. If this flag is not set, the `mode` argument is ignored as for the usual `open()` system call.

- `O_EXCL`: Return an error if `O_CREAT` is specified and an object of the same name already exists.

- `O_TRUNC`: If the object already exists, truncate to zero length.

The successful return value of `shm_open()` is a valid file descriptor.

When the shared memory object is no longer needed, it can be removed with `shm_unlink()`. Note that this will occur only when all processes using it have called `munmap()` or terminated. The object can also be removed from `/dev/shm` from the command line.

While `shm_open()` creates (or attaches to) the shared memory object, upon creation its size has to be set with:

```
#include <unistd.h>
#include <sys/types.h>

int truncate (const char *path, off_t length);
int ftruncate (int fd, off_t length);
```

In order to use the shared memory segment, one has to memory map it with:

```
#include <sys/mman.h>

void *mmap (void *start, size_t length, int prot , int flags, int fd, off_t offset);
int munmap (void *start, size_t length);
```

Depending on your **Linux** installation, programs using `shm_open()` will have to link with the Posix real time library; e.g.

```
gcc -o shm_examp shm_examp.c -lrt
```

Here's an example of a program which creates a shared memory object, and leaves it resident for other processes to attach to. (Make sure to remove the segment when done with it to avoid a memory leak.)

```
/* compile with -lrt */

#include <unistd.h>
#include <stdlib.h>
#include <fcntl.h>
#include <sys/mman.h>

int main (int argc, char *argv[])
{
    int shm_fd;
    void *shm_area;
    size_t size = 8192;

    shm_fd = shm_open ("/my_shm", O_CREAT | O_RDWR | O_EXCL, 0666);

    ftruncate (shm_fd, size);

    shm_area = mmap (NULL, size, PROT_READ | PROT_WRITE, MAP_SHARED, shm_fd, 0);

    /* Do something with it now */

    munmap (shm_area, size);

    /* shm_unlink ("/my_shm"); */

    exit (0);
}
```

## 30.4   Labs

### Lab 1: Shared Memory

Construct one or more programs to pass messages to each other in shared memory.

The receiving program may terminate when it receives the message from the sending program.

Make sure the shared memory is released when no longer needed.

You may write more than one program, or write one program that can do multiple actions based on the arguments.

Two solutions are given; one for System V IPC and one for POSIX IPC.

The solutions are written so that they take an argument, which can be either `create`, `remove`, `send`, or `receive`, which controls their action.

Don't forget to compile with `-lrt` for the POSIX IPC solution.

# Chapter 31

# Semaphores

We'll learn how to create and use semaphores to protect critical regions of code from simultaneous access by more than one process. We'll learn how to control semaphore operations.

## 31.1   What is a Semaphore?

**Semaphores** are used by processes to signal each other, and to avoid race conditions between asynchronous tasks which share resources.

Semaphores are counters often used to control shared resources or protect critical sections of code, and can implement an (advisory) locking mechanism.

There are only two operations that can be performed on a semaphore variable (**sv**):

- **wait (P) (down)**

- **signal (V) (up)**

They work so that:

- **sv** is **true** when the critical section is available.

- **P(sv)** decrements the counter until it reaches zero. This is often called the **down** operation instead of **wait**.

- **V(sv)** increments the counter. This is often called the **up** operation instead of **signal**.

A semaphore variable is a counter, and can have any non-negative value, not just 1 and 0. To give an example, suppose you want to permit up to **n** users to have access to some facility at once, but no more than that. You would initialize the counter to **n**, and then decrease it every time a new user joins in. When the semaphore value reaches 0, no further users are added until one user releases it (increments the value by unity) thereby permitting a new user to have access.

The System V semaphore implementation is complicated because it deals with **semaphore sets** instead of just individual objects. Thus the semaphore function calls are more painful than those for the other System V IPC mechanisms, and much messier than those in the POSIX implementation. Furthermore, System V semaphores should never be used in multi-threaded programs.

Semaphores will not be removed unless done so explicitly. **ipcrm** can be used to remove System V semaphores, and POSIX semaphores can be directly removed from the **/dev/shm** directory.

## 31.2   System V Semaphores

The functions for dealing with **System V** semaphores are:

```
#include <sys/types.h>
#include <sys/ipc.h>
#include <sys/sem.h>

int semget (key_t key, int nsems, int semflg );
int semop (int semid, struct sembuf *sops, unsigned nsops );
int semctl (int semid, int semnum, int cmd, union semun arg );
```

**nsems** is the number of semaphores (usually 1). If a semaphore is being accessed (not created) its value is ignored.

The **semflg** argument to **semget()** contains the usual permission bits (such as 0644) which may be combined with IPC_CREAT when creating a new object. If IPC_EXCL is also specified, failure results if the object already exists. If IPC_CREAT is not specified the entire argument is ignored.

If IPC_PRIVATE is given for the **key**, a new segment can also be created. If neither IPC_CREAT or IPC_PRIVATE is specified, one one attaches to a previously existing segment.

The successful return value of **semget()** is a valid semaphore identifier (generated from the **key** argument) to be used as an argument for the other functions.

The members of a new semaphore set are **not** initialized; this must be done with **semctl()**. (**semop()** can **change** the value of the semaphore, but not set it to a specific value.)

The value of the semaphore can be changed using the `semop()` function which uses a data structure of type:

```
int semop (int semid, struct sembuf *sops, unsigned nsops );

struct sembuf {
    short sem_num;    /* semaphore number: 0 = first */
    short sem_op;     /* semaphore operation */
    short sem_flg;    /* operation flags */
}
```

`sops` is a pointer to an array of semaphore operations, of dimension `nsops` (usually `nsops = 1`). For the **down** operation `sem_op = -1`, and for the **up** operation, `sem_op = +1`. A value of `sem_op = 0` means we want to wait until the semaphore's value becomes 0, and not return for positive values.

The final element in the `sembuf` structure, `sem_flg`, can be `IPC_NOWAIT` (which returns `EAGAIN` if resources are not available) or `SEM_UNDO` (which releases the semaphore if the process terminates.) This means whatever changes the process did to the semaphore will be undone.

Further control of the semaphore queue is done with the `semctl()` function, which affects the `semnum` member of the semaphore array instructions according to the `cmd` argument, which operates through the last argument:

```
int semctl (int semid, int semnum, int cmd, union semun arg )

#if defined(__GNU_LIBRARY__) && !defined(_SEM_SEMUN_UNDEFINED)
    /* union semun is defined by including <sys/sem.h> */
#else
    /* according to X/OPEN we have to define it ourselves */
union semun {
    int val;                    /* value for SETVAL */
    struct semid_ds *buf;       /* buffer for IPC_STAT, IPC_SET */
    unsigned short *array;      /* array for GETALL, SETALL */
                                /* Linux specific part: */
    struct seminfo *__buf;      /* buffer for IPC_INFO */
};
#endif
struct semid_ds {
    struct ipc_perm sem_perm;        /* permissions .. see ipc.h */
    time_t sem_otime;                /* last semop time */
    time_t sem_ctime;                /* last change time */
    struct sem      *sem_base;       /* ptr to 1st semaphore in array */
    struct sem_queue *sem_pending;   /* pending operations to be
                                            processed */
    struct sem_queue **sem_pending_last;  /* last pending operation */
    struct sem_undo *undo;           /* undo requests on this array */
    unsigned short  sem_nsems;       /* no. of semaphores in array */
};
```

**Note:** The `semun` structure may or may not need to be defined explicitly in your code, according to which version of **glibc** you are using, as the library maintainers tried to remove this feature, but ran into opposition from those whose code it broke, and put it back in. The intent was to make the use of the argument more flexible.

cmd can have the following values:

Table 31.1: **System V semaphores semctl() parameters**

| Value | Meaning |
| --- | --- |
| IPC_STAT | Retrieve semid_ds structure and put in buf. |
| IPC_SET | Set values of the sem_perm member of the semid_ds structure to that in buf. |
| IPC_RMID | Remove the semaphore (immediately). |
| GETALL | Retrieve the semaphore values in the set and put in array pointed to by arg.array. |
| GETNCNT | Return value of semncnt for member semnum. |
| GETPID | Return value of sempid for member semnum. |
| GETVAL | Return the value of val for member semnum. |
| GETZCNT | Return value of semzcnt for member semnum. |
| SETALL | Set all all semaphore values in the set to those pointed to by arg.array. |
| SETVAL | Set the value of semval for member semnum. Used to initialize to a known value, passed as val. |

Note that using IPC_RMID **will** actually remove the semaphore set immediately! Any processes subsequently addressing the semaphore set will return with an errno set to EIDRM.

semctl() returns 0 on success, -1 on error (errno is set).

The following limits are associated with semaphore sets:

Table 31.2: **System V semaphore limits**

| Parameter | Value | Meaning |
| --- | --- | --- |
| SEMMNI | 128 | System wide maximum number of semaphore sets. |
| SEMMSL | 250 | Maximum number of semaphores per ID. |
| SEMMNS | 32000 | System wide maximum number of semaphores, = SEMMNI*SEMMSL. |
| SEMVMX | 32767 | Maximum value for a semaphore. |
| SEMOPM | 32 | Maximum number of operations per semop() call. |

Here's an example of a minimal program that sets up a semaphore, initializes it, goes into a critical section of code, and when done marks the semaphore object for removal:

```
#include <stdio.h>
#include <sys/ipc.h>
#include <sys/sem.h>
#include <unistd.h>
#include <stdlib.h>
```

```
/* data types */
union semun
{
    int val;                     /* value for SETVAL */
    struct semid_ds *buf;        /* buffer for IPC_STAT, IPC_SET */
    unsigned short int *array;   /* array for GETALL, SETALL */
    struct seminfo *__buf;       /* buffer for IPC_INFO */
};

int main (int argc, char *argv[])
{
    int semid;
    union semun sem_union;
    struct sembuf buffer;

    semid = semget ((key_t) 261, 1, 0666 | IPC_CREAT);

    /* initialize the semaphore */

    sem_union.val = 1;
    semctl (semid, 0, SETVAL, sem_union);

    buffer.sem_num = 0;
    buffer.sem_flg = SEM_UNDO;

    printf ("Entering critical section\n");
    buffer.sem_op = -1;
    semop (semid, &buffer, 1);
    /* do something */ sleep (5);

    printf (" Leaving critical section\n");
    buffer.sem_op = 1;
    semop (semid, &buffer, 1);

    /* only the last process to use the semaphore should do this */

    semctl (semid, 0, IPC_RMID, sem_union);

    exit (0);
}
```

## 31.3  POSIX Semaphores

**POSIX** semaphores are created, opened and removed with:

```
#include <semaphore.h>

sem_t *sem_open (const char *name, int oflag, ...);
int sem_unlink (const char *name);
int sem_close (sem_t *sem);
```

Although **Linux** doesn't require it, `name` should start with a / and have no others embedded. When the semaphore exists it will be visible under `/dev/shm`.

The `oflag` argument to `sem_open()` is used only when creating a semaphore; when attaching to one that already exists it is ignored.

If the value `O_CREAT` is specified, the semaphore is created if it does not exist. If this is combined with `O_EXCL` an error is returned if an object of the same name already exists.

When `O_CREAT` is specified, the `mode` argument contains the usual permission bits, and the fourth argument contains the initial semaphore value (usually 1.) If this flag is not set, both the third and fourth arguments are ignored.

If `sem_open()` fails it returns a value of `SEM_FAILED`.

When the semaphore object no longer needed, it can be removed with `sem_unlink()`. Note that this will occur only when all processes using it have called `sem_close()` or terminated. The object can also be removed from `/dev/shm` from the command line.

So far we have described only **named semaphores**. It is also possible to use **unnamed semaphores**, which are usually local to a process (which can have multiple threads.) To do this one declares (or allocates) a structure of type `sem_t` and then uses

```
int sem_init (sem_t *sem, int pshared, unsigned int value);
int sem_destroy (sem_t * sem);
```

to initialize and destroy the semaphore object, instead of the earlier set of functions. If **pshared** is 0 the semaphore is local to the current process; otherwise it may be shared.

Semaphore control is done with the following functions:

```
int sem_wait (sem_t * sem);
int sem_trywait (sem_t * sem);
int sem_timedwait (sem_t *sem, const struct timespec *abs_timeout);
int sem_post (sem_t * sem);
int sem_getvalue (sem_t * sem, int * sval);
```

where:

`sem_wait()` is the **down** operation; the caller is suspended if the semaphore counter is zero, until an **up** operation gives it a non-zero value. The counter is then atomically decreased. This function always returns 0.

`sem_trywait()` is the non-blocking version of `sem_wait()`. If the semaphore count is 0 it returns `EAGAIN`.

`sem_timedwait()` puts an upper limit on how long the **down** operation should block, with the time value set using the usual structure:

```
#include <time.h>
struct timespec {
  long    tv_sec;  /* seconds */
  long    tv_nsec; /* nanoseconds */
};
```

sem_post() is the **up** operation; it atomically increases the semaphore counter. The function never blocks.

sem_getvalue() retrieves the current semaphore value and puts it in *sval.

Depending on your **Linux** installation, programs using these semaphore functions will have to link with the Posix real time library; e.g.

```
gcc -o sem_examp sem_examp.c -lrt
```

Here's an example of a program which creates a semaphore and protects a critical region while another process could attach to it and have to wait. (Make sure to remove the semaphore when done with it to avoid a memory leak.)

```c
/* compile with -lrt  */

#include <stdio.h>
#include <stdlib.h>
#include <unistd.h>
#include <semaphore.h>
#include <fcntl.h>

int main (int argc, char *argv[])
{
    sem_t *mysem;
    int i;

    mysem = sem_open ("/my_sem", O_CREAT | O_EXCL, 0666, 1);

    for (i = 0; i < 4; i++) {
        sem_wait (mysem);
        printf ("Entering critical section, %d, pid=%d\n", i, getpid ());
        sleep (3);
        printf (" Leaving critical section, %d, pid=%d\n", i, getpid ());
        sem_post (mysem);
        sleep (3);
    }
    printf ("PROTECT region exited for pid=%d\n", getpid ());

    sem_close (mysem);
    sem_unlink ("/my_sem");

    exit (0);
}
```

## 31.4  Labs

### Lab 1: Semaphores

Write one or more programs that protect a critical section with a semaphore.

The critical section can be as simple as a sleep().

You may write more than one program, or write one program that can do multiple actions based on the arguments.

Two solutions are given; one for System V IPC and one for POSIX IPC.

The solutions are written so that they take an argument, which can be either `create`, `remove`, or `protect`, which controls their action.

Don't forget to compile with `-lrt` for the POSIX IPC solution.

## Lab 2: Semaphores and Shared Memory

Modify the shared memory lab to use semaphores to have the programs pass messages to each other in shared memory.

The first program should get some input from the user, stuff it into shared memory, and release the semaphore to signal the second program.

The second program should read the message and display it, then release the semaphore to let the first one know that he's ready for more.

You may write more than one program, or write one program that can do multiple actions based on the arguments.

Two solutions are given; one for System V IPC and one for POSIX IPC.

The solutions are written so that they take an argument, which can be either `create`, `remove`, `send`, or `receive`, which controls their action.

Don't forget to compile with `-lrt` for the POSIX IPC solution.

# Chapter 32

# Message Queues

We'll learn how to create and use message queues to send information from one process to another.

## 32.1 What are Message Queues?

**Message Queues** constitute an **IPC** method in which linked lists of messages are used to send data from one process to another without using pipes.

Messages may be sent and received according to priority or type, rather than in purely first-in, first-out **FIFO** order.

In System V, messages may be retrieved in any order according to type; in POSIX, highest priority messages are always dealt with first.

## 32.2  System V Message Queues

The functions for dealing with **System V** message queues are:

```
#include <sys/types.h>
#include <sys/ipc.h>
#include <sys/msg.h>

int msgget (key_t key, int msgflg );
int msgsnd (int msqid, void *msgp, int msgsz, int msgflg );
int msgrcv (int msqid, void *msgp, int msgsz, long msgtyp, int msgflg);
int msgctl (int msqid, int cmd, struct msqid_ds *buf )
```

The `msgflg` argument to `msgget()` contains the usual permission bits (such as 0644) which may be combined with `IPC_CREAT` when creating a new object. If `IPC_EXCL` is also specified, failure results if the object already exists. If `IPC_CREAT` is not specified the entire argument is ignored.

If `IPC_PRIVATE` is given for the `key`, a new segment can also be created. If neither `IPC_CREAT` or `IPC_PRIVATE` is specified, one one attaches to a previously existing segment.

The successful return value of `msgget()` is a valid message queue identifier (generated from the `key` argument) to be used as an argument for the other functions.

Adding or retrieving messages to/from a message queue is done with `msgsnd()` and `msgrcv()`.

In these functions the second argument (`msgp`) points to the message itself, which which must start with a **long** non-negative integer value which is used for message selection, and which can be passed to the `msgtyp` argument of the receive function.

`msgsnd()` returns 0 on success, -1 on failure (`errno` is set).

`msgrcv()` returns number of bytes received on success, -1 on failure (`errno` is set).

In older **libc** implementations the second argument, rather than being cast as a void pointer, was required to be used this way:

```
int msgsnd (... , struct msgbuf *msgp, ...)
int msgrcv (... , struct msgbuf *msgp, ...)
struct msgbuf {
  long mtype;     /* message type, must be > 0 */
  char mtext[1]; /* message data */
  };
```

Here, the structure `msgbuf` must start with a **long** `mtype` and the array `mtext` is of size `msgsz` (in bytes) which must be non-negative. (Thus it is a **long** shorter than `msgbuf`.) This old prototype can be recovered if one uses the preprocessor definition, `__USE_GNU`

Message reception selection is controlled by the value of `msgtyp`:

Table 32.1: **System V message queue message types**

| Value | Meaning |
|-------|---------|

| msgtyp = 0 | First available message is retrieved. |
|---|---|
| msgtyp > 0 | First message with the same message type is retrieved. |
| msgtyp < 0 | First message with a type same or less than absolute value of `msgtyp` is retrieved. |

Further control is obtained through use of `msgflg`, which may be made up of the following:

Table 32.2: **System V message queue message flags**

| Flag | Meaning |
|---|---|
| IPC_NOWAIT | Return immediately if no message of the type is on the queue. |
| MSG_EXCEPT | If `msgtyp` ¿ 0, read the first message with a different type. |
| MSG_NOERROR | Truncate the message text if longer than `msgsz`. |

Further control of the message queue is done with the `msgctl()` function, which applies instructions according to the `cmd` argument on a structure of type `msqid_ds`:

```
struct msqid_ds {
    struct ipc_perm msg_perm;
    struct msg *msg_first;  /* first message on queue */
    struct msg *msg_last;   /* last message in queue */
    time_t msg_stime;       /* last msgsnd time */
    time_t msg_rtime;       /* last msgrcv time */
    time_t msg_ctime;       /* last change time */
    struct wait_queue *wwait;
    struct wait_queue *rwait;
    unsigned short msg_cbytes; /* current number of bytes on queue */
    unsigned short msg_qnum;   /* number of messages in queue */
    unsigned short msg_qbytes; /* max number of bytes on queue */
    pid_t msg_lspid;          /* pid of last msgsnd */
    pid_t msg_lrpid;          /* last receive pid */
};
```

cmd can have the following values:

Table 32.3: **System V msgctl() flags**

| Value | Meaning |
|---|---|
| IPC_STAT | Retrieve `msqid_ds` structure and put in `buf`. |
| IPC_SET | Set values of the `msg_perm` member of the `msqid_ds` structure to that in `buf`. |
| IPC_RMID | Remove the message queue **immediately**. |

Note that using IPC_RMID **will** actually remove the queue immediately! Any processes reading or writing to the queue will return with an errno set to EIDRM.

The following limits are associated with message queues and are set in /usr/include/linux/msg.h:

Table 32.4: **System V message queue limits**

| Parameter | Value | Meaning |
| --- | --- | --- |
| MSGMNI | 128 | Maximum number of ID's |
| MSGMAX | 8192 | Maximum size of message (bytes). |
| MSGMNB | 16384 | Default maximum size of a message queue. |

Here's an example of a minimal program that sets up a message queue, sends a message, clears the buffer, and then receives it, and when done marks the message queue for removal:

```
#include <stdlib.h>
#include <stdio.h>
#include <string.h>
#include <unistd.h>
#include <sys/ipc.h>
#include <sys/msg.h>

#define BUFSIZE 132

int main (int argc, char *argv[])
{
    int msgid;
    struct
    {
        long my_msg_type;
        char some_text[BUFSIZE];
    } some_data;
    some_data.my_msg_type = 1;

    msgid = msgget ((key_t) 1234, 0666 | IPC_CREAT);

    strcpy (some_data.some_text, "A MESSAGE");
    printf ("You are sending: %s\n", some_data.some_text);

    msgsnd (msgid, (void *)&some_data, BUFSIZE, 0);

    memset (some_data.some_text, 0, BUFSIZE);
    printf ("Message is cleared, is now: %s\n", some_data.some_text);
    sleep (5);

    msgrcv (msgid, (void *)&some_data, BUFSIZE, 0, 0);
    printf ("You received: %s\n", some_data.some_text);
```

```
        msgctl (msgid, IPC_RMID, 0);
        exit (0);
}
```

## 32.3  POSIX Message Queues

**POSIX** message queues are created, opened and removed with:

```
#include <mqueue.h>

mqd_t mq_open (const char *name, int oflag, ...);
int mq_close  (mqd_t mqdes);
int mq_unlink (const char *name);
```

Although **Linux** doesn't require it, `name` should start with a / and have no others embedded. When the message queue exists it will be visible if the **mqueue** filesystem is mounted (which must be done by root), as in:

```
$ mkdir /dev/mqueue
$ mount -t mqueue none /dev/mqueue
$ ls -l /dev/mqueue
total 0
drwxrwxrwt  2 root root   60 Feb  9 09:56 ./
drwxr-xr-x 13 root root 5900 Feb  9 09:56 ../
-rw-rw-r--  1 coop coop   80 Feb  9 09:56 my_mq
```

The `oflag` argument to `mq_open()` must include either `O_RDONLY`, `O_WRONLY` or `O_RDWR` and can be combined with:

- `O_CREAT`: Create the message queue if it does not exist. In this case the `mode` argument contains the usual permission bits. If this flag is not set, the `mode` argument is ignored as for the usual `open()` system call.

- `O_EXCL`: Return an error if `O_CREAT` is specified and an object of the same name already exists.

- `O_NONBLOCK`: If this flag is set, calls to `mq_send()` and `mq_receive` will fail (with **errno** = `EAGAIN`) if either resources or messages are not currently available, rather than block and wait.

The successful return value of `mq_open()` is a valid message queue descriptor, which is essentially a file descriptor.

When the message queue is no longer needed, it can be removed with `mq_unlink()`. Note that this will occur only when all processes using it have called `mq_close()` or terminated. The object can also be removed from `/dev/mqueue` from the command line, or from wherever else the **mqueue** filesystem may be mounted.

When a message queue is created, one more argument must be given to `mq_open`, a pointer to a structure of type:

```
struct mq_attr {
   long   mq_flags;      /* message queue flags         */
   long   mq_maxmsg;     /* maximum number of messages  */
   long   mq_msgsize     /* maximum message size        */
   long   mq_curmsgs     /* number of messages currently queued  */
   long   __reserved[4]; /* ignored for input, zeroed for output */
};
```

If NULL is passed in, default attributes are established. (mq_maxmsg=10, mq_msgsize=8192) Values can be examined and set with:

```
int mq_getattr (mqd_t mqdes, struct mq_attr *mqstat);
int mq_setattr (mqd_t mqdes, const struct mq_attr *restrict mqstat,
              struct mq_attr *restrict omqstat);
```

However, the only structure member that can be modified with **mq_setattr()** is **mq_flags**; the maximum number of messages and the maximum message size can not be changed once the message queue is established. (The **__restrict** attribute is in indication of this in the second and third arguments, which are pointers to the new structure value and the old one.)

Thus, overriding the default attributes must be done before the **first** call to **mq_open()**, which creates the object.

System-wide limits are exposed in the **/proc** filesystem:

```
$ ls -l /proc/sys/fs/mqueue
total 0
dr-xr-xr-x 0 root root 0 Jun 19 11:23 ./
dr-xr-xr-x 0 root root 0 Jun 19 07:50 ../
-rw-r--r-- 1 root root 0 Jun 19 11:23 msg_max
-rw-r--r-- 1 root root 0 Jun 19 11:23 msgsize_max
-rw-r--r-- 1 root root 0 Jun 19 11:23 queues_max
```

Only a root user can modify these hard limits.

Sending and receiving messages is done with:

```
#include <mqueue.h>

int mq_send (mqd_t mqdes, const char *msg_ptr, size_t msg_len, unsigned msg_prio);
ssize_t mq_receive (mqd_t mqdes, char *msg_ptr, size_t msg_len, unsigned *msg_prio);
```

Upon sending the buffer pointed to by **msg_ptr**, its length (**msg_len**) must be no greater than the maximum message size; failure rather than truncation results. Upon reception, the buffer must be greater than or equal to the maximum message size.

**mq_send()** returns 0 on success; **mq_receive()** returns the number of bytes in the successfully received message, which is removed from the queue.

The argument **msg_prio** is the priority of the message, with higher values meaning higher priorities (the highest being one less than **MQ_PRIO_MAX** = 32768.) Upon sending, messages are inserted in the queue according to priority. Upon reception, the highest priority message is always received, and that priority value will be returned in `msg_prio`.

Messages are received in **FIFO** order, and it is not possible to receive a message lower than the highest priority one available.

Timeouts for both sending and receiving can be enforced through:

```
#include <mqueue.h>
#include <time.h>

int mq_timedsend  (mqd_t mqdes, const char *msg_ptr, size_t msg_len,
            unsigned msg_prio, const struct timespec *abs_timeout);
ssize_t mq_timedreceive (mqd_t mqdes, char *restrict msg_ptr, size_t msg_len,
            unsigned *restrict msg_prio, const struct timespec *restrict abs_timeout);

struct timespec {
  long    tv_sec;  /* seconds */
  long    tv_nsec; /* nanoseconds */
};
```

Depending on your **Linux** installation, programs using `mq_open()` will have to link with the Posix real time library; e.g.

```
gcc -o mq_examp mq_examp.c -lrt
```

Here's an example of a program which creates a message queue and waits for other processes to attach to it and send messages. (Make sure to remove the message queue when done with it to avoid a memory leak.)

```
/* compile with -lrt */

#include <stdlib.h>
#include <stdio.h>
#include <fcntl.h>
#include <mqueue.h>

int main (int argc, char *argv[])
{
    struct mq_attr attr = {
        .mq_maxmsg = 10,
        .mq_msgsize = 4096,
    };

    mqd_t msg_fd;
    char buffer[4096];

    msg_fd = mq_open ("/my_mq", O_RDWR | O_CREAT | O_EXCL, 0666, &attr);

    while (1) {
        if ((mq_receive (msg_fd, buffer, attr.mq_msgsize, NULL)) == -1)
            exit (-1);
        printf ("Message Received %s", buffer);
```

```
        }
        mq_close (msg_fd);
        exit (0);
}
```

## 32.4  Labs

### Lab 1: Message Queues

Construct one or more programs that communicate with each other by using message queues. Run them in separate windows.

The sending program should take lines of input until being given the string "end".

The receiving program should print out the messages sent.

You may write more than one program, or write one program that can do multiple actions based on the arguments.

Two solutions are given; one for System V IPC and one for POSIX IPC.

The solutions are written so that they take an argument, which can be either **create**, **remove**, **send**, or **receive**, which controls their action.

Don't forget to compile with **-lrt** for the POSIX IPC solution.

# Index

www.ingramcontent.com/pod-product-compliance
Lightning Source LLC
Chambersburg PA
CBHW080357060326
40689CB00019B/4040

9 781449 906023